QUEER AS CAMP

Queer as Camp

Essays on Summer, Style, and Sexuality

Kenneth B. Kidd
and Derritt Mason
Editors

FORDHAM UNIVERSITY PRESS
New York 2019

Fordham University Press has no responsibility for the persistence or accuracy of URLs for external or third-party Internet websites referred to in this publication and does not guarantee that any content on such websites is, or will remain, accurate or appropriate.

Fordham University Press also publishes its books in a variety of electronic formats. Some content that appears in print may not be available in electronic books.

Visit us online at www.fordhampress.com.

Library of Congress Cataloging-in-Publication Data available online at https://catalog.loc.gov.

Printed in the United States of America

21 20 19 5 4 3 2 1

First edition

CONTENTS

Charlie Hailey

Twenty-five years ago, I lived in a 1964 Bambi with an autographed portrait of Divine. Barely six by thirteen feet on the inside, the trailer was Airstream's smallest model, and the headshot, a standard 8 × 10 glossy, held court in this cocoon of space from its perch at the top of the bed. It was a gift to the trailer's owner who had camped across North America, designing and constructing projects, and mentored me in the art of building that year after Hurricane Andrew. Lodged in the post-disaster jungle near Homestead, my wife and I showered outside, cooked on a hibachi in the driveway, and slept on an already crowded sofa bed with a dog and cat displaced by the hurricane. The trailer was a shell in and out of which we made room for living. We were camping, not necessarily thinking about the meaning of camp, but living its paradox as well as its potential. And we did have a few pink flamingoes around the trailer hitch.

According to legend, or at least the company's advertising copy, Wally Byam, the founder of Airstream, named the Bambi model in 1961 on one of his global caravan tours to support the company brand, transporting at great expense his polished aluminum trailers across oceans, rivers, and deserts, as he also promoted "international goodwill and understanding among the peoples of the world through person-to-person contact."[1] Nearing the end of his African Caravan in Angola, Byam heard about a small deer celebrated as *O'Mbambi* for its stability and strength. You have to wonder at Byam's intention, already tinged with colonialism, and there is a degree of shrewdness at finding in the Umbundu dialect a naming convention that might temper his appropriation of one of Disney's most beloved characters. Long associated with camps and camping, nostalgia sells trailers as well as movies. And Wally and Walt, even if only one was an avid camper, fashioned themselves as dreamers whose visions moved unnervingly between hegemony and happiness, but it was Michael Eisner, Disney's former CEO, who articulated a corporate zeitgeist of camp when he wrote how summer camp defined not only ways of living but also ways of working. His recollections convey longing for his time at Keewaydin in

Vermont: "The world is not camp, and that's too bad."[2] But there is more to this conflation of world and camp: Camps are worlds unto themselves and two decades into the twenty-first century the world is full of camps.

You might recall the Storm of the Century in March 1993. If you were in Florida, particularly at the peninsula's southern end where we were, you didn't have much warning, and it came at night in what seemed a craven affront to Hurricane Andrew's lingering damage. It blew up the east coast as a so-called hundred-year storm that now appears commonplace. We already felt vulnerable in this bristling landscape amid the Everglades' relentless humidity, legions of tradespeople camping next to bars, wary homeowners living alongside gutted houses, and a first attempt at making our own home as a couple. In a short time, the trailer had become our memory theatre, a place we could navigate—had to navigate—in complete darkness. It was a microcosm of what we came to know as home, a minimum dwelling with few amenities but many freedoms. It was also one of many thousands of trailers scattered across Dade County. And for us—I'm not sure we realized it at the time—this camp carried all the contradictions that you might expect from a road-weary capsule assembled in America's heartland, polished so that it reflected its sub-tropical context, named after a Disney character, decked with a drag queen's headshot, driven around the country for decades by a counterculture architect, and now occupied by two twentysomethings voluntarily living in a landscape of catastrophe. Like a postmodern camper's kit.

Camp is multivalent. It is noun, verb, and adjective. It houses both individual and community. Carried along by this semantic range, its practices cover wide geographic territories as well as multi-disciplinary fields. Camp connotes desire and freedom, privation and need, fear and power. It is idea and practice—a way of thinking as well as doing. It is why pragmatist and transcendentalist alike convened at the Philosopher's Camp in the Adirondack Mountains. It is how Christopher Isherwood melds philosophical demonstration with intuition.[3] The praxis of camp is performative and self-reflective, and its inflections range from summer camp to protest camp, from Sontag's "Notes on 'Camp'" to Agamben's "What Is a Camp?" And camps readily move between the political and the personal.

When Occupy Wall Street set up camp in the quasi-public space of Zuccotti Park, its simple directive was to "occupy public space" and "to let these facts be known."[4] Occupy camps were scenes of disclosure that revealed the sometimes messy—at times ambiguous—process of consensus and, more broadly, being in the world. Camping in public spaces is unavoidably theatrical, and the occupy meme camps that sprang up from

OWS's genetic code were also exercises in applied aesthetics, combining self-expression with the practicalities of self-organizing and day-to-day living. Though criticized for what was perceived as a lack of tangible results, the camp itself was the goal all along. It demonstrated a vision of everyday life where coexistence was the norm. The camping collectives cut across class, race, gender, orientation, and those with homes and those without. Occupy camps drew as much attention to their diverse community and to the agility of camp as they did to their declared goals. Which is to say the camp's the thing, and camping is about discovering who we are, who you are.

Camp is method. Though at times highly subjective and individualized, it is a repeatable process, whether the outcome is actual place-making—like pitching a tent, parking a trailer, or participating in communal events—or more conceptual constructions of identity, style, or philosophy. More than that, it is consistently repeated: We keep going back to summer camp, we return to campgrounds year after year, we even reuse the same fire pits, and along the way we refine our individual awareness of things—what Sontag called sensibilities, which reside supplemental to culture and apart from normative society alike. Camp occurs outside daily life. Camping is a kind of play-acting, a dramatic—sometimes radical—departure from home, even if your tent is pitched in the backyard. And camp, as a sensibility, operates in a similarly differential space between stable meaning and "pure artifice."[5] Both camping and camp work within paradox—impermanence and stability, mobility and fixity, displacement and place, *unheimlich* and home. The "necessary paradox" that Sontag introduced to define camp is already inherently at work in practices of camp, and camping and camp share more than linguistic similitude and reach a deeper methodological affinity in Isherwood's camp, Sontag's camp, Byam's campers, and Charles Eliot's summer camp. Eliot, Harvard's longest-serving president, saw camp as an educational opportunity without equal: "I have the conviction that a few weeks in a well-organized summer camp may be of more value educationally than a whole year of formal school work."[6] Whether in pedagogy, research, or simply setting up a temporary home, camp as method is rigorous without being rigid—adapting procedure to situation, tweaking templates based on patterns we discover, fashioning new methods out of old, crafting identity and making a place for ourselves.

In 1964, when Susan Sontag sat down to write her notes, our Bambi rolled off the assembly line in Jackson Center, Ohio. She didn't go camping or climb into an Airstream trailer to write, but when she set the fifty-eight pegs that held up the tent of her jottings, Sontag created her own critical space and set up camp similar to when a camper sites, clears, and makes a home away from home. There are as many forms of camp as there are campers, and there is a similarly varied, though intertwined, set of approaches to camp as a subject of inquiry. The discipline of camp studies harbors a wide field of meaning, cutting across many disciplines and playing with method—too many and too much for the comfort of some academic discourses. But that's what camp accommodates—a plurality of voices, a diverse set of experiences, and deep connections to place and identity. Just as Sontag's alternative methodology combined "pathos" with objective distance, camp's fugitive treatises work between practical didacticism and campfire reverie, by turns edifying and lyrical, formalized and informal.[7] In its own refreshingly varied and insightfully rich set of camp studies, this important volume adds to a burgeoning—if under-the-radar—field.

We felt the storm before we heard it. Bambi's skin vibrated with the low beat of a tympanum. The trailer shifted and rocked with each squall, with each surge of wind, like a bassinet, but one that wakes you up rather than lulls you to sleep. It was made for the slipstream of Eisenhower's national road system, not for Mother Nature's roiling windstorms. We could see the shadow of the main house backlit by veils of lightning, and between thunderclaps, naked as newborns, we ran toward the relative security of concrete block. Embedded within post-disaster recovery, our time in the Bambi was a test case, an experiment in living together, backyard camping next to the house we were repairing, and—quite simply—living outside. Bambi was the riveted proscenium for our domestic platform, less staged but still a bit self-conscious like Thoreau's Walden. Remember the episode where he pulled all the things out of his cabin and didn't want to move them back inside? Camp is like that.

NOTES

1. Wally Byam, "Wally Byam's Creed & Code of Ethics," WBCCI/The Airstream Club Caravans, http://wbccicaravan.wbcci.net/about-2/members/. Accessed March 12, 2018.

2. Michael D. Eisner, *Camp* (New York: Warner Books, 2005), 61.

3. Isherwood wrote about camp that "you have to feel it intuitively." See *The World in the Evening* (New York: Random House, 1954), 106. He continues: "Once you've done that, you'll find yourself wanting to use the word whenever you discuss aesthetics or philosophy, or just about anything. I can never understand how critics manage to do without it."

4. See Declaration of the Occupation of New York City.

5. Susan Sontag, "Notes on 'Camp,'" 1964, *Against Interpretation and Other Essays* (New York: Farrar, Straus and Giroux, 1966), 281.

6. Charles Eliot, *Directions: Youth Development Outcomes of the Camp Experience*, 1922 (American Camp Association, 2005).

7. Charlie Hailey, *Campsite: Architectures of Duration and Place* (Baton Rouge: Louisiana State University Press, 2008), 57.

QUEER AS CAMP

Camping Out: An Introduction

Kenneth B. Kidd and Derritt Mason

> Camp depends on where you pitch it.
>
> —PHILIP CORE, *Camp: The Lie That Tells the Truth*

Queer as Camp: Essays on Summer, Style, and Sexuality has many origins, but the idea for a scholarly book as such emerged at the 2015 meeting of the Children's Literature Association (ChLA). There we shared our memories of summer camp and the sense that our camp experiences had been formative as well as enjoyable. ChLA meets in June and (like many academic conferences) feels a bit like summer camp, which helped prompt our recollections. Kenneth's family ran private summer camps in central Texas, Friday Mountain Boys' Camp and Friday Mountain Girls' Camp, and after attending as a camper in the 1970s and early 1980s he became a counselor-in-training (CIT) and counselor. Derritt spent sixteen years at a private all-boys summer camp in Algonquin Park, Ontario, Canada, from 1990 through the mid-2000s, first as an eight-year-old camper and, in his last summer, as the camp's Assistant Director. In between, he was a CIT and counselor, section director, and co-leader of a 36-day canoe trip.

Queer-identified adults, we laughingly recalled that our respective camps offered the usual mix of homosocial structure and homoerotic longing but no sexual encounter. No salacious tales of sleepovers gone sexy for us, not even camp-specific revelations of identity. And yet we still found camp a space of queer encounter and formation. What, we wondered, made our summer camp experiences feel queer, and/or, what was it like for us to be queer *at* camp? How might camp function as a queer time and/or place? And how does Camp, the aesthetic practice or sensibility, play on the stages of camp? What returns us to the intersections of camp, Camp, and queerness; what makes those intersections so compelling? *Are* they so compelling? At the least, they can be very funny, as with Daniel Mallory Ortberg's "Notes Home from Camp, by Susan Sontag," which first appeared on the website *The Toast*. We happily include Ortberg's spoof in this volume. Sontag's "Notes on 'Camp'" (1964) has been influential but also daunting, and it's delightful to imagine with Ortberg the somber Sontag as a young camper, analyzing and enduring Camp at camp.

As the book began to materialize, we experimented with some strategies for thinking about camp/Camp interplay as well as the weave of the personal and the professional in this collection. Youthful curiosity and experience are foundational to camp and Camp experience both, and while this is a volume of scholarship, we don't want to lose sight of such. A more properly academic introduction will follow, but first, a listing exercise, followed by a dialogue between us about our own camp experiences and their aftershocks. As Richard Dyer writes in "It's Being So Camp as Keeps Us Going," "It is easy, and usual, to offer a list of camp things at the beginning of discussions of camp, so that we all know what we are talking about" (112). Sontag, of course, offered such a list, as have many after her (Ortberg included). As Dyer also points out, such lists can be misleading, "since camp is far more a question of how you respond to things rather than qualities actually inherent in those things" (113). We were also thinking of the camp packing list, a genre unto itself, appropriated here as a packing list for our planned volume rather than, say, a list of such crucial camp items as bug repellent, sunscreen, and underwear with sewn-in labels. Here's what we managed:

Sing-alongs	"Native" pageantry	Excitement
Campfires	Archery	Boredom
Canoeing	Speaking in tongues	Not-home, not-school
Swimming	Living unlived lives	Animals
Arts & crafts	Cultural appropriation	Family, "family"
Skinny dipping	Sex, of all kinds	Nostalgia
Camp masculinity	Hetero- and gender normativity	Longing
Lesbian scouting	Sexual subversiveness	Nature
Homosociality	Drag	Making memories

No doubt we've forgotten something crucial, and we invite you to correct and supplement. Lists are fun and instructive, but we decided the essays in this volume constitute a better list, as it were, reflecting on camp and Camp with candor, insight, and often humor. Eleven of the thirteen essays appear here for the first time, while two (Kent and Eveleth) are reprints with minor modifications. The essays are "amusing, parodic, incisive, scholarly, nostalgic, historicizing, self-reflexive, steely, and serious," to quote one of our anonymous reviewers; they "offer different affective and generic ways into the concerns" of the volume.

We also experimented with dialogue about our own experiences with queerness and Camp at camp, in our view a more successful exercise shared here in the hopes of striking some useful but informal introductory notes.

DERRITT MASON: I think I often felt queer at camp because I was so ill-fitted to its intensely hypermasculine, heteronormative environment. Having secret crushes on other boys certainly contributed to my feeling queer, but mostly it was the product of not being masculine in the camp-appropriate sense. To be frank, I was (and still am) awful at most camp activities. I always preferred drama to anything outdoors, and I was particularly enthralled by camp's "playing Indian" pageantry, which Philip J. Deloria and Sharon Wall have written about so brilliantly. Otherwise, however, I was a relatively weak paddler and swimmer. I'm allergic to horses. To this day, I loathe Ultimate Frisbee, that godforsaken summer camp staple. I grew to enjoy canoe tripping, but portaging those awkward, cumbersome packs through mosquito-infested swamps was a version of hell. I cried through most of my four-day canoe trip as an eight-year-old, and returned home with back and legs pock-marked by itchy, scabby bug bites. Everyone in my cabin except me spent the last night of camp vomiting up the orgiastic quantities of food they had devoured at the final banquet. I hated my first summer, but my parents forced me back for another, promising I could call it quits if I still despised it after my second attempt.[1]

Despite its stifling gender normativity, my camp environment was also intensely homoerotic, replete with male bodies on constant display in various phases of undress, and circumstances that enabled and encouraged close contact between boys. In her excellent historical overview of summer camping in Ontario, Wall notes that "from the perspective of camp administrations, same-sex attachments were one of the long-recognized dangers of camp" (203). Camp, in other words, permits intimate contact that always risks shifting into the sexual, although it never did for me. It certainly did for D. Gilson, however, whose "Notes on Church Camp" appears in this volume. In his autobiographical account of attending Pentecostal camp on the north shore of Lake of the Ozarks, Gilson describes a series of fleeting sexual episodes with his pastor's son. I'll confess to feeling envy at D.'s erotic bible camp experiences because my own summer camp experience was so chaste. No one in my close group of friends was particularly adept at flirting or hooking up. I was always jealous, though, when I did see it happen—it was a marker of coolness and social status, one aggressively encouraged, celebrated, and often modeled by camp staff. As Wall points out: "Staff romances were a matter of common knowledge among campers and may have gone some way towards instilling the excitement—not to mention emphasizing the normativity—of heterosexuality" (208). The camp hookup and all of its attendant sociality, excitement, and intimacy felt so painfully inaccessible to me.

In my twenties, I had a brief dalliance with a fellow staff member following a stint at a different, specifically queer camp, and I immediately texted several friends from my childhood camp: "I FINALLY had a camp fling!" Reading (and re-reading) Gilson's account, however, I still feel cheated of an admittedly nostalgic coming-of-age rite of passage. This is one of many "unlived lives" that structures my sense of self as a queer person, the likes of which Adam Phillips explores in *Missing Out: In Praise of the Unlived Life*. "We can't imagine our lives without the unlived lives they contain," Phillips writes eloquently in the preface (xiii); he insists that "we make our lives pleasurable, and therefore bearable, by picturing them as they might be" (xvii). At my childhood camp, I only outed myself as gay to a select handful of close friends during my final two summers. My queer camp romance was so satisfying, in part, because it had given me brief access to one of the lives I had so desperately yearned to live.

KENNETH B. KIDD: So much is familiar in Derritt's account: the sense of not quite belonging in this hypermasculine, heteronormative world; the pervasive homoeroticism and homosociality; the desire to have and/or be these ideal male bodies, instead of my own pimply and overweight self; the wretchedness of sports (and for me the compensatory focus on nature study and "handicrafts"); the inappropriate theatricality of playing Indian. And above all, a retroactive and ongoing jealousy about "real" gay experience that others presumably enjoyed at camp clandestinely. The unlived life ever beckons.

There were other wrinkles. For starters, my camp was a family business. My grandfather, a long-time Scoutmaster and amateur boyologist, started the camp on the property of a distinguished University of Texas historian,

Walter Prescott Webb. On top of that, the site had been a boy's boarding school in the nineteenth century, so the place was loaded with significance. My grandparents were often on site, and my uncle and cousins ran everyday activities. One cousin was the tennis coach; another was my cabin counselor. I loved and resented this family togetherness. I loved that my cabin mates knew it was my family's place. I think it protected me, although I also was good at making people laugh. I don't know how much I benefited from being "Captain" Kidd's grandson. But I know my feelings of queerness were wrapped up with being a Kidd kid. A little like being a PK (pastor's kid).

Yet, when I was a CIT, a friend and fellow CIT was apparently caught doing *something* with a handsome horsemanship counselor from Oklahoma. The camp director—my uncle—fired them both immediately. They left within the hour, and I never saw my friend again (Google searches have since turned up nothing). Family against family? My first lesson in homosocial panic. Maybe there was more to the story; I've never quite wanted to ask.

DM: Like Kenneth, I navigated parts of my camp experience using humor. During my third summer, when I was ten years old, I made some friends who reoriented my initial distaste for camp. None of us were particularly "cool"; the dynamic worked. Over the years, my cabin mates affectionately teased me about that fact that I was crappy at most camp activities. I continued to fail at canoe tripping with particular vigor. Failure is a longstanding queer art, according to Judith (Jack) Halberstam, and it is undoubtedly the most finessed of all my camp-acquired skills. My body itself rejected canoe trips, developing oozing skin conditions and cultivating fungi with impressive efficacy. My narrow shoulders refused to carry heavy loads that seemed so easily managed by my friends. Sun-scorched and peeling, my skin screamed at me daily for subjecting it to something for which it was so evidently ill-equipped. Nonetheless, my fifteen/sixteen-year-old cabin mates and I capped our time as campers with a 36-day trip in the wilds of Northern Ontario. For the duration of this trip, my friends jovially dubbed me "a bitch on portages but good in the tent," because I made them laugh despite my many inadequacies. (We do, I should probably say, remain friends to this day).

KK: Like Derritt, I hated camp at first. Gradually, that hatred turned into love. I spent the last week of my first term of camp (at age 7) in the infirmary, ostensibly sick but mostly homesick, and delighting in the spoiling of my grandmother and the evasion of regular camp life. I read, slept in, and read some more. I watched my mates ride by on horseback. Eventually, the term ended, and I went home. I didn't come back for two years, and that was a little scandalous in our family because all the Kidd kids *loved* camp, or such was the story. When I did return, however, I had a better time, attending five summers out of a possible eight. I never warmed to sports activities or rifle shooting, although I did eventually earn a sharpshooter's badge (not something I list on my c.v., especially as the rifle lessons were certified by the NRA). I became a CIT and then the camp's nature counselor, more my cup of tea. I loved taking care of the animals, hiking to local springs, and explaining how to identify the four poisonous snake species on location. I liked that we did something different each day. Plus, the nature counselor was expected to be eccentric, as was the case with the long-term nature counselor at the girls' camp, Uncle B, a confirmed bachelor and the only male counselor in the place. At the boys' camp, I upheld the tradition of weirdness. By that point, though, I adored most things about camp, and found ways to avoid what I didn't.

I was also an "honor camper" three times. Each year, one honor camper was selected from each cabin by secret ballot. Each week, we voted on a different quality, like trustworthiness, honesty, or reliability. At the final campfire, the honor campers were identified and led off for a secret, mysterious meeting, in which my cousin intoned solemnly about integrity and doing right by others. I forget the details. But I remember being chosen. And wondering if it was deserved or the result of family privilege. I still have my plaques.

DM: Sadly, my camp had no "honor camper" ceremony—if only "honesty" or "reliability" were more established measures of success than the annual canoe race I would never win! At my camp, only feats of masculine athleticism could earn you immortality through your name's inscription on various plaques in the camp dining hall; there were no trophies for "feminine" labor like compassion, nurturing the youngest and most needy campers, or, say, being "good in the tent." Like Kenneth, I grew to love camp, but as my cabin mates and I approached staff age, I became anxious about how I would continue to fit in. My failure at performing camp masculinity led my cabin mates to lovingly imagine on my behalf a variety of possible camp careers given that anything involving canoe-carrying (or upper-body strength, generally speaking) would be out of the question. Perhaps I could be the "Head of All Things Faggy," they proposed, a new camp activity I could create, one that might include competitive events like the "limp-wristed poodle walk." Yet, despite their homophobic impulses, a part of me delighted in the alternative camp environment my cabin mates were proposing. They were teasing me, absolutely, but in their own way my friends were making space for me by imagining a Camp camp that would include my particular version of masculinity. Through Wall's book, I learned that my camp's founder and first director once wrote that summer camp could remedy the boy "inclined to be a sissy" (178). How wonderful to envision fagginess as authorized camp activity, and a sissy like me as its leader!

Not that my camp was without its existing Campy elements: Theatrical pageantry was particularly seductive to me. A large part of this involved a monthly ceremony called "Indian Council Ring." Wall's chapter "Totem Poles, Tepees, and Token Traditions" provides a thorough overview of this ceremony and its practice across Ontario-based camps like mine, contextualizing it as part of camp's overall antimodernist impulse. As campers, we painted our faces and made paper headbands with feathers. We wrapped ourselves in blankets and walked to a special place in the forest. Staff members wore headdresses and beat drums. Female campers and staff performed a "fire dance," after which male staff members—typically in full body paint as "medicine men"—would light the fire in dramatic fashion (a car battery buried under the fire pit; a flaming arrow shot down from a surrounding hill; a large stick capped with a match-filled ping-pong ball plunged vigorously into stacks of gasoline-soaked wood). It was a rite not unlike Gilson's account of speaking in tongues at bible camp, but "without explicit reference to religion," as Wall explains: "One could taste the beauty of ritual, embrace feelings of awe, and experience the power of the communal event" (227).

The ceremony was led by "The Chief" (one of the camp directors, in resplendent leathers and five-foot headdress), who opened the evening with a peace pipe prayer to a series of deities with exotic names. We played games based on "Indian" legends. There was a water boiling contest. My favorite part was the enactment of "Hiawatha's Departure," in which the titular figure would be sent by his Chief into the woods on a type of vision quest. It was something of an honor, as a staff member, to portray Hiawatha. As a camper, I longed to play this part. Eventually, I would— and I even played the Chief himself, in my twenties. Sliding into the weighty leather costume, crowning myself with the headdress, and reciting the ceremonial script that had resonated in my mind for over a decade—it was thrilling and liberating. I felt powerful. This was a part of camp in which I shined.

In her chapter on the history of Council Ring ceremonies, Wall poses a series of arresting questions: "Did campers have any idea . . . that, as directors donned Native headdresses, federal laws attempted to bar Aboriginal peoples from appearing publicly in traditional dress? Were they ever aware that, as they enthusiastically participated in Indian rituals, Native bands in western provinces were prohibited from holding their own sundance and potlatch ceremonies?" (246). My answer—and, I would venture, the answer from the vast majority of my fellow campmates and staff members—is a definite "no." These particular bans were repealed from Canada's *Indian Act* in the 1950s, but the actual histories of Algonquin Park and the region's Indigenous peoples were never part of my camp's pedagogy despite the Indigenous signifiers that were (and remain) everywhere on the camp's grounds. When I reflect upon my enthusiastic participation in Council Ring, the memories now carry mostly shame and discomfort. It was never clear to me how inappropriate (yet not atypical) it was to parody (earnestly, Campily) Indigenous culture on stolen land. Joshua Whitehead's essay in this collection confronts this appropriation, which extends far beyond the official spaces of summer camp. Council Ring was a fundamental part of camp's "green space" where I underwent my own kind of queer self-fashioning and transformation, much like the characters in the young adult novels Whitehead cites. Such queer selves, however, are almost always being constructed by white settlers and are contingent on the erasure of Indigenous lives and histories.

KK: Reading the excellent histories of North American summer camp by Leslie Paris and Abigail A. Van Slyck, I realize just how typical was our camp of the traditional private summer camp: same rituals, same stories, same organizational structure. Same feelings of specialness; same playing Indian; same fixation on tanned bodies; same rhetorics of self-improvement. The sameness was belated, too, meaning that Texas got the summer camp memo later than much of the country. Summer camping had its start on the East Coast, then spread to the Midwest, Far West, and the South. Friday Mountain was founded in 1947, but even then not much was new about its philosophies or activities. I'm struck now by how generic it was, even as it felt intensely singular and special. Turns out, camps are a lot alike.

Thankfully, Friday Mountain didn't involve much canoeing. We did have one overnight under the stars, but we got to our site on horseback and the biggest excitements were the late-night, spin-the-bottle striptease games (yep), and the fried egg breakfasts the next morning. And while no one suggested the limp-wristed poodle walk, we did sometimes play a game called "Poor Pussy." Maybe you know it? Apparently it's not just a weird Texas tradition. A camper, usually younger, pretends to be a sweet little cat. He sidles up to another camper, usually older, purring and meowing and trying his feline best to make the other boy laugh. The challenge is to keep a straight face, pet the cat gently and say, three times and with composure, "poor pussy!" If instead he laughs, the older boy turns pussy and the game starts anew. One of my favorite boys at camp was remarkably talented at this game. He was the cat's meow (sorry, not sorry). Someone must have known about the classical cat duet, *"Duetto buffo di due gatti"* ("The Funny Duet for Two Cats"), attributed to Gioachina Rossini but with elements from C. E. F. Weyse's "Cat Cavatina." And at least once, performed by choirboys trying to keep a straight face (Google it).

Now that proper academic introduction. *Camp* has a complex etymology and signification, its spatial and performative meanings richly intertwined. *Campo*'s Latinate origins, Charlie Hailey reminds us in *Campsite*, are found in *campus*, referring to the level field (51). Speaking of the campus connection, Hailey is a noted scholar and theorist of architecture who also happens to be Kenneth's colleague at the University of Florida. Like our contributors, we have learned much from Hailey's work and are grateful for his delightful preface to *Queer as Camp*. As Hailey notes in *Campsite*, not a few campuses begin as camps and vice versa. *Camper* means "to camp," to pitch or make place away from more settled territory. In Greek texts, Hailey points out, there's a lexical connection between *camp* and *chora* or chorus. *Camp* also connotes a cause or position and a body of adherents; *camp* can refer to a field of debate or investigation. Meanwhile, theorists of Camp as an aesthetic practice trace such not to Sontag's "Notes on 'Camp,'" nor to Christopher Isherwood's *The World in the Evening* (1954), which ties camp to its young protagonist's sexual awakening (Booth 66), nor even to various works of modernist and pornographic Camp,[2] but rather to *se camper*, eighteenth-century French for "displaying oneself through military finery and posturing," and subsequent iterations in English. According to Dennis Denisoff, the "first English definition of camp as a conscious act of artifice appears in J. Redding Ware's 1909 dictionary *Passing English of the Victorian Era*, where he defines it in full as 'Actions and gestures of exaggerated emphasis. Probably from the French. Used chiefly by persons of exceptional want of character'" (100). Denisoff adds that the earliest known *British* use of the category, in the form of "campish," can be found in an 1869 letter by Frederick William Park, commenting on his own public drag performance (100).[3] In his introduction to *Camp: Queer*

Aesthetics and the Performing Subject, Fabio S. Cleto quotes Michael Allen along similar lines: "In the days when actors wandered from village to village they often lived in rough tents. This was camping. When one actor moved in to share the tent of another he was said to be camping with him" (Cleto 29).

Camp's many meanings are in play in this book. As we've indicated, our first desire is to think about summer camp as a queer time and/or place. Halberstam explains that "queer uses of time and space develop, at least in part, in opposition to institutions of family, heterosexuality, and reproduction," while also emerging "as an outcome of strange temporalities, imaginative life schedules, and eccentric economic practices" (*In a Queer Time* 1). In both historical and contemporary iterations of summer camp, we can note a tension between camp as a space for enforcing rigid and linear narratives of normative growth and development, and a space that makes room for these same narratives to be undercut. Paris points out that summer camp upholds the idea of childhood innocence while helping to negotiate the child's transition to heteronormative "romantic preparedness" (161). Her research shows further that male same-sex behavior at camp is often downplayed as mere boyishness, while Wall notes how girls' same-sex "crushes" have been similarly dismissed as childlike and immature (204). If camps often discourage same-sex intimacy, they also create space for such intimacies. Wall writes: "Whatever directors thought of the purifying influence of pine trees and sparkling lakes, the freedom and spaciousness of camp in some cases facilitated, rather than inhibited, sexual experimentation" (214).

Organized camping in the United States is generally dated to 1861, when Frederick William Gunn, headmaster of The Gunnery School in Connecticut, took his entire student body for a two-week excursion into the wilderness.[4] Many early summer camps were extensions of boarding schools, but character-building, "boy work" institutions like the YMCA and the Boy Scouts also established camps as a male character-building strategy. On the one hand, summer camp was and remains a normative institution, especially when linked with character-building in all its gendered and racist glory. On the other hand, summer camp offers an alternative to mainstream society and might be understood as a limited critique of such. In their respective studies of North American summer camp, Paris, Van Slyck, and Wall underscore the seductions alongside the limitations of its antimodernist energies. "As much as it seemed a rejection of modern society," Wall writes, "the camp was ultimately part of that society, helped individuals adjust to it, and, at times, even fuelled the culture of commodification and consumption that lay at the heart of modernity itself" (5). Camps allowed for experiments in alternative living in what Van Slyck calls a "manufactured wilderness." In the 1930s and 1940s, progressive and radical summer camps developed in the northeastern United States, extensions of socialist and other left-wing urban communities. As Paul C. Mishler reports in *Raising Reds*, such camps helped promote and extend the work of urban reformers and often took on a utopian and experimental tone. Many were affiliated with Jewish cultural organizations; some, notably Camp Wo-Chi-Cha in New York, experimented with interracial camping, a daring practice in the 1940s (Mishler 94–95). Such camps thrived through the late 1940s, falling victim to social conservatism and McCarthyism in particular. Across and beyond this period, more progressive and/or socially oriented camps have coexisted with privately owned camps, which tend to be more traditional (if not outright conservative) in philosophy and demographics—like the camps that Kenneth and Derritt attended.

Camping has since exploded and further diversified, although thematically political camps are harder to find than they were in the early twentieth century. The American Camp Association reports some 12,000 summer camps in the United States alone, with nearly a thousand more in Canada. If originating in and especially popular in North America, summer camp is a global affair. Certain iterations loom large in the cultural imagination— Scout Camp, band camp, bible camp—but camps engage diverse interests and activities, from sports to language learning, computing, forensic science, and weight loss. Some camps are specialized; some are free-form or have an elective curricular structure. Even so, the association of camp with escape and pleasure persists in most camp situations. Former Disney CEO Michael Eisner even claims in his memoir of Camp Keewaydin that "nobody fails summer camp" (xi).

Although summer camp is typically imagined as an institution that trains young people in the art of growing up, a recent surge of adult camps invite grown-ups to abandon responsibilities and indulge in the pleasures of childhood. Camp is also a space for *adult* play and nostalgia. Club Getaway, for instance, is a self-styled "camp for adults" that's more resort than camp (though that distinction can be fuzzy), set on 300 acres in the Berkshire Mountains in Connecticut. The 2017 season included a three-day event called Camp John Waters, hosted by none other than the legendary film director and Pope of Trash, and featuring such events as *Hairspray* Karaoke, Bloody Mary Bingo, and Burlesque Lessons. Other adult summer camps are more earnest in their nostalgic appeals, popular even with adults who didn't, in fact, go to camp as children. The notion of summer camp for adults, incidentally, may be newly accentuated but it is not new; recall the "philosopher camps" of late nineteenth and early twentieth-century America. The philosopher camp was "a laboratory for experimentation and speculation"; one such site in the Adirondacks, Putnam Camp, "would host early experiments in the pragmatic method," notes Hailey (*Campsite* 243).[5] The recent iteration of this phenomenon seems to be, in part, a way of living those "unlived lives" we flagged earlier, of bringing— to channel Kathryn Bond Stockton's *The Queer Child*—childlike pleasures into "lateral contact" with adulthood: 5 PM is cocktail hour instead of cabin cleanup (11). Adulthood for the win.

For Giorgio Agamben, working from a different set of interests, the camp more broadly is "the space that opens up when the state of exception starts to become the rule" (39). As such, camp can represent a radically good or a radically bad alternative to the usual order of things—a utopian experiment in living, but also potentially a draconian suspension of justice and the law, a site of bare life. These possibilities exist on a spectrum. Summer camp is associated with utopian experiments in free will and creative living, but can be tinged with anxiety and fear, whereas sites such as internment camps, labor camps, and prison camps represent bleaker possibilities yet may retain hopeful features. In *Camps*, a sequel of sorts to *Campsite* and a self-described "field manual" of camps, Hailey builds on Agamben and identifies three categories of camp: camps of autonomy, in which some free will is exercised; camps of control, in which people are policed and brutalized; and camps of necessity, in which victims of war, famine, or other extreme situations are rendered aid. "Camp spaces no longer just serve recreational and strategic uses but now accommodate an increasingly diverse set of occupants," he notes, "including detainees, refugees, migrants, pilgrims, activists, tourists, hedonists, and avatars" (*Camps* 2). Summer camp is generally removed from camps of control and necessity but can shade into such.

We title the book *Queer as Camp* rather than *Queer at Camp* to indicate that camp can be queer or queer-encouraging: It's not just a matter of queer behavior or identity in some neutral space. Camp is not only a location, and queer is not only an identity. We have in mind the television serial *Queer as Folk*, with "folk" functioning as an analogue for queer. Moreover, "folk" signifies appropriately given summer camp's utopian premodern aspirations. Wall, for example, describes an early-twentieth-century "quest of The Folk" in Nova Scotia, Canada, "a search for identity and meaning" that "popularized an image of an unpretentious fisherfolk as the province's true cultural identity" and resonated ideologically with the concomitant emergence of the first Canadian summer camps (4–5). We like the reversibility of our title, too. As commentators on camp aesthetics and practices note, the theoretical and practical intersections of queer and camp are at once overdetermined and underexplored—all the more so when *camp* designates both special places and cultural practices. David Bergman reminds us that queer theory, and especially the transformative work of Judith Butler, was inspired by studies of drag performance and Camp culture.[6] *Camp* arguably predates *queer* as a cultural term. Calling camp and queer "cognate terms," and noting that both work as all parts of speech, with "no static grammatical functioning" (12), Cleto remarks further that "camp is queer as a mode of being, as posturing a body, as a modality of distribution within social spaces and with the economy of the social contract, and as a mode of communication—indirect, oblique, and secondary, unstable and improvised according to its specific, *hic et nunc*, relation to the other" (30). Camp depends also on *how*, *when*, and *why* you pitch it.

As we've said, the intersection of camp sites and Camp aesthetics is a secondary but vital concern for *Queer as Camp*. The place of Camp in queer culture and queer studies is complicated, and this volume treads lightly on debates about its meaning and significance. Writing in reference to film especially, Paul Roen calls camp "any brazen triumph of theatrical artifice over dramatic substance. Camp is a phoniness that glories in itself" (9). Allan Pero puts it even more colorfully, in his playful "A Fugue on Camp": "Camp is a histrionic Heisenberg delighting in realism's decay" (28). Camp theorizing invites but also frustrates definition; it encourages and indulges in list-making, the proliferation of examples and ideas. As Cleto notes, the "impossibility" of defining Camp is linked with Camp's slipperiness or fungibility: "Tentatively approached as a *sensibility*, *taste*, or *style*, reconceptualized as *aesthetic* or *cultural economy*, and later asserted/reclaimed as *(queer) discourse*, camp hasn't lost its relentless power to frustrate all efforts to pinpoint it down to stability, and all the 'old' questions remain to some extent unsettled" (2).[7] A particularly unsettled and unsettling question concerns the ideological work of Camp. If Camp can disrupt or destabilize, it can also uphold the order of things. Michael Trask argues that Camp is aligned with postwar liberal academic style more generally, marked by an "appreciation for contrived experiences" (2) plus "a rhetoric of skepticism and a mood of detachment" (26). "Camp," he explains, "might be seen as the evil twin of the pragmatist stance that saturated academic life in the mid-twentieth century, for camp takes pragmatism's slogan, 'whatever works,' and turns it inside out. Camp's slogan might be 'whatever doesn't work'" (7).

In this volume we are interested in the places where Camp touches down on summer camp and vice versa. Summer camps, of course, are semi-permanent spatializations of camping activities (hiking, cooking, sleeping outdoors). Paris notes the intriguing use of the term "campy" to emphasize the authenticity of a summer camp against criticisms of modernization (for example, conveniences such as indoor plumbing and comfortable beds); she reports also that new activities had to be rationalized as sufficiently "campy." An elite Adirondack girls' camp thus advertised itself in 1931 as "*a Real Camp*, in the campiest way" (Paris 67). While "campy" in this sense guards against artificiality, it also performs authenticity in a highly artificial way, perhaps approaching Camp as imitation and thus artificiality.

On the flip side, Camp, often described as a style or expressive mode, can also become a location or place of presentation. "In terms of architectural method both old and new," writes Hailey, "camp describes an idea and inscribes the schematic zone for its development—its 'becoming.' Consequently, camp relates to method both in its concrete procedures and through its more abstract mental activities of making place" (*Campsite* 57). Hailey credits Sontag with the development of a "third sensibility" for Camp, one freed from the "standard dichotomy of literal and symbolic meaning" and bound up with "the paradox of a mobile fixity and an unstable permanence" (57), a useful description for "queer" also. In other words, Camp becomes a "vernacular architecture"—a habitation or shelter for the marginalized. Camp and camp connote "home-away-from-home" and thus "homely *unheimlich*," proposes Hailey (*Campsite* 59)—recalling Agamben's description of camp as a "dislocating localization" (44).

That's not to say that camp and Camp are identical or are necessarily aligned. Even when it generates queer practices or opportunities, summer camp can be relentlessly heteronormative. Summer camp drag antics are not always or even usually Camp. Critics of Camp sometimes claim that it has been straightened or that it was never sufficiently queer in the first place; we might say the same of much summer camp discourse. Consider the recent *Camp Camp* (2008), a camp miscellany made up of hundreds of submitted photographs and solicited camp reminiscences. Ostensibly a snapshot of summer camp culture in the 1970s and '80s—the "definitive formative experience for our generation," claim the editors, akin to "Woodstock, Pearl Harbor, and the Boston Tea Party" (!) (11)—*Camp Camp* plays with the queer possibilities of camp. Camp, opine the editors, "was the place many first kissed, got to third base, or cross-dressed" (13).

Camp Camp acknowledges some rather homoerotic activities at camp, such as boner contests and even teabagging (55). But *Camp Camp* is more appropriation than exploration of the Campiness of camp. It's the kind of book we might find in a hipster gift shop. Not that academic discussions of Camp and camp rise above appropriation! In fact, the lesson of many of our contributors is that summer camp allows for a relaxation of norms but not typically to the point of radical critique or social transformation—in part because camp is temporary, a respite from rather than a permanent alternative to the status quo. And Camp may or may not make good on its radical potential; or rather, its radicality may inhere more in style than action, as some Camp theorists propose.

Popular culture abounds with texts that, like *Camp Camp*, inhabit the intersections of summer camp and queerness. Outside of those addressed in this volume, we might also point to a few recent notable texts: Maggie Thrash's graphic memoir *Honor Girl* (2015), a tale of forbidden same-sex camper/staff desire; Nick White's 2017 novel *How to Survive a Summer*, the story of its young narrator's experiences at anti-gay conversion therapy camp; *Mask Magazine*'s July 2017 Camp issue, which includes a number of compelling autobiographical pieces (see, for example, A. J. Stepney's "Heartbreak at Camp Mariah" and Aimee Lutkin's "The Camp Witch"); and Melanie Gillman's *As the Crow Flies* (2017), a web comic now available in print that stars Charlie, a Black, queer thirteen-year-old at Christian camp.

Summer camp is also Campily (and hilariously) established as a queer time and place in the cult film *Wet Hot American Summer* (2001), which stages two of summer camp's most enduring taboos—same-sex and camper/staff sexual contact—and upends narrative convention with delicious irony. The former taboo plays itself out when camp staff McKinley (Michael Ian Black) and Ben (Bradley Cooper)—whom audiences have already viewed engaging in clandestine intercourse—are spotted participating in a secret commitment ceremony by aggressively hetero bros J. J. (Zak Orth) and Gary (A. D. Miles). "McKinley and Ben are fags together!" J. J. and Gary exclaim. "What are we gonna do?" Later, the pair bursts into the dining hall during mealtime, shouting menacingly: "Hey! McKinley and Ben! This is for you!" McKinley and Ben visibly ready themselves for the ridicule that would befit a setting where heterosexual norms are typically violently enforced. However, as Jack Babuscio indicates, ironic incongruities are crucial to Camp cinema, and this is precisely what the film delivers: Instead of launching into a homophobic tirade, J. J. and Gary haul a large box marked "Crate & Barrel" into the dining hall and present it to the couple. "It's a chaise lounge," explains J. J. "We didn't know if maybe you guys already had one. We have the receipt if you do." Delighted, Ben replies: "It goes with the chenille throw cloth Beth's sister gave us!"

Elsewhere in the film, we observe an art and crafts lesson-cum-therapy session as a group of young campers coach emotional activity head Gail (a then 37-year-old Molly Shannon) through a turbulent divorce. Her most empathetic camper is Aaron, played by 12-year-old Gideon Jacobs with the gentle resolve of a seasoned analyst. Viewers witness a deepening intimacy between the pair, expressed through lingering eye contact and fleeting touch. At the end of the film, they leave camp together hand-in-hand, announcing their engagement to camp director Beth (Janeane Garofalo). "I hope you like shrimp cocktail, because we want you to be the guest of honor at our wedding next week!" says Gail. Smiling and laughing, Beth replies: "But I hope it's not Jumbo shrimp, because I'm allergic to oxymorons!"

Instead of shutting down these queer taboos, *Wet Hot American Summer* allows them to freely and hyperbolically proliferate, their Campy, ironic subversiveness enabled and heightened through the film's setting. Camp is a sexually overwrought space that polices the queerness it invites, the film seems to argue; what would it look like, *ad absurdum*, were camp's queerness given free rein? *Wet Hot*'s legacy endures in two recent Netflix spin-offs: *Wet Hot American Summer: Ten Years Later* (2017) and a prequel, *Wet Hot American Summer: First Day of Camp* (2015). The latter features many of the same actors, now fourteen years older, reprising their roles and lending the series another layer of temporally dissonant Camp. We're reminded of Halberstam's argument in *In a Queer Time and Place* that queer communities queer age, dissolving the boundaries between child, adolescent, and adult (2). The *Wet Hot* prequels and sequels function in a similar fashion, resignifying camp as a space that, alongside recent trends in adult camping, confounds generational categories.[8] This collection follows *Wet Hot American Summer* in that we, too, want to encourage camp's queer proliferations.

We have tried to underscore the white privilege and even structural racism of summer camp, but have not done enough in that direction, and we fail entirely to offer critique of such in Camp productions and criticism. Both Camp and camp lean decidedly white despite their intersectional possibilities. *Wet Hot American Summer* is a case in point; there's not a single Black character in the cast. In "Slave Chains and Faggots and Camp . . . Oh My!," Noah Fields reminds us that Camp theorists "have consistently failed to address race" despite the interventions of Black queer Camp dramatic works such as Robert O'Hara's *Insurrection: Holding History* (1999), a revisionist "history" of the Nat Turner rebellion, which Fields calls "an episodic, time-bending, campy fantasia, a counter-narrative against the mainstream master-narratives about slavery." In the context of such work, *Wet Hot American Summer* looks only narrowly progressive, offering challenge to conventions of gender and sexuality in the context of summer camp narrative but falling short of the imaginative historical and political refashioning accomplished by O'Hara. If we were to start fresh, we would solicit work using Black queer Camp theory to illuminate summer camp texts, including works like the aforementioned *As the Crow Flies*. We hope this collection, in its deficits as much as its strengths, will inspire more work on queer camp and Camp.

Queer as Camp is divided into two parts. Essays in Part I focus on particular camp sites, historical and/or contemporary, with an eye toward their queer tendencies and cultivations. Many of these essays have a personal dimension, written out of participation and engagement with those sites. The essays in Part II give more priority to representations of fictional camps or camping situations in narrative film, fiction, and drama. Essays in both sections consider camp/Camp relation, in varying degrees. Contributors generally follow our practice of distinguishing camp from Camp, but also seek to explore their overlap conceptually and rhetorically.

Essays in Part I examine camp as a queer place and/or the experiences of queers *at* camp—usually both. In some cases, queerness inheres more in the camp structure or institution, whereas in others queerness emerges in and even against camp settings. In her richly historicized chapter, Annebella Pollen examines three British and pacifist camping enterprises that developed in reaction to the Great War as well as to the militarism and imperialism of Boy Scouting: the Order of Woodcraft Chivalry, the Kindred of Kibbo Kift, and Woodcraft Folk. These woodcraft-oriented movements, which also developed in relation to one another, offered radical visions of society and sexuality alike while encouraging non-normative, often highly aesthetic practices of art, craft, costume, and photography. Of the three, the Woodcraft Folk, a breakaway group from the Kibbo Kift, has been the most enduring and now boasts some 15,000 members. It is telling that some leaders in these movements were sexologists or sex educators. While these camping organizations were remarkably forward-looking, they also sometimes endorsed conservative positions, illustrating how camping leans both progressive and conservative.

Writing at the other end of our historical moment of camp, Flavia Musinsky reports on Vermont's Indian Brook, a contemporary American camp with which she has been involved for a number of years. Musinsky approaches Indian Brook as an unusual experiment in queer pedagogy, in practice if not also in name, one born of Quaker traditions, progressive education, and feminist politics. Musinsky describes how camp staff are committed to the ongoing interrogation and critique of gender and sexual norms through themed programming, discussion, and rules encouraging campers to avoid "body talk." As forward-thinking as Indian Brook strives to be, Musinsky points out that the implementation of queer pedagogy in a summer camp environment entails challenges and failures. A single-sex girls' camp, Indian Brook has struggled, in particular, with the inclusion of nonbinary and transgender campers and staff. Nonetheless, Musinsky's case study illuminates a rare example of a traditional summer camp that seeks to think queerly in its day-to-day practices, and she effectively demonstrates how camp gender politics continue to evolve since the rigid sex-segregation of the pre-WWII era (Wall 201).

We are pleased to reprint (with a new introduction) Kathryn R. Kent's "'No Trespassing': Girl Scout Camp and the Limits of the Counterpublic Sphere," which first appeared in *Women and Performance: A Journal of Feminist Theory* and was then reprinted in the groundbreaking collection *Curiouser: On the Queerness of Children* (2004), edited by Steven Bruhm and Natasha Hurley. Bruhm and Hurley describe Kent's essay as a "theoretical memoir" (xxxii), binding together as it does snapshots from her own Girl Scout experiences with analysis of how Girl Scouting as an institution—in Kent's words, "usually regarded as a stable part of the faded wallpaper of white, middle-class banality"—is nonetheless bound up with lesbian/queer identities.

Summer camp has long functioned as a site for cultivating Jewish identity. In *How Goodly Are Thy Tents* (2003), Amy L. Sales and Leonard Saxe report on their ethnographic study of twenty Jewish summer camps across the United States, underscoring how camp not only teaches Jewish history and heritage but also prepares Jewish kids for future leadership roles. In her contribution to our volume, Alexis Mitchell emphasizes the role of Jewish summer camp as a complicated site of sexuality, social bonding, and citizen-making. Mitchell considers her experience with one such camp as a queer teen, an experience that later inspired her film *Gabey and Mike: A Jewish Summer Camp Love Story* (2016). Mitchell's film takes its cue from the song "Gabey and Mike," about a doomed boy friendship/love affair, which Mitchell heard and sang at camp. She discovered later that the song, a campfire mainstay in the 1990s, was written by a Toronto folk duo called Mermaid Café, comprised of the queer musician now known as Peaches and her then-girlfriend. Mitchell's film restages the story of Mermaid Café—a love affair between girls—in the space of the Jewish summer camp, in order to explore why this song was so popular among kids not themselves queer and in fact often hostile to queers. Mitchell explains her approach to creating *Gabey and Mike*, emphasizing the importance of the Camp aesthetic for reimagining the Jewish summer camp as a potentially if not routinely queer-affirming place. Mitchell's chapter similarly aims to decipher the paradoxes of camp and Camp through an experimental weaving of personal anecdote and scholarly critique. She likens the Jewish summer camp's rituals of heteronormative belonging to those of Birthright Israel trips.

As he reports in his lyrical contribution, D. Gilson learned to speak in tongues at a Pentecostal bible camp on the Lake of the Ozarks in Missouri. In one week of camp, thirteen-going-on-fourteen Gilson learned both queer sex, through furtive encounters with the pastor's son, and also code speaking, the code of Pentecostalism running alongside and through "a code of boys." Gilson traces how his sense of aesthetic and narrative possibility was bound up with an emergent queer self. The Campiness he learned at bible camp, Gilson reports, was foundation for an "aesthetic evangelicalism" that continues to this day, formative to his identity as a poet and critic no less than his sexual awakening. For Gilson, Pentecostalism offered training in aesthetic and life management in coordination with, rather than against, queer desire.

Mark Lipton recalls queer experience at camp and its ongoing reverberations through an "assemblage" styled after Deleuze and Guattari. Lipton ranges over and across summer camp, Camp studies, bare life, and critical theory in a manner both confessional and theoretical. His essay, like Gilson's, can also be described as a theoretical memoir. He ruminates on Camp X-Ray on Guantanamo Bay, he rages against Sontag, he bemoans the sanitation of Camp, the loss or downplaying of its political radicality; so too with camp, now a safe place for affirmative gayness rather than a risky proposition, in his view. Lipton aligns summer camp with concentration camps to play up how camp "as a material, spatial, mobile, and metaphorical concept always invokes exaggerated identities." His assemblage refuses to settle down into essay form; instead, it pushes in many and sometimes competing directions, like camp itself.

Closing out Part I is Paul Venzo's meditation on the Australian summer holiday as a camping experience conducive to queers and queer experience.

Thousands of Australians, Venzo notes, camp out in seaside holiday parks during the extended vacation period of Christmas, New Year, and the school holidays, ending with Australia's national holiday on January 26. Like Lipton and Gilson, Venzo experiments with form so as to render camp as much as analyze it: a series of vignettes drawn from personal experiences punctuate the discussion. Venzo suggests that the holiday park partakes both of summer camping and Campiness in its decidedly performative rituals and extravagances—for Venzo himself, a self-identified queer observer-participant, but also for the multiethnic boys and men on scene whose stylized, even theatricalized performances of masculinity seem site-specific or inflected.

Without leaving behind the personal or experiential, Part II of *Queer as Camp* attends more explicitly to cinematic and literary engagements. While scholars have addressed the complex place of Camp in literature—see, for instance, the 2016 cluster of essays on "Camp Modernism" in *Modernism/modernity*, edited and introduced by Marsha Bryant and Douglas Mao—no one has yet sketched the history of summer camp representation, either on its own or in relation to Camp. We don't do that either, but we hope the chapters in Part II suggest some possibilities for examining Camp and camp representations together. We open with an essay short by Tammy L. Mielke and Andrew Trevarrow on the queer camping/Camping of Walt Disney's 1958 animated film short *Paul Bunyan*. While Disney's feature-length films have been considered from feminist and queer angles, this popular short has been neglected. *Paul Bunyan* retells the North American tall tale of the outsized lumberjack and his blue ox buddy, Babe. Mielke and Trevarrow show how Disney's short expands upon the tale's queer and Camp elements, playing up male homosociality and cross-species bonding and inviting queer identification in the process.

Ana M. Jimenez-Moreno reads Camp against camp in her analysis of Soon-Teck Oh's *Tondemonai-Never Happen!* (1970). This experimental, complex play—which baffled critics when it premiered—explores the double ostracization of a gay Japanese-American imprisoned in an internment camp. Camp theatricality serves as a means of resisting American nationalism in the play, proposes Jimenez-Moreno, even as it also forestalls a gay identity. Jimenez-Moreno draws on the work of Richard Dyer and Jack Babuscio concerning the role of Camp as queer male subversion. Because the spaces of home and camp artfully converge on stage, suggests Jimenez-Moreno, the play's audience experiences a feeling of imprisonment, reflective not only of internment camp horrors but also the broader strictures of queer, national, and ethnic belonging.

The ease with which summer camp utopia slides into dystopia can be seen in some horror films, which exploit the putative "horrors" of sexuality and gender and pick up on the camp's sinister associations with control, oppression, and trauma. Camp theorists like Babuscio have flagged how "the horror genre, in particular, is susceptible to a camp interpretation," especially those films that "make the most of stylish conventions for expressing instant feeling, thrills, sharply defined personality, outrageous and 'unacceptable' sentiment, and so on" (121). The horror film is already "an exercise in controlled bad taste," according to Roen, and a "camp horror film should not only be cheap, but also sleazy and vulgar," preferably with a transgressive plot and a "bizarre and grotesque sexuality" (13). In his essay, Chris McGee considers one such film, *Sleepaway Camp* (1983), part of a brief run of summer camp horror films in the early 1980s and now something of a cult classic with Camp effects. *Sleepaway Camp* tells the story of Angela, who won't go swimming or shower in front of other girls because (spoiler alert) she has a penis. Such is revealed late in the film, for maximum shock effect, as is Angela's identity as the perpetrator of a series of camp murders. McGee argues that the film certainly invites transphobic responses, but also exposes and deconstructs anxieties about the gendered body. In his view, the film is more concerned with "the horror of the male gaze" than with transgender possibility.

Kyle Eveleth examines another potent if more joyful reworking of camp narrative: Miss Quinzella Thiskwin Penniquiquill Thistle Crumpet's Camp for ~~Girls~~ Hardcore Lady Types, the setting for the wildly popular *Lumberjanes* comic series. A direct affront to the traditional scouting novel's sexism, racism, and imperialism, *Lumberjanes* features an array of racially diverse, queer protagonists who confront a range of Camped-up villains, including "supernatural foxes, eagles, sea-monsters, and possessed Scouting Lads." *Lumberjanes*'s campy hyperbole, Eveleth contends, serves to expose the artifice of camp culture and "begin deconstructing it as a farce." What distinguishes *Lumberjanes* from other ironic camp productions, Eveleth argues, is its ability to balance critique with a celebration of all things camp.

Building on their earlier collaborative work on Camp aesthetics and children's culture, Kerry Mallan and Roderick McGillis claim much the same for Wes Anderson's critically acclaimed 2012 film *Moonrise Kingdom*, which beautifully integrates camp and Camp. Set in 1965, on the fictional

New England island of New Penzance (itself a kind of camp environment), *Moonrise Kingdom* chronicles the romance between an eccentric and unhappy "Khaki Scout" named Sam and an equally eccentric and unhappy girl named Suzy. The two run away, cutting their own path across the island. The other Scouts—not fond of Sam—leap into pursuit, along with Suzy's parents, a wayward sheriff, and other singular characters. The escape is temporary but blissful; Sam and Suzy swim, kiss, and dance in their underwear, vowing eternal love and creating their own queer space and time. The Scouts close in, and Sam is nearly turned over to child protective services (he is an orphan), but meanwhile a northeaster blows in, threatening to level the island and its campers. Anderson turns Scouting into "something of a drag show," note Mallan and McGillis, Camping it up through nostalgic evocations of image and sound. At times quiet and dreamy, at times over the top, *Moonrise Kingdom* "makes the familiar look different, and opens the possibility of arriving at a better place," hold the authors.

As we've acknowledged, summer camp, for all its positives, is notoriously appropriative of Indigenous life, part of a broader apparatus of assimilation, whitewashing, and genocide. That's true of the camps both Kenneth and Derritt attended, and as Musinsky indicates in her chapter, the progressive camp Indian Brook has worked to confront its name, which references and elides the Indigenous peoples on whose land the camp sits. Deloria offers a comprehensive account of the consequences of "playing Indian," and Paris, Van Slyck, and Wall also address the issue in their respective studies of summer camp. In our final contribution to the volume, Joshua Whitehead tackles camp's colonial legacy vis-à-vis a trend he notices in some young adult literature: The "green space" of camp often operates as an "Indigiqueer idyll" that bolsters the queer transformations of white settler protagonists. Whitehead weaves together queer theory, the work of Indigenous scholars Gerald Vizenor and Qwo-Li Driskill, and young adult novels by John Donovan and Emily Danforth to ask, "what if Indigiqueerness were to reclaim the camp, to reterritorialize it?" Going beyond critique, Whitehead draws on Lee Edelman's *No Future* to offer a theory of "Indiginegativity": a performative self-annihilation that embraces the Campy ferality of summer camp's "Indian" to engage in aesthetic acts of decolonization. Typically a site of Indigenous erasure, camp for Whitehead becomes a space for enacting Two-Spirit survivance.

Many of our contributors are queer-identified, and speak about their own queer relations with camp and Camp both—and of course, we developed *Queer as Camp* out of our own such investments. But camp is not necessarily a queer time or place, we know. And queer experiences at camp—or camp's queer structures—don't always produce queer-identified people. Like school and other social institutions, camp is a many-splendored thing, with unexpected qualities and trajectories. It is easier to describe as what it is not: home, school, regular life. Camp offers some relief from those things, and *potentially* helps us envision non-normative options for life and love, sometimes in a Campy manner. This volume points to some of the queer histories and textures of camp with Camp. That said, we've only scratched the surface, and we hope you will undertake your own camp/Camp adventures.

See you next summer!

NOTES

1. DM: When I think back on my first few years at camp, I relate so thoroughly to this passage from Wall's book that I'm quoting it in full here: ". . . incompetence with camp skills could create awkward, humiliating, and even devastating experiences. For boys not fond of physical activity or simply more interested in other things, the all-male and physically demanding experience of camp may have felt more like an ordeal to be endured than a manly adventure to be anticipated. For the skinny boy who dreaded the drudgery of the canoe trip, the bed-wetter forced to share a cabin with five or six others, or the homesick camper who simply missed the familiarity of family, parts of camp life could be experienced as sheer misery" (211).

2. See especially Scott Herring's contribution to the 2016 cluster on Camp Modernism in *Modernism/modernity*.

3. In *Camp*, Mark Booth locates a French usage in the 1863 *Capitaine Fracasse*, by Théophile Gautier.

4. For more information on the camping movement, see Macleod, Chapter 13, and Eleanor Eells, *History of Organized Camping: The First 100 Years*.

5. Putnam Camp, founded by Henry Bowditch, William James, and Charles and James Putnam, famously hosted Jung, Ferenzci, and Freud in their 1909 visit to the United States.

6. "For Butler," writes Bergman, "the hyperbolic, parodic, anarchic, redundant style of camp is the very way to bring heterosexist attitudes of 'originality,' 'naturalism,' and 'normality' to their knees" (11).

7. Cleto himself calls camp "queer discursive architecture" (35), as justified by the camp's "politics of deterritorialisation, recontextualisation, and stratification" (31).

8. In a 2014 *New York Times Magazine* essay entitled "The Death of Adulthood in American Culture," film critic A. O. Scott remarks that we can

now conceive of adulthood "as the state of being forever young. . . . Grown people feel no compulsion to put away childish things: We can live with our parents, go to summer camp, play dodgeball, collect dolls and action figures and watch cartoons to our hearts' content." Scott implies that "adult camp" is one indication and consequence of contemporary shifts in the construction of age.

Notes Home from Camp, by Susan Sontag

Daniel Mallory Ortberg

Dear Mother, and to a lesser extent Father,

Many things in the world have not been named; and many things, even if they have been named, have never been described. One of these is the sensibility—unmistakably modern, a variant of sophistication but hardly identical with it—that goes by the name of Camp Kenwood at Winnipesaukee.

To snare a sensibility in words, especially one that is alive and powerful and swarming with first-summer city kids, one must be tentative and nimble. The form of jottings, rather than an essay (with its claim to a linear, consecutive argument), seemed more appropriate for getting down something of this particular fugitive sensibility. It's embarrassing to be solemn and treatise-like about Camp Kenwood. How can a piece of writing capture the spirit of summer camp? How can, to put it in terms you will understand, an *indoor kid* write about the most wholly outdoors of activities, namely Camp?

Camp taste is, above all, a mode of enjoyment, of appreciation—not judgment. Camp is generous. It wants to enjoy. There is pudding with almost every meal (rice pudding at breakfast). We are not permitted to leave the table without cleaning our pudding cups and singing our respective cabin's anthem with the greatest show of enthusiasm one can muster at six-thirty AM in New Hampshire. It only seems like malice, cynicism. (Or, if it is cynicism, it's not a ruthless but a sweet cynicism.) Mother, I have been changing my socks nightly, I can assure you. Camp taste doesn't propose that it is in bad taste to be serious; it doesn't sneer at someone who succeeds in being seriously dramatic. What it does is to find the success in certain passionate failures. This is why I refuse to consider my one-woman performance of *Death Comes for the Archbishop* at last Friday night's talent show a failure—I was able to wrest a certain sweet dignity from it, and in that sense I was a success.

Camp taste is a kind of love, love for human nature. It relishes, rather than judges, the little triumphs and awkward intensities of "character." I am making friends here, and no longer wish to come home; several of the girls in Bunk Seven have tastes and interests not altogether foreign to my own. They understand the polyphonic voice and are not altogether lost to my theories on Heidegger. Camp taste identifies with what it is enjoying. People who share this sensibility are not laughing at the thing they label as "a camp," they're enjoying it. Camp is a tender feeling. In this respect it is altogether unlike P.S. 119. My camp friends tell me they will write to me during the school year. I wonder.

The way we live now is as follows: reveille at six, breakfast at six-fifteen, morning activity time from seven to nine-thirty, free swim from nine-thirty to ten, bunk inspection from ten to ten-thirty, free play from ten-thirty to noon, lunch at noon, ropes course or guided hikes at one, quiet time from three to four, arts and crafts hour until five ("One should either *be* a work of art, or *wear* a work of art," Mr. Kittridge, the craft director, is fond of reminding us), dinner at five-thirty, evening entertainment (skits, singalongs, etcetera) from six-thirty 'til eight, lights out at nine-thirty.

Not only is there a Camp vision, a Camp way of looking at things; Camp is as well a quality discoverable in objects and the behavior of persons. There are Camp and Non-Camp ways of behaving. Crying over a letter from home is distinctly Non-Camp. Sharing any baked goods found in a care package is Camp. Jumping the Bridge portion of the ropes course without a harness is Camp. Not having a date to the talent show is Non-Camp. There are "campy" movies, clothes (thank you for sending me another pair of denim shorts; my usual severe all-black ensemble has served only to make me an object of fun and I have not had occasion to wear my cape even once), furniture, popular songs (have you heard the one about the little lady from Nantucket?), novels, people, buildings (particularly the Game Equipment Hut). . . . This distinction is important. True, the Camp eye has the power to transform experience. But not everything can be seen as Camp. My bunkmate Rachel, for example. She is hopeless, and I hate her. I wish very much I were bunkmates with Denise, who brought seven different colors of lip gloss with her and is the most popular girl in the cabin.

Random examples of items which are part of the canon of Camp:

Amateur astronomy

Having a crush on Terrance, the *goyishe* swimming instructor

Cutting out the sides of your camp t-shirt and then tying up the cut ends into little ribbons such that part of your midsection is visible to the naked eye

Athletic socks (no frills)

Getting a sunburn on your first day

Capture the Flag (the actual capturing of the flag is of little importance)

Bellini's operas

Visconti's direction of *Salome* and *'Tis Pity She's a Whore*

The old Flash Gordon comics

Running out of batteries for your flashlight because you stayed up so late talking to the other girls after Counselor Debbie snuck out to visit her boyfriend across the lake

Swan Lake

I have no pictures to send you. Using a camera appeases the anxiety that the work-driven feel about not working when they are on vacation and supposed to be having fun. They have something to do that is like a friendly imitation of work: They can take pictures. You will have to take me at my word when I say I am getting plenty of sun and fresh air and have successfully completed the swim test.

I have not yet jumped off onto the Blob. I have yet to see a convincing argument for making the leap. Time, that old tattle-tale, will tell.

Best,
Your daughter, Susan Sontag

P.S. The end-of-summer bus arrives at the station at 7 PM next Tuesday night. Please don't embarrass me in front of my friends.

PART I

Camp Sites

"The most curious" of all "queer societies"?

Sexuality and Gender in British Woodcraft Camps, 1916–2016

Annebella Pollen

In the years during and after the Great War, disaffected with the apparent militarism and imperialism of Boy Scouts, British pacifists established rival outdoor youth organizations. These new organizations returned to some of the founding ideas of Scouting in the form of the "woodcraft" system of outdoor education pioneered at the turn of the twentieth century by Ernest Thompson Seton and latterly absorbed into Baden-Powell's organization. To these ideas each of the new organizations—the Order of Woodcraft Chivalry, the Kindred of the Kibbo Kift, and Woodcraft Folk—added their own distinctive philosophies, drawing on psychology, spirituality, art, and politics, to provide idiosyncratic camping experiences across genders and ages. Camp in this context was more than leisure, and more than an escape from encroaching industrialization—it was a personally and socially trans-formative space, rich with utopian possibility.

The British woodcraft movement's subversions represent a distinctive and elaborate queering of the Boy Scout ideal. Through their futurist visions and revivalist performances, members acted out their radical ideals for a hybrid new/old world. Alongside these activities, each group devel-oped detailed and sometimes unorthodox ideas about "sex instruction" and "sex equality" interlinked with complex theories of camping. As such, new ideas about social relationships ran through woodcraft organizations' vision and were played out under canvas. In the temporary worlds of primitivist camps in the heady period of change after the Great War, alternatives to so-called civilized life could be tried on for size. Gender and sexuality became prime sites where the limits of experimental practices were tested and contested, and aspects of these challenges continue in the organizations' twenty-first-century manifestations.

Through an investigation of woodcraft theories and practices, this essay examines the movement as a case study of oppositional ideals in the interwar period, when camping and experiments in living intertwined. While woodcraft organizations in Britain have always been much smaller in scale than numbers of Scouts and Guides, and their founding ideas were far from mainstream, their position as aspiring cultural revolutionaries meant that they inhabited a space—literally and figuratively—as outsiders. This essay presents views from the three most prominent woodcraft organizations, each founded during or shortly after the Great War. The Order of Woodcraft Chivalry was the first pacifist coeducational breakaway from Scouts. Founded in 1916, it was at its most productive in the 1920s and 1930s with public projects including the progressive Forest School for children and Grith Fyrd craft training camp for unemployed men. The organization recently celebrated its centenary; it is now a very small cluster of descendants of early members. The flamboyant, artistic Kindred of the Kibbo Kift was established as an all-ages, mixed-gender alternative to Scouts in 1920 but only lasted just over a decade as a woodcraft organization before being radically remodeled into an economic campaign group (The Green Shirts) and latterly a short-lived political party (The Social Credit Party of Great Britain and Ireland). Finally, Woodcraft Folk was founded in 1925 following a schism in Kibbo Kift over political direction; it continues to thrive as an outdoor-focused and democratic organization with around 15,000 adult and child members in groups spread across the United Kingdom.

Camping as an Oppositional Practice

Camping may seem to be an innocuous leisure activity, merely providing a low-budget holiday; as such, it could be of little social or political consequence. Yet camping has also been described as essentially socialist in character. In G. A. Cohen's analysis, as a system based on collective property and mutual giving, camping demonstrates in miniature "that society-wide socialism is equally feasible and equally desirable" (11). Camps are clearly diverse in their organization and ideologies, but they have nevertheless been characterized as extraordinary and exceptional places; as philosopher Giorgio Agamben has put it, the camp is "a piece of land placed outside the normal juridical order" (1). For their capacity to stand outside conventional social structures, camps have become utilized for protest and as sites where the building blocks of society can be symbolically deconstructed and remade. Angela Feigenbaum, Fabian Frenzel, and Patrick McCurdy, for example, have argued that the collective nature of camps has been particularly effective in forging "communities of understanding." In their conception, camp is a "unique structural, spatial and temporal form that shapes those who live, work, play and create within it" (8). A further essential aspect of camp—its transitory nature—necessarily results in a shift in everyday practices. To use the anarchist Hakim Bey's terminology, camps encapsulate a "temporary autonomous zone" where intentional communities can form "pirate utopias." The temporary nature of camping allows for the suspension of norms and the trying on of new worlds for size. As camping historian Matthew de Abaitua writes, "Camping promises nothing permanent. It is a way of trafficking between what was and what could yet be" (60).

The romantic promise of camping has long held an allure for reformers at odds with the modern world. Since the writings of Henry David Thoreau in the mid-nineteenth century, a substantial body of literature has been produced in Britain and America espousing the ostensibly moral value of withdrawing from urban life with only the most basic means of survival on hand. Full of motifs of savages, Indians, gypsies and the like, such discourse contains much that can be critiqued as privileged colonial fantasy, but the experience of going back to the land clearly had (and has) anti-establishment potential. The "pastoral impulse," as Jan Marsh has described it, was particularly prevalent from the 1880s in Britain among socialist campaigners, who saw the countryside disappearing from view and reconfigured it as an idea. "Country" became an oppositional and idealized space in positive relationship to the rapidly expanding, polluted, and industrialized city (Williams). For those late-Victorian reformers who campaigned for all-round social improvement, new enthusiasms for cycling, hiking, and camping were part of a broader urge for the simplification of life. Campaigns for fresh air and radiant health were a core part of these left-wing desires, which aimed to reform all aspects of life, from new ways of eating and dressing to new forms of social relationships.

Key proponents of these lifestyles, which espoused anti-industrial and alternative causes from vegetarianism and self-sufficiency in food production to the revival of handicrafts, included John Ruskin, William Morris, and Edward Carpenter. Carpenter, in particular, offers a bridge between the late nineteenth-century practices and their manifestation among alternative youth organizations in the 1920s. Carpenter's writings were wide and included transcendental poetry, tracts denouncing industrial civilization as a social ill, and those promoting a wide variety of loving relationships, including same-sex, unconstrained by convention (Rowbotham). For his pioneering ideas and lifestyle—he maintained an openly gay relationship with his working-class lover, George Merrill, at their smallholding in the north of England—Carpenter became something of a guru among the socialists and feminists who were challenging convention across a range of causes, in particular in relation to the emerging discipline of sexology.

In the early decades of the twentieth century, Carpenter and his friend and colleague, the physician Havelock Ellis, became figureheads for the emergent "sexual science" informed by new psychological studies, which aimed to take seriously a wide range of sexual experiences and to develop a new vocabulary for their understanding. In the context of highly charged anxieties about "degeneration" and "deviance," prostitution and venereal disease, the radical position of sex reformers on abortion, divorce, and same-sex relationships remained far from mainstream. As Alison Oram notes, interest in sexology in the years up to the Great War was not respectable and was largely confined to intellectual elites and "radical fringe groups" (219). In this context, it is clear to see that woodcraft organizations, especially in relation to their role with children, were unusual in having frank "sex-instruction" built into their educational programs.

The extent to which these practices can be described as a form of queering depends on one's understanding of the term. As an expansive definition, David Halperin has argued that queer is "whatever is at odds with the normal, the legitimate, the dominant" (62). As I will argue, while British woodcraft organizations may not have been exclusively concerned with sexual behavior, let alone what might be understood as queer sexual behavior, their activities nonetheless challenged conventional approaches to sexuality as part of their broader challenge to social norms. In thinking of woodcraft organizations as queer, I draw on Matt Houlbrook's argument that "thinking queer" is a historical methodology. As such, it moves away from simply seeking to restore an LGBT history; instead, it performs the work of critical history in disturbing categories. Houlbrook applies this method to interwar Britain, a period that he characterizes as one of "massive social, economic, cultural and political upheaval" (135), when emergent attempts to characterize and pathologize sexual orientations, roles, and practices were particularly insecure. The examples that Houlbrook examines are, like woodcraft organizations, studies of transgressive behavior that resist cultural convention. He persuasively argues, "thinking queer is too useful to be confined to the study of the queer" (136).

Sex and Gender in Woodcraft Organizations in the Interwar Period

I. O. Evans, a former Scout and subsequently an enthusiastic member of several woodcraft organizations, compiled a book of the philosophies and practices of the British woodcraft movement in 1930, which included a chapter outlining woodcraft approaches to sex. Evans summarized that, until recent years, youths had only "ignorant filthy gossip" for guidance, leaving them "to blunder experimentally amidst the most frightful perils." He added, happily, that this period was on its way out, and noted, significantly, that "its passing synchronizes with the rise of Woodcraft" (177). To Evans, woodcraft organizations were at the fore of open-mindedness. Sex education in organizations such as the Order of Woodcraft Chivalry and Kibbo Kift was "very thorough-going." By contrast, he noted Baden-Powell's alarmist attitude to "self-abuse" and how Scouts' "reactionary" attitudes to gender segregation were shared by the Guides. Both organizations held that gender mixing was "most undesirable" and that gender separation should be "strictly enforced" (178).

Woodcraft organizations formed in opposition to Scouts put mixed-gender camping at the heart of their project. Reassuring those who feared a loosening of morals as a result of intermingling, Evans noted, "the standard of behaviour in coeducational Woodcraft groups is remarkably high" (185). Any who engaged in sexual misconduct, Evans believed, would surely be expelled. He also noted, amusingly, that mixed camping is hardly "sexually exciting" (180). Should "morbid sex-cravings" emerge, the best solution, he proposed, is "an honourable love affair." He even went so far as to suggest that a socially concerned and morally keen woodcrafter would make a more "devoted lover" (181).

In this, Evans was not advocating sex before marriage; that would be beyond the pale in organizations that courted, at least some of the time, public respectability. In Evans's summaries, conventional approaches to marriage and parenthood were enshrined in woodcrafters' eugenically informed attitudes to the development of the human race (in this context meaning the positive development of healthy bodies across generations rather than sterilization of the so-called "unfit"). For all of their relatively open-minded approaches to sex education and gender equality, Evans nonetheless expected woodcraft relationships to be "innocent" and chaste. Perhaps playfully, he concluded that it was possible for "the two sexes" to "camp in adjacent tents as safe from improper behaviour as though encased in iron armour and chained to the ground, they dwelt behind walls and locked doors in camps miles apart from one another and with an angel with a flaming sword standing between" (186). Despite Evans's idealistic overview, sex education, gender segregation, and gender roles played out rather differently on the ground and under canvas in woodcraft organizations.

The Order of Woodcraft Chivalry

The Order of Woodcraft Chivalry was founded in 1916 by British Quakers. Ernest Westlake, an amateur geologist, and his son, Aubrey, a doctor and conscientious objector who had run Scout groups as a form of public war service, combined their shared interests in nature, progressive education, and classical poetry into an organization that they felt offered a more imaginative and less militaristic camp experience (Edgell). They did this by returning to the ideas of Ernest Thompson Seton, a British-born, American-resident youth leader whose turn-of-the-century Woodcraft Indians scheme had inspired Baden-Powell. The Order adapted elements from Seton to create a system that took the English knight rather than the Native American as its mythic ideal, and which included adults as well as children, and girls as well as boys. Based from 1920 at Sandy Balls, their private campground on the edge of the New Forest, the group's colorful, ceremonial camp practices attracted thousands of members in the interwar years.

The group was committed to outdoor life, a belief in the capacity of children to self-govern, and a biologically inspired developmental model of recapitulation, popularized by child psychologist G. Stanley Hall. This scheme—shared in the 1920s by all woodcraft organizations—proposed that children should perform, or recapitulate, all successive stages of cultural evolution, from the undeveloped "primitive" to a "civilised" maturity. Order members developed distinctive schemes for the theory's application, both in the progressive schools that were organized along woodcraft lines, and in their extensive literature. This was informed by intellectual inspirations from the "New Psychology" of Freud and Jung to Quakerism, the mystic science of Neo-Vitalism, classical myths, symbolism, and poetry. The Order believed that profound social, cultural and spiritual change was needed to correct the multiple ills of war-torn society. Militarism, materialism, and mass pleasures were destabilizing modern life and only a return to the best of the past could consolidate the new future they intended to shape. To this end, the Order designed folk-revival dress, regalia, and language to be used in group ceremonies and camps. These were structured not just to provide social gatherings but to model a new way of life.

As with all woodcraft organizations, camping was an essential transformational activity. Ernest Westlake argued that "civilisation"—modern, urban life—had made daily experience too comfortable (Edgell 72). Camping was a practical and moral re-education in simplicity and hardihood. Significantly, it was far from the corruption of the city, characterized as the root of all evil. Camping was also particularly important for young people. Order member Dorothy Revel argued, for example, "Motor cars, telephones, wireless sets, central heating, and other expensive adult luxuries are absolutely out of their place for children." She argued, "They need to know the basic necessities of life [. . .]. They want earth-contact" (*Woodcraft Discipline* 14–15). A 1928 Order publication argued that camping was a symbolic ritual through which utopian ideals could be realized. Its author, Dr. H. D. Jennings White, noted, "I am a member of the Order of Woodcraft Chivalry because I see in it the germs of an organisation for the conscious creation of superhumanity" (13). This vision was a moral, physical, and spiritual rebirth; nothing less than "the creation of a new race of men here on earth, with the light of science in their eyes; with the love of beauty in their hearts; with order, control, and foresight in their actions; with a vitality and health in their bodies which we have never felt and can but dimly imagine; and with a spirit more tolerant, more daring, and more gracious than we shall ever have" (13).

Alongside its extensive writings on camping, the Order explored personal development. The membership was well-disposed to examine such issues as it boasted psychiatrists, medical practitioners, and radical educators among its leading figures. How these ideologies might be combined with children's activities was hotly debated, particularly among more conservative members who saw the Order as a wholesome outdoor venture to implement new practical educational ideals, and the progressives who saw the Order as a crucible for radical life experiments. These debates crystallized around theories of nudism, sex reform, and sex education for children.

The first controversy focused on Harry "Dion" Byngham, a natural health journalist and mystic disciple of Blake, Whitman, and Nietzsche. Like many in the early days of the Order, Byngham was excited by the myths of the Ancient Greek Bacchae, whose ecstatic revels, he felt, offered a template for living a joyous life close to the earth. The Order's visual symbol was the Bacchae's Thyrsus, a phallic ivy-wreathed wand topped with a pine cone. Byngham's application of Dionysian ideas challenged the organization's attempts at respectability. For example, his advocacy of gymnosophy, or social nudism, resulted in risqué articles and naked photography of Byngham and his girlfriend as pan pipe-playing nymphs in the pages of *The Pine Cone*, the official Order journal. Byngham's cohabitation before marriage was also a source of consternation. His last hurrah involved dancing naked with his lover as the embodiment of ecstasy in front of representatives of the national press. For this flagrant challenge to sexual propriety, Byngham was ultimately expelled (Edgell).

Another prominent and controversial member was the aforementioned Jennings White, a psychologist and one of several Order members of the British Society for the Study of Sex Psychology. Historian Lesley Hall has explored the function and membership of this eccentric group, established in 1914, who challenged received wisdom on homosexuality, obscenity, divorce, abortion, and birth control. She notes that members included clergymen, anthropologists, psychiatrists, progressive educationalists, nudists, and the occasional lecher (78). Jennings White attempted to apply a program of radical sexual reform within the Order, including trial, open, and even promiscuous group marriages. While these ideas were warmly received by only a few—and were viewed with utter horror by Christians and Quakers—they expressed his broader hope that the Order would form the basis for a new social utopia.

Theodore Faithfull was another sexologist member of the Order. Formerly a veterinary surgeon, Faithful shifted his sights post-war to psychology and established an independent experimental woodcraft school in Norfolk from 1920. Under his headship, with Revel on his staff, Priory Gate developed innovative and sometimes controversial methods. A hardy, primitive outdoor experience was at the heart of the provision, including, in addition to camping, naked exercise, extensive hikes, and the hand-making of many items by the children, such as their own clothes. Some aspects of the curriculum were highly controversial in their own time, including the use of children as naked models in school drawing classes; indeed, some remain outside current orthodoxy. Faithfull penned a series of radical psychological publications in the interwar years, including *Bisexuality: An Essay on Extraversion and Introversion*. Here bisexuality was understood as the psychological coexistence of essentialist masculine and feminine characteristics within all persons rather than sexual attraction to men and women. In this and his other works, Faithfull detailed his woodcraft experiments and argued that gender mixing and outdoor living in the Order positioned child members as the bisexual "vanguard."

Faithfull encouraged nudity as a means of fostering pride in the body and satisfying natural curiosity. Nudity for sunbathing and swimming was part of the simplification of life and the harmony with nature that underpinned woodcraft philosophies, but in the hands of members with interests in Freudian psychology, it also prevented repressive tendencies in children, which were believed to lead to morbid desires, blocked energy, and arrested development. Revel argued that these issues could also be avoided by adult nudity; she stated, "it should be possible to all who are not suffering from repressions to bathe in water or take sun baths together naked without experiencing any emotion, pleasant or unpleasant, due to nakedness" (*Cheiron's Cave* 74). Revel argued for frank sex education in her books, *Cheiron's Cave: The School of the Future* (1928) and *Tented Schools: Camping as a Technique of Education* (1934). She argued, "The whole subject needs to be treated naturally and in the daylight. The parents should be able to speak plainly. If they show they have not recovered from the prudery in which most of the present adult generation was reared, the child will inevitably copy their attitude" (*Cheiron's Cave* 132).

Like Baden-Powell, Revel had outspoken views on children's masturbation. Historian Sam Pryke has characterized the discussion of masturbation as "something of an obsession" (17) in early Scouts; advice given on the subject was strident and regular. Founding publications claimed that the practice would lead to lunacy. Although this approach was moderated by the 1920s, masturbation was still considered to be a problem to be solved. Revel, as a woodcrafter, took a more liberal perspective, noting the damage done in claiming the practice to be a sin, but she still sought to eliminate the habit. She argued that it resulted from fundamental unhappiness and that the root of the dissatisfaction—of which masturbation was merely the symptom—should be pursued.

The subject was dealt with comprehensively in 1930, when the Order undertook a study of their experiential philosophy of "learning by doing" on the education of children, producing an internal report examining how the principle could be applied to practical and moral contexts, from the experience of travel to the condition of poverty. Among the experiential areas discussed was that of sex. The report offered a plain-spoken assessment of the child's interest in sex at various developmental stages, and argued for the normalization of masturbation. It stated, "after puberty masturbation may be described as a dirty and babyish habit"; nonetheless, it is "practised by many who cannot be classed as abnormal in any way either physically or mentally." The report also included a draft Order policy to promote "greater freedom in sexual behaviour," with the declaration that "Sex is the greatest expression of our unity with one another and with all life, and it cannot be neglected with impunity." Proposals were floated for companionate marriage, cheap and easy divorce, the eradication of stigma around illegitimacy, widespread information about contraception, and the "advocacy of nakedness as far as appropriate and practical." With the exception of the last point, rooted in its own time and place, each recommendation sounds eminently sensible around ninety years later. Such advanced thinking, however, was quickly moderated by other editorial hands. A second version reinserted monogamous marriage and suggested that contraception should be avoided until after the birth of preferably two children, due to the unhappiness and sterility that would surely result. The final word was that "Low-grade sex morality is anti-social and wholly inconsistent with the Order's ideal of Chivalry" ("Order of Woodcraft Chivalry").

Within the Order, then, a range of experimental sexual propositions were mooted. Some were outlandish and remain unconventional today, yet many sound reasonable to the twenty-first-century liberal ear. Even within the experimental and temporary worlds constructed in 1920s camps, however, concerns over reputation and respectability challenged the application of new ideas. When Revel married fellow Order member Norman Glaister, another radical psychiatrist and sexologist, in a "troth-plighting" ritual, for example, they wrote their own mystic vows and wore rustic homemade tunics and flowers in their hair. They even cut their wedding cake with a woodcraft axe. These were symbolic gestures of resistance, however, as the Order had collectively agreed that the marriage must be legally consecrated before the ceremony could take place. Order camps offered a place where challenging new ideas about sex and relationships could be entertained, but these were contained within the limits of convention whenever the play turned serious or threatened to leave the boundaries of the site.

The Kindred of the Kibbo Kift

Among the Order's early advisors was John Hargrave, a precocious young Scout leader and author and illustrator of popular books and articles on woodcraft technique. Hargrave, also of Quaker descent, had joined the Boy Scouts shortly after its inception as a teenager and had risen to Staff Artist by 1914. In 1916, after two years' service as a stretcher-bearer, Hargrave was appointed Commissioner for Woodcraft and Camping. His war experiences, however, ruptured his faith in the movement and he used his senior position to corral support for a splinter section who valued the backwoodsmanship and ceremony of Scouting but deplored its militarism. By 1919, with the publication of his anti-establishment tract, *The Great War Brings It Home*, Hargrave's oppositional position was sealed, and he was ultimately expelled. As had surely been his plan, he took many disaffected Scout supporters with him. In 1920, he created the Kindred of the Kibbo Kift (see Figure 1).

Hargrave's new organization—whose name was an archaic English colloquialism meaning "proof of strength" and had nothing to do with the white supremacist group with which it unfortunately shares its initials—proposed a program that went far beyond Scouts' improving leisure (Pollen). Kinsfolk—as members were known—committed themselves to world peace, world government and the reorganization of industry, education, and the economy. Hargrave was a highly charismatic figure with an immense capacity for self-promotion. As well as being a talented writer and artist, his employment in advertising gave him extensive knowledge of propaganda and persuasion. Through these skills he was able to attract the endorsement of high-profile thinkers, including sexologist Ellis, biologists

Figure 1. Kibbo Kift boys and men In the Touching of the Totems rite, 1925. (© Kibbo Kift Foundation. Courtesy of the London School of Economics Library.)

Julian Huxley and J. Arthur Thompson, and novelist H. G. Wells. Each
was concerned with the need for physical, social, and cultural renaissance
post-war. As such, Kibbo Kift's political reconstruction, combined with
all-ages activities in camping, hiking, and handicraft, presented an endeavor
worthy of support.

A core Kibbo Kift ambition was the development of physical, mental,
and spiritual health; that commitment was underpinned by faith in eugenic
improvement. Members were expected to better themselves through exercise and hardihood, and make informed decisions about pairing up. The
organization was open to men and women—indeed, this coeducational
aspect was one of the principal points of attraction for its substantial suf-
fragette membership—and the establishing of Kibbo Kift marriages and
families was encouraged. The children of the organization, it was expected,
would carry Kin philosophies forward and ultimately lead a new Kibbo
Kift world. As part of their drive to reform all aspects of life, books by
sexologists, including Edward Carpenter, were featured on recommended
reading lists.

Kibbo Kift's combination of the forward- and backward-looking is a key
characteristic, and one that can be seen in all aspects of the group's style and
ethos. Primitivist outdoor practices stood side-by-side along with cutting-
edge ideas about birth-control and technology. Camping enabled people to
develop valuable survival skills that would be needed after the expected
collapse of civilization; more fundamentally, it tapped into something
essential and authentic. As Hargrave put it, "In camp all affectations, fads,
and civilised veneers drop away and reveal us exactly as we are" (*Confession*
91). He continued, "It is a necessary break-away, a ritualistic exodus, from
Metropolitan standards of civilisation, from pavements, sky-signs, shops,
noise, glitter, smoke. It is a vital urge" (93).

Despite camp offering a radical crucible for social transformation,
some aspects of the existing order penetrated Kibbo Kift practices. One
of these was Kibbo Kift's organizational method. Despite its original
appeal to socialists, Hargrave had a powerful personal need to remain the
unchallenged head of his organization, and he justified his dictatorial
position through recourse to emergent political ideas about the ineffec-
tiveness of democracy. Similarly, despite the commitment of the organization to tear down "taboos" and to be at the forefront of coeducation,
Kibbo Kift was strongly conventional on matters of gender and sexuality.
It had a membership equally split in numbers between women and men,
yet few women held positions of authority. Unlike the Order of Woodcraft

Chivalry, who explicitly described themselves as feminist, Hargrave saw the women's movement as a failure, arguing that the shift in sex roles "leads to an intermediate position which tends more and more to make both sexes atonic and devitalised, to their everlasting misery." In contradistinction, noting that "this sometimes astonishes," he asserted, "The main directive force of The Kindred is in the hands of the males" (*Confession* 85).

One area in which Kinsfolk aimed to cut a swath through "taboos" was in sex education. Hargrave's pre–Kibbo Kift publications took a Scout-like tone on matters of "continence" (masturbation). He believed that boys raised on "open-air woodcraft methods" (*Great War* 323) would not be overwhelmed by sexual desire in adolescence. Woodcrafters' experience of nakedness in camp, their proximity to reproduction and fertilization in nature, and their understanding of "totems and taboos" learned through primitivist play were expected to stand them in good stead. Hargrave felt "instincts" had become confused as a result of urban sophistication, and he urged a return to more "natural," "primitive" approaches to love than simpering and giggling courtship on "motor-buses and tube stations" (*Great War* 323). Despite his calls to transform sexual relationships, Hargrave also proclaimed, "The Kindred is strongly hetero-sexual and dislikes any blurring of the edges of the male and female qualities. It has no place whatsoever for the masculine type of woman or the effeminate type of man" (*Confession* 84).

Other Kibbo Kift members also had frank opinions on matters of sex. Arthur B. Allen, the leader of the Kibbo Kift teachers' group, trialed a Kin policy for "sex-instruction" in classrooms. He described, "No Kin Teacher will stand up in front of a class with 'And now children, I am going to tell you where you come from when you are born.'" He argued, "To do so is to put the Kindred on a level with all the other woollies who succeed in making the child conscious of his own penis and then leave him in a worse mess than before." Instead, Allen proposed that "honesty towards the child is the Kin policy. When a child asks, 'Where do kittens come from?', tell him" (173). Allen noted two dangerous forces in contemporary society. One was the "sex hysteria" of Mrs. Grundy (a figurative term connoting an upholder of prudish convention), and the other was "sex-rot" (including voyeurism in racy theatre shows, male same-sex relations, rape in marriage, and pedophilia). Kinsfolk needed to battle both. As a reward for speaking so frankly about sex, he warned, "We shall be attacked, sullied, libelled, dishonoured. We shall be accused of immorality, of free love, of license.

Our camps will be called brothels and our women whores." He continued, "But we know that it is not so. Our conduct will have to be our weapon and it must never falter. No shadow of a shadow must fall across the path of a single Kinsman, no moral aberration must be permitted in any one of our lives" (176).

While official documentation regularly celebrated Kin marriages and the birth of Kin children, other kinds of relationships were inevitable. In one notable case, a young Kinsman, Angus McBean, a shop assistant and an aspiring theatre designer and photographer, tested the limits of Kin morality. McBean would become one of the most celebrated photographers of the British stage in the mid-twentieth century, a lover of many men on London's queer scene—including Quentin Crisp—and would be imprisoned with hard labor for same-sex relationships in pre-liberation times. His first homosexual experience, however, was in Kibbo Kift, with an older and more sexually experienced man who moved in similar naturist, social reform, and mystic circles. Roland Berrill and McBean—who was, at the time, in an unconsummated heterosexual marriage—understandably conducted their relationship out of view, given the condemnations of homosexuality in official Kin discourse. Later in life, McBean noted that when he revealed his orientation to Hargrave, the leader "didn't seem at all surprised" (Woodhouse 52). Indeed, McBean's experimental approach to sexual identity and queer desire is writ large in his photographs, where he styled images of Kinsmen in theatrical costumes cut away to reveal exposed buttocks, in ritualistic naked poses on sacred sites, and in meditation on the chalk phallus of the Cerne Abbas giant (see Figure 2). In his own Kibbo Kift appearances, he experimented with the minimum of clothing, flamboyant dress, and full make-up (see Figure 3).

Kibbo Kift inhabited a curious position in relation to convention. On the one hand, it was radical in its philosophy and appearance. Its aesthetic style drew on the artistic avant-garde, and Hargrave and his followers saw themselves as "intellectual barbarians" opposed to the "mass-mind." Yet they mostly stood apart, in income, education, and connections, from cultural elites and could be scornful of "overcivilised," "refined," and Bohemian people. As such, members' moral and political compasses were not always easy to predict. The organization attracted suffragettes but had aspects that were anti-feminist; it challenged taboos about sex education while reinforcing popular myths about sexual behavior; it planned to revolutionize all aspects of political and cultural structures while maintaining conservative personal relationships.

Figure 2. Naked kinsman on Silbury Hill (Wessex Pilgrimage), 1929. (Photograph by Angus McBean. © Kibbo Kift Foundation. Courtesy of Donlon Books.)

Figure 3. Angus McBean applying Holy Fool stage makeup in camp, c.1929. (© Kibbo Kift foundation. Courtesy of London School of Economics Library.)

Woodcraft Folk

Kibbo Kift began as a socialist alternative to Scouts, yet, as it developed, some policies and practices changed fundamentally. In the mid-1920s, new economic theories of wealth distribution were added to the group's aims. These ideas of Social Credit came to dominate Hargrave's interests, and by the early 1930s he turned his back on woodcraft. Kibbo Kift was transformed into a new organization marked by political street marching and paramilitary stylings. The majority of members, originally enthused by the outdoor aspects, left. The split resembled an earlier rupture that also halved Kin membership. A 1924 schism had divided those who endorsed Hargrave as their unchallenged leader and those who wished to camp and campaign democratically. The crisis resulted in a motion of no confidence in Hargrave, and the socialists who led the charge walked out.

Within a year, two defectors founded their own group, Woodcraft Folk. Borrowing many aspects from Kibbo Kift—including camp ceremonial practices—the Folk also added a stronger left-wing political direction. Leslie Paul, a young writer and the organization's first leader, developed most of the Folk's early philosophy, including the education of working-class children the application of socialist principles to outdoor living. Camping in the Folk offered an opportunity to try out a socialist world in microcosm. *The Course of Instruction*, designed to inform leaders of Folk methods, stated: "Camping does not need justification. We do not need to enter into a profound analysis of the 'why' of camping. We camp because we like it. But camping in a woodcraft fashion is more than a pastime, it is an art and an educational adventure" (2). As such, its function was said to provide healthy outdoor opportunities for young and old to experience self-reliance and communal responsibility.

In 1934, the Folk declared, "Modern civilisation stands condemned for its ugliness, falsehood, greed, dirt, disease, disorganisation, poverty, war. Surely a new way of life can be found?" Training for this "New World Order" was to occur through "example, practice and research" into earth kinship, world unity, and "knowledge of self and sex" (2). Sex was mentioned to show the radical and progressive-minded nature of the organization; it was also an acknowledgment that children in the Folk would be unlikely to receive such information elsewhere. As outlined in *The Course of Instruction*, most child members came from working-class homes and "will have not even an elementary understanding of life." On sex, "the child's knowledge will be chiefly smatterings of gossip, invariably distorted" (2).

The Folk were well aware that their core principle of coeducation was seen as scandalous. As such, they argued, "Neither licence nor taboo must spoil this comradeship. [. . .] We have had to fight hard to secure this new relation between the sexes and we must be self-disciplined enough to safeguard it" (3). Unlike Kibbo Kift, the relation between the sexes was intended to be equal. As *The Course* put it, "We wish to see a frank and free comradeship springing naturally and unforced from our delight in each other and our common way of life" (2). Such frankness also applied to the instruction given to children about sex; the Folk's aim was "to avoid giving children a crippling sense of guilt over the habit, to avoid completely veiled warnings about purity, and to give advice only when asked for it" (*Training of Pioneers* 23). Folk leaders were pointed toward *Experiments in Sex Education*, a 1935 book produced by the Federation of Progressive Societies and Individuals, an organization that united social reformers and woodcrafters in its espousal of sexual freedom and socialism.

By and large, sexual relationships were less of a preoccupation in the Folk than they were in other woodcraft organizations, and they became even less of a priority after the Second World War. This was in part due to Paul's departure as leader and a drive by his successors to cast off aspects—from fanciful costume to archaic language—that had brought accusations of cultishness. Successive improvements in British education also meant less pressure to fill gaps in an inadequate curriculum. Instead the Folk maintained their core specialism: an education based on peace, democracy, and internationalism, with the emphasis on creating cooperative and socially engaged citizens. New campaigns were added as they arose in left-wing British politics. These included, from the 1980s onwards, an expanding interest in tackling sexism in the wider world as well as in the organization.

As a part of this broad agenda, the Folk established a working group to examine restrictions to gay rights in the late 1980s at a time when the introduction of the notorious Clause 28 of the Local Government Act, which prohibited councils from "promoting" homosexuality, was galvanizing the gay rights movement in Britain. This group was the subject of controversy among those who might be described as the old guard. The former General Secretary, Henry Fair, who had first joined the Folk in the 1920s, stated in 1988 that he was "appalled" to learn of the Gay and Lesbian Support Group, arguing that if the tabloid press heard of it, "they would have crucified the movement." Fair warned that it was not an area that the Folk should explore. He clarified, "I'm not saying that there's not a problem there. But it's a problem that should be dealt with by an adult organisation [. . .]. It is not a problem that should be dealt with by an organisation that professes itself to be a children's organisation" (136).

Shortly after the founding of Gay and Lesbian Support, a women's group was established to develop anti-sexist educational resources. By the early 1990s a further group, styled Men for Change, argued that men could and should play a role in recognizing and challenging non-sexist behavior as individuals and within organizations. Despite the group coinciding with the emerging men's movement of the period, inspired by publications such as Robert Bly's influential *Iron John*, the desire was not to establish a sepa-ratist space in the Folk to explore essentialist ideas about masculinity but to acknowledge that changes in attitude could only come if men and women worked together.

The probing self-scrutiny of these documents shows that members' recognition that the Folk, for all of its longstanding attempts to create an egalitarian space, might be reproducing the gendered asymmetries of the wider world. These included the historic woodcraft tendency of girls to select for themselves symbolic names of flowers, while boys chose beasts. Female and male domestic and public roles tended to be replicated in camp duties. Men for Change noted, regretfully, "the Folk is no different to the Labour Party and the Trade Union movement. Gender issues have come onto our agendas relatively recently and still contain potential for conflict, unease and confrontation. Yet simply passing anti-sexist policies is not enough—policies need to be followed by positive actions." To this end, they drew up a manifesto, organized meetings, and circulated reading lists that included resources developed by other youth organizations alongside Marxist-Feminist studies of gender and sexuality. Their efforts show that the Folk was determined to include radical approaches to sex and gender within its remit of "education for social change."

The need for the Folk to examine its own behavior is reflected in attitudes of members to gender equality. In her short, commissioned history, Mary Davis suggested that it was not just older members who tended to object to efforts to eradicate sexism in the Folk from the 1980s; there were some who saw such concerns as merely "middle-class fads." This she reflected on with some surprise, as unlike the labor movement more broadly, the Folk had always had women leaders (114). Davis happily noted the Folk's full support for tackling racism, sexism, and homophobia by the date of the millennium, but she also noted that it was a late starter; some more traditionally cautious organizations had already led the advance.

These discussions show how issues were raised, debated, and made mate-rial as the organization matured. In the twenty-first century, the Folk has forged forward with campaigning on sexuality and gender and once again holds a pioneering position. As part of its longstanding membership of International Falcon Movement—Socialist Education International (IFM-SEI), a European alliance of left-wing youth organizations, they have developed an important collection of educational materials called *Rainbow Resources*. Produced in 2011 and now in its second edition, these build on what IFM-SEI describes as "over forty years" of working with young people on issues of gender and sexuality. More specifically, the material grew from the regular IFM-SEI initiative, Queer Easter, instituted in 2001, which brings together young people from across Europe to discuss sexual identity, heteronormativity, and homophobia. The work undertaken in these projects aims "to curb heteronormative and cisnormative attitudes before they have a chance to be fully developed" (4). In particular, the guide was produced in response to a paucity of such material for under twelves. In the context of the wider aspirations of international socialist education, the emphasis remains on understanding gender and sexuality as "part of our struggle against all forms of exclusion and discrimination" (4).

Conclusion

Woodcraft organizations in Britain emerged as part of a network of social reform practices, linked by pacifism and socialism, as reactions to the Great War. As such, their interests overlapped with oppositional political and intellectual ideas more broadly, including feminism and sexology. While each of the three woodcraft organizations had differing emphases, and each approached sexuality, gender roles, and sex education in different ways, all were agreed that mainstream solutions to social problems needed radical revision.

Woodcraft camps offered temporary spaces away from the city; they were organized not only against the so-called civilized world but also against the dominant Boy Scout mold. Women and girls were included to disrupt male domination; models drawn from popular ideas about Native American methods of organization were internationalist and anti-imperialist in aim. Each had differing philosophies of camping but its centrality to all woodcraft organizations was a rejection of urban sophistication, comfort, and decadence. Instead, woodcraft espoused collective living, physical hardihood, and natural health; all were territories informed by leftist lifestyles.

Woodcraft organizations were highly unorthodox in their own time. In a newspaper article entitled "Queer Societies" from 1925, Kibbo Kift achieved the dubious honor of the uppermost position among "three thousand" niche societies operating in London. Described as "the most curious," Kin practices were described as "weird rites" and were thoroughly ridiculed (7). In the 1950s, William Eager, a historian of boys' clubs, also used the term "queer" to describe woodcraft organizations, dismissing them as "long-haired enthusiasms labeled with high-fallutin' names, of which the friendly, sporting, sensible and humorous working-boy would fight shy." For Eager, woodcraft aims were merely "Fads, fancies and fanaticisms," nothing less than a form of "queer feminism which would affiliate Boys' Clubs to Girls' Club Federations."

While queerness in these instances was used to designate strangeness, queerness in woodcraft organizations can also be understood another way. In Houlbrook's use of the term, to queer is to challenge the prevailing social order and to embrace the disruptive. What made these organizations strange was, in many cases, their experimentation with appearances, ideas, and practices that were outside of their time and place. In this, they were self-consciously rebels and agitators. They operated within but largely against interwar moral expectations of sex, gender, and beyond; they queered dominant thinking and they aspired to be a thorn in the side of dominant youth organizations. Devoted to the training of children, their sexual politics mounted a standing challenge to respectability in their foundational years, yet many of the ideas pioneered as radical interventions—not least coeducational camping—have now become mainstream practice. In some outdoor youth education programs in the twenty-first century, gender and sex roles remain contested territories. Gay youth, for example, have only been accepted into Boy Scouts as recently as 2013; gay adults were only permitted to lead—and even then with some provisos—in 2015. Woodcraft organizations were founded in explicit contradistinction to Scouts one hundred years ago. In the radical queer resources assembled by Woodcraft Folk in the present day, this opposition shows itself to be still alive and well.

Queer Pedagogy
at Indian Brook Camp

Flavia Musinsky

It is July 18, 2010, and the evening activity at Indian Brook Camp in Plymouth, Vermont, is "Gender and Sexuality Night." First, Big, and Senior Lodge campers are gathered in the upper lodge, and several staff facilitators begin by defining sex, gender, and sexuality, reflecting on their personal relationships with these topics. Campers are then asked to brainstorm the ways in which society defines "real" men and women, and after compiling a list, they are split into groups for more intimate discussions.

Over the course of that summer, I observed many such instances, some explicit and others more subtle, in which campers and counselors navigated the complexities of sex and gender in a female, single-sex community. Like many traditional American summer camps, Indian Brook is bound by cultural and legal constructions of gender identity as binary and predicated upon biological sex—campers and staff must be female-bodied to attend or work at camp—and it has historically been a space in which girl/womanhood is celebrated. Unlike other single-sex camps, however, Indian Brook does not insist that campers and staff identify as girls or women, and actively works to disrupt normative understandings of sex and gender using a variety of practices. Simultaneously questioning the confines of gender and celebrating the empowerment of women, all while organizing on the basis of sex, Indian Brook often finds itself in the midst of apparent contradiction, generating a complexity that can at times be fruitful, and at others limiting. The way Indian Brook navigates this complexity can be understood as a form of queer pedagogy in practice, one that strives to deconstruct norms upon which societies rely to maintain the dominant order, yet which is intrinsically characterized by im/perfection (Bryson and De Castell 1993), messiness, and sometimes, failure.

Queer pedagogy combines queer theory and critical pedagogy, and aims to critique, question, and ultimately deconstruct the norms upon which societies rely to construct notions of difference (Shlasko 2005). In particular, it strives to subvert and deconstruct processes of heteronormativity and traditional models of gender and sexuality, as is evident in its efforts to challenge the male/female and homosexual/heterosexual binaries, and the silence created around marginalized identities (Luhmann 1998; Rasmussen, Rofes, & Talburt 2016; Quinlivan and Town 1999). Though it may involve queer curricula such as anti-sexist and anti-homophobic educational initiatives, queer pedagogy generally signifies any practice that works toward an interference with dominant processes of normalization (Britzman 1993). Put into practice, queer pedagogy is inevitably untidy as it strives, yet often fails, to transgress and/or transcend the limiting contexts within which it unfolds. By the very nature of its project, queer pedagogy is a challenge to the world in which it finds itself, and thus—in order to occur at all—as Susanne Luhmann writes, "queer pedagogy must learn to be self-reflective of its own limitations" (121). Indian Brook does not explicitly name its work as a form of queer pedagogy in practice—that term is my own framing of what I saw occurring there. However, as I hope to show, this learning-by-doing rather than coming from a pre-formulated theoretical position is a part of what makes Indian Brook such a powerful example of queer pedagogy in action, entailing a constant process of questioning and self-examination.

Though there are cases of queer pedagogy having been attempted in single-sex schools (Reay 1990; Kruse 1992), there is not much literature on its practice in single-sex summer camps. As Charlie Hailey notes in his comprehensive study of camp environments, camps are fundamentally liminal spaces—spatially and temporally—that allow for experimentation with habitual social structures. Summer camps in particular have historically existed as gendered spaces, with girls' summer camps often serving as sites of "practical feminism" where social constraints and expectations placed on girls are tested (Hailey 2009). Camp would thus seem to be an ideal environment in which to question and explore the boundaries placed upon gender, sex, and sexuality, and Indian Brook serves as a unique example of this, as a space in which campers explicitly interrogate categorical understandings of sex and gender all while being organized around those very categories. A practice rooted in Indian Brook's interweaving of Quaker tradition, progressive education, and feminist politics, it continues to evolve to the present day.

Indian Brook and Farm & Wilderness

Farm & Wilderness was established by Kenneth and Susan Webb in 1939 in Plymouth, Vermont, with the founding of Timberlake, a camp for boys. Indian Brook followed in 1941 as a response to the demand for a sister camp to Timberlake, and preceded the five camps that emerged soon after. Influenced by John Dewey and the progressive education movement, the Webbs aimed to create a program where children could not only participate in farm work and wilderness trips, but also live in a community built upon Quaker values of simplicity, service, honesty, equality, and non-violence.

Though Farm & Wilderness camps differ programmatically and organizationally, some elements and traditions remain constant. Recorded music, television, and electronic devices of any kind are not allowed at camp, in order to promote a community based on living free from the typical everyday barrage of media and technology. All camps practice silent meeting each morning, an established practice of Quaker tradition through which campers can enjoy a moment of peace and reflection apart from the usual bustle of camp. There is an emphasis on living sustainably and within nature, and campers live in open cabins, use composting toilets, and abide by leave-no-trace policies on wilderness trips. Many families have a long history at Farm & Wilderness, with generations of children attending or working at the camps. Farm & Wilderness is a very large community as a whole, but each camp has its own history, values, and traditions.

Indian Brook is the largest of the Farm & Wilderness camps. Its website describes Indian Brook as "a place for girls to find friendship, adventure, and support in a non-competitive environment" (Farm & Wilderness). It is open to girls between the ages of 9 and 14, and has a high camper-to-staff ratio, with most staff of college age or in their early twenties. The majority of Indian Brook staff members teach daily activities and live in cabins supervising a group of campers, with the exception of those hired as supervisors and "support staff," positions that involve less direct participation with the campers.

Campers are divided into three age groups: First Lodge (9–10 years), Big Lodge (11–12 years), and Senior Lodge (13–14 years). Activities focus on community building through collective work and aim to teach campers tangible skills (carpentry projects, barn and garden work, outdoor living skills), as well as less structured entertainment chosen by campers (water-front, rock climbing/ropes course, creative arts, nature adventures, and so on). Though there is unstructured free time, each day is full of activity and follows a general schedule, with the exception of occasional "special days," which are less structured or follow a particular theme. Additionally, all campers are required to go on a wilderness trip, the length of which is dependent on their age (two nights for younger campers and four to six nights for older campers).

In the summer of 2010, I worked as a full-time counselor at Indian Brook, living in a cabin with eight 13-year-old girls and a co-counselor. At the same time, I was conducting qualitative research on the community's understand-ings and practices with respect to gender. As a participant-observer, I drew primarily on ethnographic and grounded theory approaches, taking notes on anything I witnessed that was expressly related to gender and sexuality and conducting interviews with several staff members; later, I organized the data into themes and concepts, which allowed for a theoretical understand-ing to emerge; in other words, my observations over the summer informed the conclusions I came to about Indian Brook (Bogdan and Biklen 2006). In what follows, I describe and discuss the findings of my research, articulating the ways in which Indian Brook challenges and sometimes succumbs to the confines of its being a single-sex institution.

Indian Brook as a Single-Sex Space

Indian Brook exists as an intentionally single-sex community that has his-torically celebrated girlhood and womanhood, placing importance upon being a community for and by women. Many proponents of single-sex education feel that organizing as a group of same-sex individuals allows for the acknowledgment of shared similar experiences and struggles because one only needs to be *perceived* as a woman or man—based on observed or imagined physical markers of sexual difference—in order to *be* a woman or man (Haslanger 2000). This is reflected in an interview I conducted in the summer of 2010 with Sarah Waring, who was at the time Program Director of Farm & Wilderness, responsible for general event programming as well as the placement and organization of campers within each of the seven camps. In the interview, she discusses the importance of Indian Brook's being a single-sex community, commenting:

> One thing we know about single-gender programming—and I use that term knowing it's not particularly appropriate—[is that] classically and historically . . . women don't have a place to express themselves and feel safe. For both men and women, learning about one's own strengths and weaknesses in a single-gender community *feels* different than out there in the real world. In particular, it's been important for women to get that, because it's a male-dominated world. There is something important about having a space where [we] don't have to have men and boys around. (Waring)

Waring recognizes the problem of referring to Indian Brook as a "single-gender" community, as it is clearly single-*sex*, not single-*gender*, but also highlights the importance of a community in which men and boys are for the most part not present, and the way this "feels different" from other spaces; presumably because it acts as a safe space, necessary for women in a male-dominated world.

Others have argued that single-sex institutions reinforce essentialist conceptions of sex and gender—namely, the notion that biological sex always informs gender identity (Tsolidis 2006)—and thereby invalidates those individuals whose gender does not "match" their sex. When one must qualify as either a boy or a girl to be part of a single-sex group, transgender, intersex, and gender-bending people who exist beyond this dichotomy are rendered invisible (Jackson 2009). Furthermore, single-sex institutions can reinforce gender differences and foster stereotypes of traditional femininity and masculinity, roles that are ultimately detrimental. Wendy Kaminer, for instance, makes this observation: "Whether manifested in feminine décor or in an approach to teaching that assumes a female penchant for cooperative, or 'connected' learning, stereotypical notions of femininity often inflect institutions for women and girls . . . accepting the limits of femininity rather than challenging them" (34).

Though Indian Brook values remaining a single-sex space, it has evolved over time to include programming that attempts to ameliorate the problematic aspects of single-sex institutions described above. Waring explains that Indian Brook's identity and structure have evolved with the changing emphases of feminist thought, saying that in the early '90s, Indian Brook was "pretty hardcore feminist, a place where feminists and those strong in their sexual orientation were finding their voices. The need for that to be one of the primary focuses of program became less important as society changed around F&W—social justice issues shifted." This process has resulted in and from a dynamic conversation between distinct views of what feminism can be or accomplish.

Indian Brook was established following first-wave feminism, the primary concern of which was to ensure that women and men had equal rights; the camp was created as a way to offer girls the same experiences that boys were having at Timberlake Camp, established two years earlier. Two decades later, second-wave feminism called for the liberation of women from traditionally female roles and expectations; at Indian Brook, this manifested in programming, with a strong focus on female empowerment. Third-wave feminism emerged in the 1980s and continues to the present day (Rand 2017; Iannello 2010), questioning the notion of "woman" and, more broadly, gender, as a unified construct. The emphasis of third-wave feminism can be seen in Indian Brook's current programming, which both explicitly and implicitly questions normative understandings of gender and sex themselves. At the same time, the camp remains, to an extent, organized around such constructions. Working to retain the potential benefits of being a single-sex institution while avoiding falling prey to its possible limitations entails careful and critical attention on the part of campers and staff to Indian Brook's place in larger conversations around feminism, gender identity, and social justice. As Rosemary C. Salomone writes: "Separating students by sex on a voluntary basis . . . need not be a surrender to the reactionary forces of separate spheres ideology, so long as programs are thoughtfully designed and administrators and teachers are adequately informed and sensitized to the issues" (14). I found that Indian Brook works to ameliorate the potentially limiting consequences of its single-sex organization by challenging normative understandings of gender and sex in a variety of ways. Some of these are explicit tactics that could be considered an enactment of queer pedagogy; others, apparently steeped in contradiction, highlight the way in which queer pedagogy in practice is often limited and imperfect.

Challenging Normativity

Indian Brook's most straightforward ways of pushing against boundaries of sex and gender are through its deliberate discussions with campers regarding gender roles, and through its challenging of the sexualization and objectification of women, an issue that is so pervasive and normalized that it is often internalized well before adolescence. In the text that follows, I highlight examples of such conversations, along with the ways they can be seen enacting facets of queer pedagogy.

Questioning Traditional Gender Roles

Open, honest, and critical discussions about gender and sexuality are an important component of queer pedagogy. The assumptions and stereotypes we make about gender and sexuality often go unexamined, and providing a space in which individuals can become aware of and question the foundation of these categorizations can be transformative (Rasmussen, Rofes, & Talburt 2016; Maher 1999). In the classroom, this may involve initiating discussions when incidents of intolerance occur, or when stereotyping appears in texts (Boldt 1996). Furthermore, the sharing of personal stories allows individuals to recognize the ways normative ideas of gender and sexuality serve to limit everyone, even those who are privileged as a result of these constructs.

At Indian Brook, campers often question traditional gender roles, and nowhere is this more apparent than at "Gender and Sexuality Night," wherein staff support campers in sharing and reflecting upon their experiences of being gendered. Staff initiate the activity by defining sex, gender, and sexuality, and then ask campers to articulate their own understandings of how society defines a "real" woman. In so doing, they open space for a critical dialogue around distinctions that are often overlooked in other areas of the campers' lives. One camper says, "It made me think about how different I am from the woman described on the list, and that when I do things or have qualities that are on the list I feel bad, like it's one or the other."[1] Another comments, "At my school there are tons of stereotypical girls—I try not to be like that because I don't want to be obsessed with my looks. I like being strange." Campers understand these stereotypes to be a product of "television, magazines, school, media in general, etc.," and share experiences where they reacted against these traditional roles ascribed to women. Their responses imply a sense of satisfaction and pride in being a girl, especially in relation to "the boys," perhaps a reaction to the fact that numerous qualities found on the "real women" list are associated with weakness, often in relation to men: "[women] don't exert themselves, are worried about how they look, rely on men for support, cannot be taller or stronger than men, have a goal to attract men, are timid and scared of mice." In many stories shared by the campers, girls are expected to be the weaker sex, and they actively work to counter this stereotype by identifying with traits of strength and empowerment.

Throughout the discussion, the idea that stereotypes are limiting emerges recurrently. At times, the facilitators try to discourage overly simplistic generalizations; a document containing the written goals of the discussion includes the bullet point: "Some of these [stereotypes] might apply to you, and some might not, and either way that's fine, we just want to think about where they come from." The purpose of Gender and Sexuality Night is not to reject those stereotypical traits per se, but rather to encourage discussion about their origins and the impact they have on our identities—a fundamental aspect of queer pedagogy. Campers thereby learn to question the validity of rigid gender roles, expand their conception of what it means to be a woman/girl, and challenge the idea of gendered identity as limited or value-laden.

When employed in single-sex institutions, queer pedagogy in the form of discussion can support students in actively addressing and challenging normative gender roles, adding beneficial complexity to institutions where sex or gender are organizing principles (Reay 1990; Kruse 1992), and acting as a means to achieve solidarity with one's gender group through the shared reconstruction and enrichment of the gender identity in question. As Anne-Mette Kruse elaborates, "The gender-identity and self-confidence of individual pupils and their gender group are supported; the sex roles, attitudes, and behavior are challenged" (15); certainly, this would seem to be the case with Indian Brook's approach.

CHALLENGING THE SEXUALIZATION OF WOMEN AND GIRLS

While it is ultimately to the advantage of *all* individuals to look critically at sex and gender, those who identify as girls and women, in particular, can benefit greatly from the push to dispute traditional notions of femininity and broaden the category of "woman," as their gender identity is tied in with subordination and oppression (Haslanger 2000); one aspect of this dynamic is the extreme pressure put on women's appearances, often to the exclusion of other qualities. Bodies are sites of constant negotiation and questioning for young girls, who often suffer from low self-esteem and body image issues as a result of the highly sexualized and objectifying gaze directed toward women.

At Indian Brook, this is addressed and challenged in two ways. First, campers are encouraged to discuss body image and their experiences dealing with constricting notions of the ideal body. Second, the camp adheres to a "No Body Talk" rule, which Laurie, the Senior Lodge Head, explains as "no talking about bodies or their appearance negatively or positively, so that we're not thinking about bodies all the time . . . outside of camp there is a huge emphasis on how we look, so at camp we want the emphasis to be on who we are." Adrienne, an Assistant Director, adds that Indian Brook "actively resists the objectification of bodies. We want it to be about celebrating bodies in a real way, not silencing them."

The "No Body Talk" rule encourages campers to recognize bodies for what they can *do*, not what they look like (or what they are clothed in), creating an environment in which campers don't need to worry about their appearance or feel that their bodies are being judged, often a much-needed respite for those who face these anxieties outside of camp. Staff also role model this idea in discussions with campers, sharing personal experiences such as: "Starting in middle school, I would be validated by my physical appearance more than anything else. Really, I wanted my friends to notice things I was *doing*—and I still deal with this. I learned that that's how I'm validated—I still think about it and it's hard to accept feedback and compliments about what I do." This staff member's comment calls attention to the fact that women primarily receive physical rather than "functional" validation. Reflecting this idea, one camper says, "sometimes in our society you have to be pretty and wear the right clothes to have your personality acknowledged."

Though campers sometimes play with the rule by sarcastically commenting on how "functional" their friends look, most understand its positive impact, and convey their relieved appreciation of camp as an affirmative space for bodies, saying, "Camp is a place where you don't want to care about what you're wearing—it's safer here"; "[At camp] I can wear a shirt 5 days in a row"; "Sometimes at camp I feel like you can wear whatever you want." From these comments, it is clear that Indian Brook encourages and helps foster positive self-image for girls both in *and* outside of camp, working to challenge the oppressive and rampant objectification of women as part of its larger project of striving to help campers question and critique traditional conceptions of sex and gender. While these practices undertaken by Indian Brook can be understood as perhaps more straightforward, or "effective," forms of queer pedagogy, its most radical practice is also its most apparently contradictory, speaking to the way in which queer pedagogy in practice entails coming up against boundaries and venturing into uncharted territory.

Contradictions & Limitations

The practice I refer to here is Indian Brook's inclusion of female-bodied campers and staff who identify as transgender, and not as girls or women.

Additionally, the camp increasingly promotes gender-neutral language, replacing terms like "ladies" and "girls" with "folks" and "friends." As it has embarked upon this deconstruction of its single-sex identity, however, Indian Brook has found itself faced with contradictions and limitations that reflect both legal restraints and cultural anxieties.

To offer a glimpse into the context and history of the decision to welcome transgender campers and staff into Farm & Wilderness's traditionally single-sex camps, I conducted personal interviews with two Farm & Wilderness staff, Sarah Waring and Courtney Porter (neither of whom currently work at Farm & Wilderness). Through our conversations, it became clear that welcoming transgender campers and staff into the community is an intentional decision based on a nuanced, critical understanding of gender and sex, which simultaneously questions constructions of gender while seeking to create a community that is primarily for women and girls.

First, I spoke with Sarah Waring about the process of assigning campers to the main single-sex camps (Indian Brook and Timberlake) in terms of biological sex and gender. Waring comments: "We were having more kids who were transgender or questioning, who wanted to know why they needed to be in a specific place . . . [we] wanted to sort of challenge the general duality that schools and camps and society in general have always imposed on them." Calling it the "same equipment" rule (which she admits is "horrid shorthand"), Waring explains that campers are assigned to camps based on biological sex; thus, a transgender boy who was born female could attend Indian Brook, while a transgender girl who was born male could not. However, Waring also states that this policy is continuously re-evaluated by the Farm & Wilderness program team, and that each camper (and staff member) is treated as an individual case—nothing is set in stone. This flexibility indicates at once Indian Brook's sensitivity to the particulars of each situation, as well as its lack of a single overarching answer to the increasing tension between supporting girls and welcoming those who don't identify as girls.

Following my interview with Waring on the placement of campers, I spoke to Courtney Porter, the Human Resources Manager of Farm & Wilderness, responsible for employing, training, and paying staff (among other administrative tasks). In our conversation, she elaborates on the hiring of staff and the legal restrictions and policy to which Farm & Wilderness must adhere. Porter confirms that, like campers, staff must be female-bodied to work at Indian Brook. However, in order to work as a cabin counselor and reside in a cabin with campers, they must have a "matching identity." At

Indian Brook, this means transgender staff may only work as leadership/support staff or in the kitchen as a cook. When asked why this is the policy, she says:

> For a couple of reasons: because it is more "safe"—I hate using that word—because even though it is more sex and gender focused at the two camps [Indian Brook and Timberlake], while parents might be progressive, some parents might not be—its about their comfort level. "Why do I have a male cabin counselor for my 9 year old girl?"—this is something a parent might say. (Porter)

In addition, Porter makes it clear that "the decisions we make from a human resources perspective we make first based on law. The most important thing about this discussion is that we have an equal opportunity policy—we cannot and will not discriminate based on sexual identity or gender." While she does not go into detail about the laws that inform the "matching identity" rule or the reasons it is not "safe," Porter later says transgender individuals cannot be cabin counselors at Indian Brook and Timberlake because "that might be confusing to our campers" (Porter).

Porter then addresses the hiring of transgender staff at Indian Brook specifically, saying, "While Indian Brook might have female-bodied staff who present as male, that was a very deliberate discussion between the staff [member] and Nicole (2010 director of Indian Brook). . . . How can we as an IB community respect who you are and how you identify, *and* what our needs and program needs are?" She adds, "We need to find a place that is accepting and open and safe for people who don't fit either gender—[and] find the best way to integrate them into our programs." This comment speaks to the struggle that Indian Brook faces as it strives to include those who do not identify as female while maintaining its cohesion as a single-sex camp; as can be seen, this challenge necessitates nuanced attention to each individual's place in the larger context.

Perhaps the most marked contradiction Indian Brook faces, then, involves its very structure, which raises the question: If the camp aims to disrupt categorical notions of identity through pointed discussion, and welcomes individuals who don't fit into the traditional sex-gender binary, isn't it illogical that it should organize itself on the basis of the very identities it seeks to disrupt? As many of the Indian Brook staff recognize, however, the situation is not quite so straightforward. Although there is not one unifying factor connecting or separating all women or all men, it would be remiss to deny the existence of "woman" and "man" as social categories with real influence. Insofar as these identities are predicated upon oppressive systems

of power, from the perspective of queer pedagogy, they are ripe for deconstruction; in her seminal work on the topic, Deborah Britzman echoes this,
writing, "[Queer pedagogy] refuses normal practices and practices of normalcy . . . [it is] interested in the imagining of a sociality unhinged from the
dominant conceptual order" (165). One powerful way to do so is through
organizing around the identities themselves, appreciating the complexity
they contain and challenging from within those elements of womanhood
and manhood that lead to inequality. In thinking through its space as a
camp for girls that simultaneously questions the very notion of womanhood, Indian Brook continually finds itself navigating a state of contradiction; I describe perhaps the most salient example of this occurring below.

Toward the end of the summer, support staff received a letter from an
anonymous Indian Brook staff member regarding the need to maintain the
aspect of Indian Brook that celebrates women and girls, even with the
inclusion of transgender members in the community. The author asks why
the "Women at Work" sign was taken down (a sign historically hung on
the lodge, removed while the building was being repainted), and does not
like the suggestion that the phrase "Say it Sister!" (used when asking a
person to speak louder) be replaced with more gender-neutral language. At
a staff meeting, Laurie, the Senior Lodge Head, brings up the letter. After
welcoming its author to speak privately with her if they want to discuss it
further, she and other support staff share their reactions. Laurie begins by
saying, "You can still be a feminist and be proud of being a woman, and
deal with the gender binary." Alex, an Assistant Director, adds: "Indian
Brook is still a girls camp—most of our campers identify as girls, but not
all of them. When we address campers in groups we should be aware [of
this]. We want campers to feel supported no matter how they identify."

The non-discrimination of individuals based on gender is a fundamental
aspect of Indian Brook but is accepted only with certain limitations that
reflect dominant ideology about gender and sex identity. While the camp
certainly challenges the common duality of female = woman and male =
man, it isn't immune to cultural pressures pertaining to sex and gender, as
is made clear by the "matching identity" rule. Furthermore, in welcoming
those who do not identify as girls or women into the space, campers and
staff must reconcile conflicting views of who and what Indian Brook is for,
as is made clear by the author of the anonymous letter. This struggle can
be seen as exemplifying the spirit of queer pedagogy in practice—indeed,
one could say that queer pedagogy is less about arriving at a conclusion
than questioning conclusions that have already been drawn, continually
problematizing tidy understandings and dealing with limitations; as Mary

Bryson and Suzanne de Castell write, "In pedagogical matters, im/perfect outcomes are necessarily the norm" (299).

Although it was not the focus of my research, I feel that I would be remiss to not address the topic of cultural appropriation in a discussion of queer pedagogy in practice at Indian Brook camp. The emphasis on reflection and questioning that can be seen in Indian Brook's stance toward issues of gender can also be seen operating in the ongoing conversation around cultural appropriation.

The term "cultural appropriation" has been the subject of considerable theoretical debate in the social sciences, but it is generally taken to refer to the "borrowing" of certain facets of a subaltern culture by members of a hegemonic culture, often without the former's consent, reworking and re-contextualizing these attributes to suit the needs and purposes of the dominant cultural group in ways that reinforce historically exploitative relationships (Rogers 2006). Cultural appropriation and reification of American Indian culture is inextricably bound up with the American summer camp tradition (Van Slyck 2006; Paris 2008) and can be recognized at Farm & Wilderness in several ways, a full discussion of which goes beyond the scope of this essay. However, insights into Indian Brook's commitment to questioning societal norms and its own positioning can be gained from examining its response to the controversy surrounding its own name.

On April 27, 2017, Indian Brook's director wrote a blog post on the Farm & Wilderness website titled "Revisiting Our History with a Modern Lens." In the post, she acknowledges the ongoing conversation at the camp around the name of Indian Brook, sharing that the Board and the Farm & Wilderness management team had been discussing the possibility of changing the name to "remain sensitive to current dynamics," and writing that "we respect how words and policies may affect underrepresented communities" (Chamberlain 2017). Finally, she articulates some of the questions that have emerged from "heartfelt" discussions including Indian Brook community members past and present: "What is the point of view of the Indian community? We should not look at this issue in a vacuum. . . . Is 'Indian' our word to use as a mostly white community? How does it look to someone new to F&W?" (Chamberlain).

Indian Brook's continual grappling with problematic conventions speaks to Luhmann's claim that "the refusal of any normalization, be it racist, sexist, or whatever, necessarily has to be part of the queer agenda" (128). The emphasis on reflection, consensus, and ongoing inquiry that is apparent in the blog post echoes the way in which Indian Brook makes sense of itself and its positioning with respect to sex and gender. In exploring how Indian

Brook navigates this process, I found that it moves forward by embracing rather than glossing over complexity, focusing on what is empowering within that, and questioning norms that would limit the potential of the campers and the space. Facing and working with the messiness of identity and difference *is* queer pedagogy in practice, which, I contend, Indian Brook embodies in its very structure. Though Indian Brook certainly struggles with many contradictions, and will likely continue to do so for the foreseeable future, the conversations that I had and witnessed with those who care deeply about Indian Brook showed me that the willingness to grapple with this complexity enriches the experience for both campers and staff, and ultimately makes the camp the unique experiment that it is. My sense is that, while Indian Brook has its own history, culture, and values, its own conflicts, confusions, and achievements, it can serve as an example to other single-sex camps and institutions, indicating a way beyond limiting boundaries of identity, even as it discovers where this way leads.

NOTE

1. At the start of the summer, campers and staff gave their permission to have group discussions recorded and to allow their words to be quoted anonymously. All uncited quotes were sourced from these discussions, whereas direct interviews are cited.

"No Trespassing"

Girl Scout Camp and the Limits
of the Counterpublic Sphere

Kathryn R. Kent

Introduction to the Reprint of "No Trespassing"

This piece elucidates the ways in which queerness of all sorts can be nurtured and sustained within what appear to be normative structures. * *In some ways, then, this essay represents an extension of my preoccupations in my book,* Making Girls into Women: American Women's Writing and the Rise of Lesbian Identity, *and, in particular, the chapter on the function of the Girl Scout handbook. But this work, what the editors of the volume in which it first appeared, Steven Bruhm and Natasha Hurley, term a "theoretical memoir," experiments with narrating and analyzing my own experiences of Girl Scout camp in the late seventies and early eighties. Such experiments have become much more common since I wrote this piece. I argue that camp provided what, in the critical parlance of the early 2000s, was being termed a "counterpublic sphere." At the same time, because of camp's unique location as an alternative private, I was questioning the limits of such dominant theorizations to account for camp as a location. I was also grappling with the still resonant question of what it means to privilege the imperatives of visibility and "outness" over spaces*

that emphasize alternative narratives of gender, sexuality, and, in this case,
"nature," to create an undefined space, camp, where all kinds of queer things
can happen without having to be immediately named as such. Not just swaths of
queer culture, but various forms of erotics, such as those I encountered at Girl
Scout camp, are disappearing under the aegis of a sanitizing, liberal, "we accept
all diversity" rhetoric that, at the same time, now openly regulates sexual
behavior rather than pointedly ignoring it. In other words, Girl Scouting offi-
cially acknowledges lesbianism exists, but that means that, in addition to affirm-
ing this sexual identity, it openly polices queer desire. What happens in the
private spaces of Girl Scout camps all over the country, I imagine, I suspect,
I hope, is possibly still more complicated.

> Marjorie opened her suitcase and took out her bugle. Swinging its cord
> over her shoulder, she remarked: "I suppose I really ought to be learn-
> ing new calls instead of looking for trails."
>   "Nonsense; you don't get points for blowing the bugle."
>   "No, but you get smiles and maybe something better from Captain
> Phillips!"
>   "What do you mean, Marj?"
>   "Don't ever repeat this, Lily." Marjorie lowered her voice. "When
> I succeeded in blowing Reveille correctly, Miss Phillips kissed me!"
> (Lavell 54)

This passage, from a Girl Scout novel written in the early 1920s, illuminates some of the most queerly productive aspects of Girl Scout camp:
It implicitly connects the public performance of a particular task or skill
with private erotic reward. Similarly, Marj and Lily's illicit conversation
during rest hour highlights the movement between secrecy and revelation, ignorance and knowledge, which Marj handles as skillfully as she
does her bugle.[1] She gains power by sharing her secret. She has achieved
what every camper desires: Through her eagerness to please and to
achieve, she has been singled out for "special attention," what I call "lesbian pedagogy," by her beloved counselor, "Miss"— or is it "Captain"?—
Phillips. This variability in address gestures toward what I will argue is the
instability, even total redefinition, of gender and sexuality, their own
public and private performative complexities, within the space of the Girl
Scout camp.
    Recently, there has been widespread discussion of the function of camp
as an aesthetic practice, a performance, a quintessentially queer phenomenon. Yet the idea of camp as a *space*, *summer camp*—and in the case of the
Girl Scouts, a highly routinized, geographically isolated location designed

to aid in the reproduction of girls—has not been explored.[2] This essay attempts to begin to theorize the relationship between the Girl Scouts, usually regarded as a stable part of the faded wallpaper of white, middle-class banality, and the formation and reproduction of nascent lesbian or queer identities and identifications in the United States.

An Introduction to Girl Scouting

GIRL SCOUT MEMORY

Since it is a rainy day, we are showing a movie in the lodge. We always screen the same one, a black and white film from the fifties on the history of Girl Scouting. I have seen it so many times that I know all the dialogue by heart. It opens with the older, distinguished-looking Agnes Moreheadesque woman, sitting on a sofa drinking tea. (One year, for my birthday, one of my Scouting friends will send me a relic, an actual piece of the film, a frame of this older woman holding her teacup, pinkie extended.) "Morehead" narrates the film within the film, made in the early twenties, of a group of Girl Scouts and their trusty patrol leader, Margaret, a girl of great bravery and aplomb. Around me girls lie on their backs, sit cross-legged, hold hands, give back rubs, giggle and groan with boredom. I am curled up in another woman's lap, yelling out the proper responses. (Since most of the movie is a reprint of a silent film, there is tinny music, and subtitles). Everyone reads the titles together, except for the little ones, who don't read yet.

Like spectators at the "Rocky Horror Picture Show," one must cheer, boo, hiss, etc. at the appropriate moments. We watch the troop help a wayward woman organize her house and wash up her children before her soldier husband arrives home from the (First World) War. Margaret, trusty patrol leader, demonstrates her ability to "be prepared" in an emergency, when she finds the telegraph man knocked out cold in his office and uses her extensive knowledge of Morse code to call for help. At last "our founder," Juliette Gordon Low," appears and nods ever so coolly at the camera. She is dressed in full uniform, with a wide-brimmed hat. She looks like a male impersonator. Or is she transgendered? She looks like a butch, her gaze so steady, so alluring. Our heroine.

Already, in this narrative, one might recognize a reinscription of spectator-ship that in some ways resembles Miriam Hansen's discussion of early film viewing practices. As Hansen describes it, early films were screened as part of a larger event, which often included live acts, music, and various audience-generated interruptions. Such conditions of spectatorship, Hansen argues, prohibited the establishment of any stable, hegemonic subject

position, and instead allowed for different "horizons of experience," counterpublic moments of collective spectatorship (*Babel to Babylon* 23–59). One
might read the Girl Scout episode described above as a similar moment of
counterpublicity. Indeed, I would argue that the Girl Scouts enables the
formation of oppositional horizons of experience even as it performs some
of the most rigidly imperialistic and anti-feminist narratives of subject-
formation. In the case of the film, a group of pre-adolescent girls feel perfectly entitled to burst into the home of a working-class woman, take charge
of her children, and clean and reorganize her household. At the same time,
this colonizing impulse is contradicted by, even as it enables, the homoerotic scene of collective spectatorship described above.

It is this peculiar slippage between nationalist narratives of white, middle-
class femininity and queer forms of subjectivity that makes the Girl Scouts
such a suspicious and thorny subject. Many might read the organization as
simply a "partial public,"[3] an extension of the values and politics of the
industrial-commercial public sphere, a "habitus" (to use Pierre Bourdieu's
term) marked by race and class. I am interested, though, in elucidating
how, through the summer camp, it could simultaneously become a counterpublic space for the inculcation and nurturance of (sometimes) anti-
nationalist, anti-bourgeois, and anti-heterosexist identities and practices. I
base my deployment (and simultaneous interrogation) of the term "counterpublic" on the work of recent political theorists, historians, and theorists
of material culture that attempts to understand how collective, oppositional
forms of meaning/identity/representation are produced and sustained. As
such theorists describe it, the counterpublic sphere is one in which "subor-
dinated social groups" construct oppositional narratives of subjectivity and
resistance (Fraser 123).

But claiming counterpublicity is difficult. Determining what constitutes
dis-identification or a break with the values of the public sphere, as opposed
to a simple imitation of them, is always subjective, tenuous, open to interpretation.[4] Definitions of the difference between "partial" public and
"counterpublic" spheres often rely on strictly demarcated criteria of what
constitutes political action, agency, and identity. Even as Hansen admits
that it may be difficult to tell "partial" publics from "counterpublics," she,
as well as Fraser, privileges an alternative public sphere as one that contains
collective representations of oppositional identity, forms of visible publicity. In the case of the Girl Scouts, I argue that the line between hegemonic
and subversive discourse is always unstable, and that this precariousness
may itself produce queer effects.

For example, if we return to Margaret, the heroine of the film discussed above, she signified within the space of "camp" as either a marker of shame or of distinction. To call someone a "Margaret" could indicate that this person was compulsive about rules and cleanliness, or it could mean that she was competent, strong, a butch under pressure. At least once during the season, sometimes twice, our camp would hold a "Margaret Scout" contest, and each living group or unit would field a participant, a child or counselor dressed up to imitate "Margaret." Parody or not? Similarly, the ritual screening of the film itself offered the camp a moment of communal interaction, a chance to spend time with one's partner or cruise a new counselor, to cuddle or be cuddled, at the same time that it reinforced the imperialist values of Scouting for girls. It is precisely such queer ambivalences and performances that I examine in the rest of this essay.

The Topography of the Camp

> At school, living under the same roof, seeing each other day after day, these girls thought they knew each other well; but there is no fellowship so close as that of out-door comrades; the vastness of the sky with its millions of stars, the loneliness of the woods and of camp life, and the close association in work and play, drew them together as they would have never dreamed it possible to be drawn. (Lavell 80)

Mark Seltzer's work on the "topography of masculinity" in the turn-of-the-century United States includes a detailed analysis of the ideological underpinnings of the Boy Scouts, the same underpinnings that Juliette Low would coopt for her own purposes when founding the Girl Scouts. As Seltzer illustrates, the early proponents of Boy Scouting feared that commodity culture was "feminizing" boys. In order to combat this weakening of the body, boys must be "made into men," removed from the feminizing domestic sphere of the home, and taken out into "nature," where through the rigors of outdoor living, they would be restored to a vigorous masculinity (Selzer 149–55).

The Girl Scouts adapted this ideology of nature and of its character-building powers.[5] But by the time I entered the organization, "nature" had acquired specific resonance. "Living in nature" became the same as "living outside the real world." A place unspoiled by urban or suburban ugliness, a place supposedly without technology, "nature" remained, as it did at the turn of the century, a retreat both from commodity culture and from its allegedly "feminizing" effects. Yet within the counterpublic of the Girl Scout camp, "feminizing" connoted instead a release from the normative definitions of gender and sexuality placed on mainly white, mainly middle- and lower-middle-class women. At the same time, nature acted as a sort of empty signifier, a name for a space in which one could escape one's family and one's school culture, a place where one's "natural" self and "natural" attractions could surface. Thus, nature and natural became interchange- able definitions, and what was "natural" at camp might be considered completely "unnatural" elsewhere.

As one of the rhetorics employed to explain intense attachments between young girls and between full-grown women (not to mention cross- generational relationships), Scouting rewrote as "natural" relationships and interactions between women that "outside the camp" might signify as "homoerotic" or "homosexual." In the "real world," people had lost the capacity for physical intimacy; here hugging, kissing, giving back rubs, and holding hands (especially on sentimental occasions, such as the last night of camp) were natural, produced by nature, by being one's "real" self. Thus, behavior that "outside" would be pathologized or ridiculed became utterly acceptable and expected under the ideological umbrella of Scouting, so much so that intense, erotic friendships and/or sexual relationships were seen as perfectly compatible with one's heterosexual existence in the "real world."[6]

Many Scouts would be outraged to hear me call this contact "sexual," let alone "lesbian," where the term connotes any self-affiliation with col- lective identity. Perhaps "queer," where queer is used to include a whole host of sexual expressions excluded by the already over-determined hetero/ homosexual dichotomy, better serves as a label for these relations between women, although it would certainly not have been more acceptable to my counselors than any other "deviant" sexual label. Yet I also have encoun- tered many women for whom "lesbian" was or has become part of their camp identity.

The rhetoric of the "natural" was also used to redefine gender identity. "Real" women were the ones who could build fires with wet wood and hike uphill for ten miles. They were independent, forthright, honorable, and butch.[7] They ran the camp, drove the vans, built the fires, and held arm- wrestling contests at the dinner table. While in the public sphere of manda- tory gender binarisms, these women might have been viewed as cross-gender identified, perhaps even as transgendered, in the counterpublic of camp they were simply camp counselors.

Girl Scout Memory

When I was in high school, my brother and father devised an ingenuous
strategy designed to regulate my body and my sexuality. Whenever we passed
a butch or transgendered woman on the street, the two of them would chortle
in unison, "There goes another camp counselor." At such moments I felt a
mixture of shame and anger, shame at this woman's inability to "fit in" and
at my own alliance with her, and anger because, while I had no names for
what my father and brother were expressing, I understood how endangered
both she and I were by our identities as "camp people," as queer.

It was more difficult to express "femininity" than "masculinity," however.
In fact, like much of the larger lesbian community in the United States, the
Girl Scout counterpublic legitimated "butch" behavior more readily than
it did "femme." But certain staff members mastered the femme role. It
meant a variety of things—the ability to keep one's temper, to rival Julie
Andrews in one's talent with leading songs, to quiet a whole cabin of
homesick children.

Much of the camp humor and play was organized around gender transgressions, but what counted as a crossing over from one gender to another
differed in the context of camp ideology. It did not simply mean "women"
dressing "as men" because this distinction did not have epistemological
currency within the camp. Instead, the most butch counselors would put
on dresses, and the femme darling would don a suit and tie, and this would
be considered a cross-gendered performance.

It is tempting to read this gender play as a prototype of Judith Butler's
assertion that there is no such thing as "femininity" or "masculinity," that
gender is always a parody of a parody, and that such gender performance
reveals this essential inessentialness (Butler, *Gender Trouble* 138). This
assumption was crucial to our "camp" humor and sensibility. Within the
camp counterpublic, however, while parody *was* a common form of expression, there existed alongside it a strong emphasis on finding and sustaining
one's "true," "natural" self. Only here, in the camp, could one truly be free.
As one camp song put it, "Hiking to rainbows, sunsets and stars / Just finding out who we are" ("Moon on the Meadow"). That one's identity might
be "performative" was only accurate as a description of how one "survived"
in the world "outside," by adopting "artificial" imitations of femininity in
order to get by.

And get by one did, until the next summer started. Finding in camp a
space in which their gender and sexual identities were recognized, emulated,

72 Kathryn R. Kent

desired, and rewarded, many of my counselors took jobs that allowed them to keep their summers free. Some were "professional" Girl Scouts (meaning they worked in the administrative structure of the local Girl Scout organization), elementary and secondary school teachers, recreation specialists (park rangers, program leaders), or seasonal employees; some were combination fruit pickers, Christmas tree loaders, day laborers, plasma donors, and school bus drivers.

While some of these occupations fell into the category of "traditionally female," others did not. While teaching school or running the YMCA's after-school program might be considered a middle-class occupation, many of the jobs my counselors took to support themselves in the off-season placed them firmly within the working class. Camp ideology romanticized the transiencies of seasonal wage-labor: the subjugation of all employment and activities to the camp schedule (whether or not to quit one's "good" job to go back to camp is often the biggest recurring dilemma in one's life) was framed within an ethos of change, transition, movement. Many of the beloved camp songs of my childhood idealize, with a characteristic wistfulness, the vagabond, the wanderer in the wilderness, the exile. With titles like "The Life of a Voyageur," "On the Loose," and "Born for Roaming," they enforce an ideology of a gypsy-like existence. For women, the realities of this hobo-esque lifestyle are obviously fraught with danger. Because of the threat of sexual violence, women have never been able to ride the rails and hitchhike the way men do (although many women have done it anyway). Within the camp counterpublic, a sort of wandering could occur, as one traveled from camp to camp, summer to summer. Each season brought new friends and lovers, and then one moved on.

This romanticization of exile and transition was also a way to transform what are conventionally perceived as the isolating, devastating consequences of a queer existence, including the loss of familial support and the discriminatory practices that bar queer and transgendered people from employment. Thus, the camp legitimized and reorganized what might otherwise be viewed in the bourgeois public sphere as the inability to "fit in." What might otherwise be regarded as simply a "failure" to attain the privileges and accouterments of middle-class status, or to assume one's position in the capitalist work ethic—what my parents often referred to disdainfully as the inability to "grow up"—the camp revalued. Being "grown up," as any queer knows, means submitting to the dual claims of bourgeois normalcy and compulsory heterosexuality—getting a "real job" and getting married (Rich, "Compulsory Heterosexuality").

Is it no wonder, then, that collectively disavowing "growing up" was part of the camp philosophy (reinforced, in part, through the immense popularity of the song, "I Won't Grow Up," from *Peter Pan*)? Leaving camp "for good" was thus a highly overvalued moment. At a certain point, one was regarded as being "too old" for camp. This was a personal decision, made by the individual herself. It connoted a final giving-in to society, a letting-go of "camp." The sense of loss one experienced at the end of every summer, as goodbyes were spoken and relationships terminated, became at this moment of retirement, a greater, more final loss that could never be recuperated, and each woman had a different sense of when the last summer at camp should be. Some quit in their mid-twenties, others in their mid-thirties. Still others were persuaded to come back to camp after several years of absence. Even after they "left for good," however, many former counselors remained within a "camp network" of friends and/or lovers, returning during the summer for visits, hosting reunions during the off-season, and volunteering within the local Girl Scout organization. Thus, one could maintain the camp spirit and live within the camp counterpublic long after one had retired, perhaps even for life.

All of these examples suggest that inside the ideology of the Girl Scouts, an oppositional space flourished, one in which compulsory heterosexuality might be suspended, gender redefined, and one's non-participation in the capitalist work-force supported and justified. As I noted above, however, there seems to be a premium placed, in much work on the public sphere, on counterpublicity as a space for those who claim a particular social identity and who assert their *right* to visibility and to representation. But what about those for whom identity-politics have no urgency, or feel too dangerous, or impossible, or simply not descriptive of their own immediacies? Is there room for a counterpublic based on practices, congregations, habits?

Furthermore, can the idea of a counter*public* adequately account for a space such as the Girl Scout camp, since it was precisely because the Girl Scout camp was perceived by its inhabitants as outside the "real world," a sort of "private public," that many of its collective, oppositional practices could occur? Certainly the camp functioned as a "public space," in terms of one's ability to cruise and flirt "out in the open" without fear of physical violence. As I have outlined, it also offered a space for the formulation of oppositional identity-practices. Yet it was precisely because the camp was *not* "public," that in fact it actively shunned publicity, that these experiences were possible. Much of the work on the utopian possibilities of the counterpublic relies, it seems to me, on the (liberal) assumption that visibility/

speech itself is inherently liberatory.[8] But is the closet itself a "counterpublic" sphere? a counterprivate? As Michel Foucault notes, "There is not one but many silences, and they are an integral part of the strategies that underlie and permeate discourses" (*History* 27).

Much of the revisionist work on the public sphere after Habermas has been based on a critique of the "private sphere" as an arbitrary class and historically specific ideology.[9] To claim the private sphere, even as a space of empowerment, is to reinscribe dangerous racist, sexist, and classist ideologies about what is a false division between social spaces, to ignore that the fantasy of the abstracted, public sphere of white male citizenship in the United States exists in part because of its own "othering" of the "private" as a feminizing, racialized space, outside the realm of the "political." I am certainly not advocating a reevaluation of this particular positioning. Yet, in our urgency to abolish the idea of the private, have we lost the ability to imagine alternative, closeted spaces as sometimes just as powerfully subject-forming and sustaining?

Returning once again to my memory of watching the same film over and over on rainy days, I find in this scenario a rich image for what happened at Girl Scout camp. In the darkened theater that was "camp," as long as the Girl Scout film was running, all kinds of other activities could take place among the trees and woods, all of them saved by the label "Girl Scout."[10] Thus, camp becomes the closet of the Girl Scout public, its own, arbitrarily designated "private," whereas space within the camp repeats these layerings: There are the things one says in public versus those things that can only be spoken in private, or written in a note, the differences in how one behaves in the space of the dining hall versus how one behaves in the hidden clearing behind it. As Sedgwick describes this phenomenon: "'Closetedness' itself is a performance initiated as such by the speech-act of silence—not a particular silence, but a silence that accrues particularity by fits and starts, in relation to the discourse that surrounds and differentially constitutes it" (*Epistemology of the Closet* 7–8). It is these unstable relations between silence and speech, secrecy and revelation, visibility and invisibility, as well as the performance of privacy within publicity and publicity within privacy, that made camp such a richly *queer* location.

Scouting for Girls

When I was thirteen, I wrote my own Girl Scout novel.[11] My "book" made the rounds of the camp that summer, passed from camper to counselor—my own little queerzine. Later, I found it simply embarrassing and put it in the back of my closet, where it lay until I began this project. The narrative describes in obsessive detail the character formation of a particular young woman, obviously modeled on myself, who is packed off to camp by her disinterested parents. It recycles a gothic plot—the main character is a girl who is always being mistaken for someone else, someone who is dead, someone who eventually turns out to be her long-lost sister. Perhaps this convention mediated the ways in which, even at thirteen, I was being "mistaken" by counselors and peers for a lesbian. The book is a blissful fantasy of an abundance of older, experienced teachers/mothers/lovers; alternatively described as "beautiful," "breathtaking," "fascinating," "talented," "athletic," "long, flowing-haired," and "short, curly-haired," these counselors take care of, instruct, punish, reward, excite, adore, and continually misrecognize and recognize a younger, femme camper.

The novel also contains scene after scene of instruction, where the protagonist "learns," in minute detail, every rule and regulation of the camp, every custom in the dining hall, every ritualized interaction, every song, every game. In the process of the heroine's instruction, the reader learns it all, too. And, as in the case of Marjorie, as the heroine masters public forms of achievement, she is rewarded with private forms of attention.

These fictionalized sites of pedagogical intensity mirror exactly the highly scripted public of Girl Scout camp life. Besides the clearly demarcated steps up the Scouting ladder from "Brownies" (ages seven to nine) to "Juniors" (ages nine to eleven) to "Cadettes" (ages twelve to fourteen) to "Seniors" (ages fifteen to seventeen),[12] the Scouting program also includes hundreds of badges and awards based on community service, religious service, and so on. All of these measures of achievement work together to ensure that a girl "becomes" a woman within a specific framework by acquiring a variety of "essential" skills.

The Girl Scout camp has its own set of progressions. Besides the hierarchized organization of the camp staff, beginning with the camp director, moving downward through the assistant camp director, directors of various program areas, unit leaders and unit counselors, the campers themselves are also highly organized. Split first into age groups, they are further divided into interest groups (horseback, general, waterfront, trips, and so on). Once they reach senior (high school) age, they may become Counselors in Training (CITs). The dream of many young campers, CITs occupy the middle ground between camper and counselors in terms of privileges and responsibilities, yet legally they are still campers, meaning officially that they cannot be left alone with children and unofficially that they are off-limits for sexual encounters with counselors.

Every activity in the camp centers around progressions as well. One starts out as a beginning horseback rider and summer after summer improves one's riding. One learns to swim and eventually, as a CIT, earns her certificate as a lifeguard. In this way, almost every increase in knowledge can be accounted for and quantitatively measured.

These progressions become part of the identities of the girls within them. Not only do the CITs and counselors memorize the characteristics of each age-group as part of their training, but the girls themselves know exactly what it means to be a "Brownie," a "Cadette," a "canoe tripper," or a "wrangler." This allows younger campers to project themselves easily "into" older identities, to perform them, so to speak, to imitate counselors and fantasize about "being on staff." Like young girls modeling themselves after movie starlets, my friends and I dressed like staff, imitated their gestures, copied their slang, and tried to "be" them, often convincing younger campers that we "were" counselors. Not only did this involve fashion choices, it also necessitated imitating and appropriating the behaviors of counselors, often in violation of the rules.

In learning how to *be* staff, in addition to appropriating privileges and actions unique to the social structure of the camp, we were also copying, at first "unknowingly," a variety of styles of self-representation, many of which signified in the world at large as "lesbian." Cutting my hair, converting to vegetarianism, refusing to shave my legs, begging for flannel shirts and Levis and hiking boots—all these activities, much to my parents' chagrin, were often associated in the late seventies and early eighties with lesbian "subculture."

In illuminating queer and traditionally female "styles" of representation, Sedgwick values "gossip" as an important method of representing the differences that constitute one's society. As she explains it:

> I take the precious, devalued arts of gossip, immemorially associated
> in European thought with servants, with effeminate and gay men,
> with all women, to have to do not even so much with the transmission
> of necessary news as with the refinement of necessary skills for making, testing, and using unrationalized and provisional hypothesis about
> what *kinds of people* there are to be found in one's world. (*Epistemology of
> the Closet* 23)

Queer-identified persons must always be aware of the people around them who may pose a threat to one's physical or economic or emotional security, or who may offer an erotic opportunity. "The writing of a Proust or a James," Sedgwick notes, is projects precisely of *nonce* taxonomy, of the making and unmaking and *r*emaking, and redissolution of hundreds of old and new categorical imaginings concerning all the kinds it may take to make up a world. (*Epistemology of the Closet* 23)

Or (my world) a Girl Scout camp. While the myriad of knots to be tied, songs to be learned, and rules to be memorized itself functioned as a kind of mapping of social space and identity, so too did the incitement to gossip and taxonomize the counterpublic/counterprivate spaces the camp provided. My novel includes numerous lessons in how to "read" scenes between women, scenes of silence, shared glances, unexplained angers, cryptic notes, desired and repelled awarenesses, scenes that require interpretation according to a varying set of codes, scenes that are predicated on established hierarchies of experience and inexperience, knowing and "unknowing," and an intricate hierarchy of influence unique to the camp and to the Scouts.[13]

For instance, much of the erotics of the exchanges of power and affection I participated in with older campers and counselors centered around convincing them to "tell" me things I wasn't supposed to know—camp gossip—which started out as questions that were fairly innocuous, such as what "Jo's" real name was,[14] how old "Leaf" was, and as I grew older, often implicitly or explicitly revolved around the various relationships/sexual adventures of the rest of the camp—who was and who wasn't, who was doing it with whom. Lists of counselors' "real" names turned into lists identifying counselors' sexual preferences, as sexual identity became a more potent "open secret" than any other marker of identity.[15] We learned the public ways in which one indicated one was queer, too—who switched the gender of pronouns in songs, who wore a baby diaper pin on her staff tie, who sat with whom in the dining hall. With access to such well-kept and well-displayed "open secrets," my friends and I felt ourselves set apart from the rest of the Cadettes, bound together in our "Harriet the Spy"–esque conspiracy of interpretation (Fitzhugh).[16] And as we began to "taxonomize" the women around us, we could ourselves evaluate, perform, and sometimes reject their styles and mannerisms. We were, in fact, encouraged, through the dominant discourse of Scouting, to do so.

Of course, both the thrill and the terror that accompanied one's "knowledge" of an adored counselor's lesbianism (often attained only after a long period of what Sedgwick has termed "willed ignorance," a performance of unknowing) sprung from the fact that as one realizes one "knew it all along," this moment of recognition threatens also to subsume the knower— "maybe I'm one, too" ("Privilege of Unknowing: Diderot's *The Nun*" 23).

Queer theory, despite its flourishing in recent years, still lacks models for the multiple ways that deviant, perverse sexualities are formed, and how they survive. For example, Teresa de Lauretis's recent work on modern lesbian subjectivity, while attempting to account for the effects of popular culture on lesbian identity, remains firmly within the psychoanalytic purview. She repeats the same old story of the construction of lesbian identity, in which a universalizing (white, middle-class) mother/daughter relationship forms the basis for a multiplicity of identities and identifications. Because of de Lauretis's inability to relinquish this model, she ends up reducing the effects of culture, ethnicity, and even, I would argue, masculinity, on lesbian subject-formation.

It was precisely my counselor's distance from my mother, like the camp's distance from my suburban tract home, that made her so alluring. Simultaneously, her slippage into nurturance traditionally defined as "maternal" was extremely pleasurable, but so was her adaptation of the role traditionally defined as "paternal." In fact, as I have argued elsewhere, lesbianism itself as an identity may spring in part from such historically specific, class- and racially marked moments of substitution.[17] In the late nineteenth-century United States, the responsibility for white, middle-class, female identity-formation, once sentimentally held to be solely the mother's affair, became the job of other counterpublics. It is this distance and slippage between mother and other, having and being, home and camp, that seems so perversely productive, and it is a dialectic (or tria-, or quadra- lectic) for which psychoanalysis, with its rigidly gendered, racialized, and class-delimited heterosexual family of origin, cannot begin to account.[18]

My counselors offered me multiple opportunities for identifications, identifications that as I have noted were rewarded and expected within the rigid structure of the Girl Scout program. Perhaps it was this emphasis on the inherent performativity of identity that made assuming a lesbian identity feel, ironically, almost compulsory to me: When at age fifteen I began to want not only to be, but to have, my counselors, I struggled against this "recognition," not so much out of internalized homophobia (although this was certainly a player) as out of the fear that I was simply succumbing to peer pressure.

In fact, if what I believe—in essence, that I was "taught" to be a lesbian, "brought up" to desire other women—has resonance, then counterpublic spaces such as Girl Scout camp may tell us something about how gay, lesbian, and queer identities and practices have been replicated and sustained in the twentieth century. Perhaps some gays and lesbians, enabled by such institutionalized spaces of pedagogy, do "reproduce" themselves.

This hypothesis has serious political and epistemological consequences: The terror/fantasy of gay and lesbian "recruitment" takes on new meaning in this context. With the paranoia around children and queers at an all-time high, to claim that sexual identities are "learned" or "taught" is to unleash the possibility that this knowledge could be just as easily used to justify its "unlearning" or to restrict our access to children.

Because of its emphasis on children, Scouting is in a particularly vulnerable position, evidenced by the recent skirmishes over whether or not gay men could be Boy Scout leaders (significantly, the Girl Scouts have a nondiscrimination policy). What would it mean to really "out" the Scouts—or is that what I'm doing here?

It may be that the Girl Scouts as a space of lesbian pedagogy has lost its originary function, that other cultural locations are now able to do the work of "bringing up girls to be gay," especially in the era of Queer Nation and even Queer Scouts. This analogy between Queer Nation and the Girl Scouts raises another question, a continuous undercurrent in my discussion of a specific or universalizing lesbian pedagogy: the problematic relationship between extremely productive sites of lesbian and gay identity formation in the twentieth-century United States and their relation to nationalism, militarism, and forms of cultural imperialism. Tomas Almaguer's critique of Queer Nation points out the dangers of a queer nationalism, which enables a homogenized, singular queer identity at the expense of racial and ethnic differences ("Letter to Jackie Goldsby").

While Girl Scout camp may have been an idyllic scene of lesbian pedagogy, it, too, relied on the homogenization of identity produced by the Girl Scouts. One was always a Scout first, in the same way that much of contemporary lesbian theory, a Girl Scout camp of its own, often relies on a homogeneity of experience and privilege. Hence my discomfort at realizing I, too, was "one of them" sprang in part from the sense that I was being recruited, that I would thus have to conform to a particular set of rules and mores. The phrase "scouting for girls" epitomizes this tension; it may be interpreted simultaneously as a metaphor for the imperialist urge to reformulate individual girls into good American women, or as a playful invocation of lesbian cruising. Is lesbian identity, as a set of practices, styles, and counterpublic identifications, itself a form of imperialism?

While the utopian collectivity posited by theorists of the counterpublic sphere seems both politically necessary and utterly attractive, we must not, in our eagerness to invoke radical democracy, forget those counterpublics or counterprivates for whom such moments of collectivity have no meaning, as well as those for whom identity is not an organizing term. Yet

I would hate my cautionary tale to be confused with something like a call for a queer rugged individualism, as it seems to me Leo Bersani's idealization of gay male subjectivity as utterly out-law might be (Bersani, *Homos*). Many calls for anti-collectivism, for gay male identity or lesbian identity as distinct, pure spaces, it seems to me, are really ways of justifying one's own misogyny, racism, classism, or AIDS-phobia, a problem that the utopian fantasy of the public sphere as a space for discursive debate among competing counterpublics seems designed to address. Yet how do theories of the counterpublic reconcile the fact that for many gay, lesbian, and queer-identified people in the twentieth century (and perhaps earlier centuries), the dramas of secrecy versus revelation, private versus public, were themselves highly eroticized, and perhaps also constitutive of such identities? Increased visibility, as Foucault's *History of Sexuality* reminds us, always means increased regulation, as much as it means anything else. In our eagerness to co-opt and exploit the means of national, not to mention global, publicity for our own queer ends (a project my essay itself participates in, as it "outs the Scouts"), let us not forget those for whom such performative gestures have no meaning, no erotic pay-off, or too great a material cost.

NOTES

*Kathryn R. Kent, "'No Trespassing': Girl Scout Camp and the Limits of the Counterpublic Sphere," *Women and Performance: A Journal of Feminist Theory*, vol. 8, no. 2 (1996): 185–202. Copyright © Women & Performance Project, Inc., reprinted by permission of Taylor & Francis Ltd., www.tand-fonline.com, on behalf of Women & Performance Project, Inc.

For their support in and out of the Girl Scouts, I thank Alison Regan, Eve Kosofsky Sedgwick, N.W., P.T., and Jane Gaines. This essay could not have been written without the encouragement/incitement of Brian Selsky, Amanda Berry, José Muñoz, and Benjamin Weaver, and the expert editing of Leslie Satin.

1. My discussion of public and private economies of revelation and secrecy relies on Eve Kosofsky Sedgwick's (*Epistemology of the Closet*) understanding of the powerful effects of silence and secrecy in the performative relations of discourse around the closet.

2. *Camp Grounds*, a recent anthology of queer writings on camp, does not include any discussion of summer camp, even as it playfully alludes to this space in its title. See *Camp Grounds: Style and Homosexuality*, edited by David Bergman.

3. In an attempt to distinguish "partial publics" from "counterpublics," Hansen, in her introduction to the work of Oskar Negt and Alexander Kluge,

defines the "partial public" as one that exists inside the workings of "industrial-commercial" capitalist subject-formation, does not function on an "identitarian model," and is "silent" in terms of public discourse (Hansen, Foreword to *Public Sphere and Experience*).

4. For a detailed discussion of this term, and relations of identification and dis-identification and its relationship to minority counterpublicity, see José Muñoz, "Disidentification" (Ph.D. diss., Duke University, 1994).

5. Ernest Thompson Seton, one of the founders of the Boy Scouts, wrote sections of the early Girl Scout Handbooks (*Scouting for Girls: Official Handbook of the Girl Scouts of America* [The Girl Scouts of America, 1920], 280–372).

6. For a fictional representation of precisely this phenomena, see Judith McDaniel, "The Juliette Low Legacy," *Lavender Mansions: 40 Contemporary Lesbian and Gay Short Stories*, edited by Irene Zahava (Boulder: Westview Press, 1994), 242–50.

7. I use the terms "butch" and "femme" to represent two forms of gender expression evidenced by my counselors, despite that fact that few, if any, of them would have labeled themselves this way, just as many would not have identified themselves as "lesbian" or as "queer."

8. The utopian ideal of a public sphere in which multiple, and often competing, counterpublics hammer out their similarities and differences presumes not only a kind of formal equality, but also an assumption that representation and self-representation are the paramount political vehicles.

9. For feminist revisions of the "private sphere," see Mary Ryan, *Women in Public: Between Banners and Ballots, 1825–1880* (Baltimore: Johns Hopkins University Press, 1990); Linda Kerber, "Separate Spheres, Female Worlds, Woman's Place: The Rhetoric of Women's History" (*Journal of American History* 75 [June 1989]: 9–39; and Gillian Brown, *Domestic Individualism: Imagining Self in Nineteenth-Century America* (Berkeley: University of California Press, 1990).

10. Cindy Patton, in analyzing the space of a supposedly "non-gay" porn cinema, describes the ways the screening of "heterosexual porn" allowed "straight" men to have sex with men without challenging their sexual identification (Patton, "Unmediated Lust: The Improbable Space of Lesbian Desires," *Stolen Glances: Lesbians Take Photographs*, ed. Tessa Boffin and Jean Fraser (London: Pandora Press, 1991), 233–40. Similarly, following Caroll Smith-Rosenberg, I would argue that it was precisely because of the ideology of female sexlessness in the nineteenth century that a legitimating space was created for "romantic friendships"; at the same time, the doctrine of sexlessness also maintained white, middle-class femininity as respectable, distanced from the supposed sexual improprieties of the working classes (Caroll Smith-Rosenberg, *Disorderly Conduct: Visions of Gender in Victorian America* [New York: Oxford University Press, 1985], 53–76).

11. This is the title of one of the earliest editions of what would become the Girl Scout Handbook.

12. Because of the decline in enrollment amongst older girls, in the 1980s the Girl Scouts added another level to this progression, "Daisy Scouts," who are five and six years old.

13. I take the term "unknowing" from Sedgwick's discussion of the performative effects of ignorance both in *Epistemology* and in her essay, "Privilege of Unknowing: Diderot's *The Nun*," *Tendencies* (Durham, N.C.: Duke University Press, 1993), 23–51.

14. By the time I was in Scouts, military titles had been replaced with "camp names," pseudonyms that counselors assumed for the summer, and sometimes for life.

15. My use of the "open secret" comes from D. A. Miller, who argues that secrecy functions as a space of both resistance and "accommodation," and that the "open secret," through its unstable status as both known and unknown, undermines the workings of regulatory power (D. A. Miller, *The Novel and the Police* [Berkeley: University of California Press, 1988], 207).

16. That Harriet is the fictional "role model" for many a queer child, and that she repeats this process of taxonimizing her world as a kind of queer reversal of adult surveillance, should come as no surprise. For a discussion of the novel and its remarkable author, see Karen Cook, "Regarding Harriet: Louise Fitzhugh Comes in from the Cold," *VLS* (April 1995): 12–15.

17. Kent, "Making Girls into Women: Reading, Gender and Sexuality in American Women's Writing, 1865–1940."

18. For two notable interventions into psychoanalysis, one that foregrounds and queers the "having vs. being" dichotomy, see Judith Butler, *Bodies That Matter: On the Discursive Limits of "Sex"* (New York: Routledge, 1993), 57–91, and Diana Fuss, "Fashion and the Homospectatorial Look," *Critical Inquiry* 18, no. 4 (1992): 713–37.

Nation-Bonding

Sexuality and the State in the Jewish Summer Camp

Alexis Mitchell

> Jew Camp. The various locations where Jewish kids 6 to 16
> are shipped off every summer to give their parents and nannies a
> break from them. They all go for years and years and learn to love it
> and are turned into good little Jewish boys and girls. Often the
> location of the first kiss, first hand job, first . . . well let's just say
> there are a lot of firsts at Jew camp.
>
> —URBAN DICTIONARY, "Jew Camp"

When I was a child between the ages of eight and eighteen years, I attended Jewish summer camp in Southern Ontario, Canada, in an area where there were at least seven other Jewish summer camps within sixty miles. I don't remember how I knew that attending summer camp would one day be my fate, but I remember begging my parents to send me away for the summers starting from the time I was six years old. In hindsight, there were likely a variety of factors contributing to my desire to escape to what I imagined to be a magical forest far away from the urban (or rather suburban) life I knew in Toronto, Canada. I was an awkward and boyish girl who grew much faster than my peers, and this put me in a prime position to be bullied. Summer camp wasn't only a place in my dreams; it was my one and only escape—a place so cemented in the consciousness of North American Jews that my parents would have sent me whether or not I begged them to, and whether or not they could afford it. Summer camp was just something Jews *did*, and my parents would have it no other way.

It is impossible to separate Judaism in North America from the space of the Jewish summer camp. As co-founder of the *Foundation for Jewish Camp*, Elisa Spungen Bildner said, "How can we talk about Jewish identity and ignore Jewish summer camps?" (Bildner, "Foundation for Jewish Camp"). Elisa and her husband Robert Bildner started the foundation in 1998 as a philanthropic project to ensure that Jewish education would continue to flourish at an informal level, and believed that summer camps were the perfect place for this to occur. Equipped with the knowledge of the history of the Jewish summer camp movement, the duo understood the camp's importance in Jewish history and education. Dating back to the end of the nineteenth century, Jewish summer camps acted as a redemptive space free from the squalor, disease, and poverty of the tenements Jews inhabited in the city. Summer camps became a corrective to the perils of industrialization and helped many Jewish children (particularly boys at the beginning of the movement) remain physically and emotionally healthy (Paris 2008; Sales and Saxe 2004; Van Slyck 2010; Wall 2009; Lorge and Zola 2006). The summer camp, in this way, has always been a biopolitical project, invested in the longevity of Jewish life. In the late 1990s, the Bildners noticed a trend among American non-Orthodox Jews: declines in "synagogue membership, attachment to Israel, donations to Jewish charities, organizational belonging, the number of Jewish friendships, and, most famously, in-marriage" (Cohen et al. 4). They were certain that the summer camp was the space to correct these trends and created a localized network for philanthropy and resources for non-profit Jewish summer camping.

This idea of "in-marriage" historically holds a lot of cultural weight within Jewish communities — and many other communities that have faced persecution. Sprung from a cultural anxiety about the historical oppression and extermination of Jewish people and communities, Jews have often privileged the perpetuation of the Jewish people through the only truly acceptable means: blood. Marriage for the purpose of maintaining Jewish bloodlines (via the mother as is the case for Jews), has been one of the main focuses of Jewish culture and identity for centuries. Therefore, even summer camps that embrace this "quiet Jewishness," as Marcie Cohen Ferris labels the camps that don't have explicit Jewish programming (such as the one I attended), still offer a contained environment for Jewish children to spend time with one another "bonding" (Cohen Ferris 2012). As Emily Shire writes, "Hooking up at camp is a hallmark of the American Jewish youth experience" ("Hooking Up at Summer Camp"), and in 2017, though the continuation of the Jewish community via sexual reproduction is perhaps less predominant, the importance placed on Jewish community bonding persists.

The summer camp I went to wasn't Jewish per se, as there was no specifically Jewish programming or education, but every person who attended the camp was Jewish, and this, to me (and my parents) was all that Jewish summer camp was—a place where I would be surrounded by the type of cultural sameness my parents obviously felt very comfortable with (they also sent me to a private Jewish day school until I was twelve years old). Summer camp wasn't exactly the place that I dreamed about. In fact, I was teased more aggressively in this "magical forest" than I was back home, but the intensity of the love that everyone around me felt for this space, made it feel like an impossible place to leave. The camp spirit, showcased through song, cheers, and a level of campy exuberance that could only be rivaled by *RuPaul's Drag Race*, made my anxiety about not fitting in even stronger. Therefore, instead of leaving, or trying to change the space and the people around me so that I felt more at ease, for the ten years that followed, I tried as hard and as vigorously as I could to belong.

Because I continued to feel outside of the culture, when things resonated with me I clung to them with an intensity performed mostly by teenage fan girls. One of these things was the music. Every year I would discover new folk bands and continue to obsess over my existing favorites. One of the most popular bands at camp was the Indigo Girls, a lesbian folk duo whose sexuality was never a topic of conversation. I remember going to my first Indigo Girls concert in Toronto in my late teens, and the audience was made up of white lesbians in their fifties and eighteen-year-old Jewish girls from the suburbs. I would have thought that in a space so rife with childish emotions, high-intensity drama, and bullying, the Indigo Girls' sexuality would be a topic of conversation, but it was neither interesting to anyone nor a deterrent from singing their songs around the campfire year after year.

I also have a very distinct memory of another song we used to sing: "Gabey and Mike." I remember walking down the camp path from activity to activity with my cabin, and we would all sing this song, line after line, year after year. I had never heard a recording of the song, so in my mind it was something someone at my camp had written that the rest of us continued to pass down from generation to generation—a Jewish summer camp oral history. I would lie in bed at night and hum the tune while furiously scribbling down the lyrics in my diary:

> *Yesterday Michael found a letter all tattered and worn from when he was young*
> *All ripped up and taped together, a painful stabbing of what they once shared*

And this is what the letter said:
I'm sorry my mom found us in bed, it's just that I was feeling lonely and I
  missed the
days when we were kids
Gabey and Mike
They were both fine young boys
Friends never mattered, they didn't seem to care
But his mom told Gabe not to see Mike anymore
The neighbors are asking, they're looking in
But they never seemed to understand, that our love was simply friend to friend
I took the chance I had to see you
My mom wasn't due home before noon.
Gabey I saw you get on the bike and I didn't know what to say or do,
  I remember when
we were kids, you were half of me and I was half of you.
The engine roared and you drove away, your mother yelled at me that day
I didn't listen I didn't hear, all I saw was that truck driving near.
Yesterday Michael found a letter all tattered and worn from when he was young
All ripped up and taped together, a painful stabbing of what they once shared
And this is what the letter said:
I'm sorry my mom found us in bed, it's just that I was feeling lonely and I missed the
days when we were kids
Gabey I saw you get on the bike and I didn't know what to say or do,
  I remember when
we were kids, you were half of me and I was half of you.
The engine roared and you drove away, your mother yelled at me that day
I didn't listen I didn't hear, all I saw was that truck driving near

A few years ago, a friend (who went to another of those Jewish camps within a sixty-mile radius), alerted me to the fact that this song was by a band from Toronto called Mermaid Café and that it was queer musician/performance artist Peaches' first band (see Figure 4 for an image of Peaches). Mermaid Café was a folk-duo comprised of Peaches and her girlfriend at the time, Andi D; they played together for only a year, but became rapidly famous amidst this circuit of Jewish summer camps in Southern Ontario, as "Gabey and Mike" was a campfire sing-a-long mainstay throughout the nineties. The recalling of this very gay song by this queer musician within the space of the Jewish summer camp, coupled with my experience of being ostracized for my (at least gender) queerness, urged me to question the ways queerness might figure within this unique space so primed for Jewish-on-Jewish "bonding." I created a film about this song and its prominence in the space of the Jewish summer camp called *Gabey and Mike: A Jewish Summer Camp Love Story*. The film situates the story of Mermaid Café and Peaches' first queer relationship within the space of the summer camp itself—and asks similar questions to the ones this paper explores: Why was a song about two gay kids in love so popular within circles of young Jewish kids in the nineties who were quite proficient at ostracizing those who were different? And what cultural trends does the song's popularity foreground within the space of the Jewish summer camp itself? The inclusion of this song alongside so many other cultural markers of queerness in the camp environment—sing-a-longs, musicals, mud-wrestling, talent shows with drag performances—creates the illusion that sexuality, in general, and queer sexuality, more specifically, might have been accepted and perhaps even encouraged within my experience of Jewish summer camp. In actuality, the inclusion of modes of queerness like the camp aesthetic honed in the musical productions, camp cheers, and love of lesbian folk rock did not queer the space of the summer camp at all. There was no celebration or even attempt to normalize queer desire, and above all, as the song's dramatic ending expresses, there were ample repercussions for expressing queer sexuality overtly.

In order to frame this tension in the film—between the openness expressed through the popularity of the song and the intensity of control exhibited throughout the culture of the Jewish summer camp, my collaborator Stephanie Markowitz and I juxtaposed these two seemingly disparate

Figure 4. Peaches performing in *Gabey and Mike: A Jewish Summer Camp Love Story* (2016) by Alexis Mitchell and Stephanie Markowitz. (Director of Photography: Ava Berkofsky)

worlds against one another. Visually, the sweet, tender, often slow-motion love story of the two characters of Gabey and Mike is interrupted by quickly edited, and slightly sinister, archival footage from Jewish summer camps in the nineties, which is organized by themes (camp musicals, camp crushes, camp bullying, and camp competition).

The juxtaposition of these worlds creates a scenario where "incongruity can transform the banal into the fantastic" (Rainer qtd. in Green 9) placing (or drawing out) the camp aesthetic within the summer camp environment. We use camp as a method knowingly, because, as Fabio Cleto notes, the "semiotics of camp are inscribed with a politics of deterritorialization, recontextualization and stratification through irony, mimicry and parody invading not only the subject matter of camp representation but the mode of representation itself" (31). Using camp to produce these specified outcomes foregrounds the failure of representations (two gay kids in love) and thus the ways we have come to understand not only gender and sexuality through these representations, but all discursive subjects/objects, which opens up the potential to re-imagine the space of the Jewish summer camp as queer while allowing us to view the complex culture produced through/ by the space as well. This paper attempts to employ a similar productive juxtaposition—weaving between the casual personal narratives, and the more formal academic criticism and analysis to make use of (the) camp's most active qualities—its impermanence. As Charlie Hailey writes, the camp can be defined as "weak architecture" as the space itself "allows for open epistemological system and a productive, though unstable, ground of reference" (59). This campy instability makes apparent the complex layers, lending to a narrative that views the space as queer, while undermining that very narrative simultaneously.

Desire and sexuality, queer or not, were omnipresent in the world of the summer camp, but this seemingly open and accepting environment around sexual exploration served a function other than the promotion of sexually open, perverse, or queer lifestyles. Through these performative gestures of acceptance around sexuality and gender, the Jewish summer camp performs an environment of immense acceptance, which limits the capacity for outsiders. By creating an atmosphere where almost anyone is meant to feel welcome, the summer camp creates a closed circle—an insular environment, where notions of belonging and group bonding among the Jewish community are central. While the feelings of ownership over the natural environment and belonging to a cohesive group of Jewish people are part of the joy people experience at Jewish summer camp, these feelings are also what feed the regulatory and imperialist framework the summer camp exhibits. The Jewish summer camp is able to forge cohesion and insularity among Jewish people inside the camp, drawing a boundary around this camp environment, simultaneously creating an outside—and outsiders. In order to explore this dynamic, I will look at how desire is produced within these spaces to forge coherence around a common bond, and to consider what this bondedness does for the summer camp and those who exist within it.

I recently spoke to a friend who attended Jewish summer camp near Yosemite National Park. This camp is known within the community of North American Jewish summer camps as having one of the most liberal attitudes toward gender and sexuality. My friend Kyle attended the camp in the early 2000s, and I spoke with him about his experiences. This camp boasts a form of Jewish engagement that's more intense than the camp I went to. My summer camp wasn't Jewish in programming or ideology; in fact, the only Jewish facets were the children who attended and the Hebrew blessings we sung before each meal. At Kyle's camp, campers recited the Hebrew blessings, celebrated the Sabbath, and partook in daily programming based on different Jewish values such as "Tikkun Olam" (Hebrew for "repair the world" and used in nature programming), the "Hebrew word of the day," and an involved celebration of "Israel Day" where campers learned cultures, rituals, and politics of the region. Though the camp does not promote one specific ideology related to Judaism, it does boast a very open and seemingly radical approach to physical intimacy and relationships. Though Kyle (now a trans man in his late 20s) was not out as gay, queer, or trans when he attended the camp, he fondly recalled stories about the camp's openness to sexuality and gender. He spoke specifically about how the camp viewed sexuality and queerness and remarked that it

> wasn't something that was tolerated, it was something that [was] built into the structure of the camp. [The camp offers] queer family camp weekends; everybody knew that the director of the camp was a lesbian and her partner was a rabbi. Everybody knew that. Everybody knew there were gay and lesbian counselors there. And it was just part of it. (Lasky)

For Kyle, Jewish summer camp did provide an escape from his life back home, the perfect reprieve from a life that was otherwise full of bullying, cliques, and alienation:

> I didn't have any friends during normal life and I was not cool and nobody liked me and I cried all the time. And I didn't know how to

change that or to be in a social situation or be in a group of people and interact and feel happy. And so at school I was just like a loser and so when I went to summer camp it was the opposite, I was cool. And people liked me and we all hung out all the time and also I got to hang out with the counselors which was the thing I liked the most, like 18, 19, 20-year-old, young women [laughs]. (Lasky)

The experience Kyle had at camp is also not unique—as both an experience of belonging as well as in the excitement produced via the relationships between counselors and campers. This is something I've reflected on in my own experiences of Jewish summer camp, and it's what many ex-campers I've spoken to have related as well. The notion of the Jewish summer camp expressed in the urban dictionary epigraph, as a space rife with sexual energy, lacks obvious complexity, but it is not outside of the experiences of many. As the urban dictionary quotation and pop culture like the film and television series *Wet Hot American Summer* suggest, Jewish summer camps are widely imagined as spaces rife with sexual energy, experimentation, and play (see Figure 5 for a still from *Gabey and Mike* that represents this kind of intimacy). I don't imagine this is because Jewish kids are more promiscuous than non-Jewish kids, but there is a culture to these spaces that has proliferated for over a century, and while the notion of sexual openness may not have been an agenda item at staff meetings in the 1920s, there are

Figure 5. "Hands." Video still from *Gabey and Mike: A Jewish Summer Camp Love Story* (2016) by Alexis Mitchell and Stephanie Markowitz. (Director of Photography: Ava Berkofsky)

certain cultural qualities that have worked their ways through these spaces and continue to have lasting effects.

From my own experiences of Jewish summer camp, coupled with what I've learned from the interviews I've conducted, the idea of sex, or sexual exploration, and camp "bonding" are used interchangeably. In "Wet Hot American Jewish Sleepaway Camp," Shire writes that the alumni she interviewed remembered discussing hookups with older counselors (and by older I mean three or four years), and said that those conversations helped them create a "special bond." She goes on to say that "part of the problem is that some counselors pay more attention to campers who dish on their sexual exploits—and campers who don't are all too aware that they're not the ones in the spotlight" (Shire). Kyle's excitement over his camp counselors is not unique. Whether it takes the form of the extreme pleasure of a teenage crush, sneaking out at night to the cabins of the opposite sex, or the excitement that comes from crushing on one's camp counselor—sex, or the idea of it, acts as the glue that holds the camp family together.

This type of group bonding occurs intensely at summer camp, where entire months are spent in the company of the same group of people. Erving Goffman calls spaces like the summer camp (along with asylums, prisons, and army barracks) "total institutions," where all aspects of life are conducted under a single authority, and each phase of the members' daily activities exist in relation to others, all of whom are treated alike and required to take part in the same activities together (xiii). The members' daily activities are tightly scheduled and assembled in a single, rational plan designed to fulfill the official aims of the institution. That these types of institutions would produce a heightened level of group bonding is obvious, but the function of the relationship between the total institution and group bonding is quite fascinating in a space whose mission is to provide personal and communal growth rather than rigid forms of sublimation and control. As Jonathan Sarna notes, the "'total environment' of the summer camp . . . offered what one historian calls 'an unparalleled venue for the transmission of values'" (35).

Another institution that produces such heightened forms of desire and functions to bond a close-knit community of people is Birthright Israel, where groups of over thirty Jewish teenagers who have never visited the State of Israel are bused around the country for two weeks. Looking at this trip provides a unique understanding of the ways "group bonding" in the total institution of the summer camp functions for the benefit of the "Jewish cause" (whether that's in-marriage, organizational belonging, or Jewish friendships and love). In his book *Tours That Bind: Diaspora, Pilgrimage, and*

Israeli Birthright Tourism, Shaul Kelner writes about the infamous Birth-right Israel trips as a "medium of political socialization [which] is deeply entrenched in the repertoire of modern Jewish practice" (6). Unlike the Jewish summer camp, Birthright Israel is quite explicit about its ideological goals: to bring groups of Jewish people to experience a version of the State of Israel that will inevitably solidify the emotional and material bonds Jewish people will have to the State. This might entail unequivocally supporting aggressive state policies including the ongoing violence and expropriation toward Palestinian people and their land, or the economic investments materially produced through capital ties like the purchasing of Israeli bonds. The type of bonding that happens during a Birthright Israel trip is unquestionably bonding with an intention. Kelner notes that when speaking to people about their experiences on Birthright, the memories they recall have more to do with what happened inside the tour bus, and little to do with Israel as a place, and he comments on how central the experience and culture of "hooking up" is on the trip and how often the trip is colloquially referred to as "Birthrate Israel" (145). These heightened sexual experiences and memories have worked quite well for the success of the Birthright Israel trip as the "tour sponsors hope that the emotions generated by the group experience will attach to the symbols of homeland and ethnic community in which this group experience was embedded" (Kelner 168).

In an article called "The Romance of Birthright Israel," journalist Kiera Feldman describes Birthright as a trip where the group is "chronically underslept, hurled through a mind-numbing itinerary" including "booz-ing and flirting with the IDF soldiers" assigned to accompany the trips, and spending a night "in a fake Bedouin tent, where participants sleep crowded together, a setup conducive to first kisses." The experience is reminiscent of the summer camp's activities and environment. In fact, Feldman describes one night of the Birthright trip in such terms:

> We had a cookout at Gvulot, the first kibbutz cum military outpost in the Negev, in southern Israel. We learned the story of Gvulot's found-ing—conquest over Palestinians—in the manner of all summer camp lessons: skits with gratuitous cross-dressing. The part of the man who prances onstage with makeshift breasts was played by Yossi Mizrahi, then a goofy 21-year-old Israeli soldier, adored by the entire Birthright group. He'd fought in Operation Cast Lead, and he liked to show us the "terrorist headbands" he claimed to have collected from the bodies of Palestinians he'd killed. The activity came to a close with a round of sweet Bedouin tea.

Here, the types of drag and camp that are ever-present in the queer bar and the space of the summer camp are utilized to their productive ends. Because "Camp sees everything in quotation marks" (Sontag 280), the objective of violence present in this series of events is packaged as something else. In this example, camp turns violence into desire by providing the group a temporary architecture for bonding over events that were, perhaps at one time, too violent to bare, but are now camp skits and drag performances.

This sounds like an extreme example, but it is the common experience on this trip, one that centers romantic lust/love in the midst of its intensive and militaristic propaganda. What better way to sell the state of Israel to its chosen citizens than to show the group that not only can the military be fun, but that they can also engage in flirty and sexual acts with soldiers and one another by using the tools of Camp/the camp to turn violence into quotation marks.

Producing lust on this trip extends quite smoothly to lust for the state. As Feldman points out, "Birthright boasts that alumni are 51 percent more likely to marry other Jews than nonparticipants." In this case, the lust between participants serves as a reminder of where they met and therefore helps to solidify the bond, not only to each other, but to the state as well. In fact, this is precisely the function of lust and love on this trip, as Feldman quotes one of the Birthright board members exclaiming: "many of our Birthright alumni come back and are ready and eager to be advocates for Israel." Birthright's method draws on a policy created by Israeli educator Elan Ezrachi called "mifgash—the encounter"—promoting relationships between Jewish Israeli teens (Israeli soldiers) and youthful diasporic Jews. As Ezrachi says, these encounters "move very fast to what we call 'hormonal mifgashim' . . . 'Things happen'" (Feldman).

The ideologies of the trip itself are actually not restricted to sexual reproduction—or furthering the Jewish bloodline materially—but are embedded in the social and sexual bonds created on this trip for everyone. After all, many philanthropic Israel-supportive organizations work to sell the state to LGBT people as well—hosting LGBT-focused trips that encourage the same kinds of lust-filled environments rife with sexual energy and promotion of "in-marriage." Gays, too, can be part of the process of nation-building because early Zionists thought the vision of the movement was encompassed in the vision of a "'new Jew,' a virile conqueror and tiller of the land who would channel sexual energy into nation building" (Feldman). This "new Jew" does not have a specified gender or sexuality (Zakim)—but does embody this image of the ideal Israeli citizen that the birthright trip is seemingly interested in producing. Thus, the focus of these trips is the forging of Jewish citizens that will bring as much excitement and sexual energy as they forged through their group bonding to the State of Israel itself. The stress is therefore less on heterosexual reproduction and child-rearing and more on recruitment of ideal Israeli citizens through the ideology that Israel and its military are spaces of openness and acceptance that bring all women, men, and trans people regardless of their sexuality into the militaristic and nationalistic fold.

Though the agenda of Birthright Israel differs dramatically from the goals and locations of the Jewish summer camp because these summer camps exist mostly in the North American wilderness, and many of them are not explicitly Zionist in their ideology or programming, we can see resonances of the type of group bonding alongside the creation of this figure of the "new Jew" within the space of the summer camp. Kelner writes that on the Birthright tour, in order to "foster relations of intimacy, tour staff attempt to create embracing, nonjudgmental environments that encourage self-disclosure" (165). Like the hookups shared with counselors in Shire's example, and the feelings of elevated excitement in Kyle's story about his counselors, both Birthright and summer camp produce a level of exuberance over the shared experiences of touring Israel or living in a cabin with a group of people for an entire summer. The Jewish summer camp is one where children of all ages feel comfortable enough to take control over their natural environments through campfire sing-alongs, cabin cheers, and color wars (yearly competitions where the camps are divided into teams, assigned a color or country, and compete for days in relay races, tug-of-wars, and mud-wrestling), and bond over their shared experiences, both at camp and home. In comparing the type of activities, openness, acceptance, and group bonding made explicit in both of these environments, it becomes apparent that the summer camp produces forms of desire alongside or through feelings of safety, excitement, and acceptance within the cabin, the campfire, and the color war.

In order to unpack what this culture of acceptance, sexual openness, and group-bonding is productive of in the space of the Jewish summer camp, it is helpful to look at the role the group plays in fostering a collective feeling of belonging. As Freud writes, "the essence of a mass consists in the libidinal attachments present within it" (67). Following him, in her book *The Last Resistance*—a collection of essays of Jewishness, Zionism, and the legacies of the Holocaust—Jacqueline Rose writes, "Love then, and devotion to the leader are what binds" (231). Rose, here, is working through an understanding of Freud's *Mass Psychology* when she asks, "So what are these love relationships or emotional ties which bind subjects en masse? They are precisely the experience of being loved; or to put it in more clichéd terms, not what I give to you, but what you give, or do for, me" (233). Jessica Benjamin echoes this sentiment when she writes, "Obedience to the laws of civilization is first inspired, not by fear or prudence . . . but by love" (5). Through an understanding of the meaning and sensations that being part of (and loved by) the group produces—a form of loyalty produced out of the need to be loved in return—it becomes apparent how desire functions within a total institution like the summer camp. Whether or not the intention of the camp is to produce a love or attachment to Jewishness and/ or the State of Israel, this is precisely what occurs in a Jewish space where bonding and belonging along the lines of cultural sameness are fostered.

There are many instances where the destructiveness of this group mentality is overtly apparent (the nation, the army, the colonizer), but the ways this functions within the Jewish summer camp is more insidious and perhaps even more complex. It is not my intention to undermine the importance of belonging—of feeling accepted in an environment free from some of the anxieties that persist in the world outside summer camp. I do hope to create some nuance around forms of acceptance via sexuality and desire, and to pinpoint what belonging in this respect produces aside from boosted self-esteem. Being accepted within the space of the Jewish summer camp is absolutely the most important and central aspect of this experience. To not belong at summer camp is to exist within a space of continuous discomfort, with no escaping the circuitous effects of this failed belonging. Therefore, ensuring "belonging" is beneficial to all—especially to camp owners who rely on the child's return the following year, and to Jewish culture and identity more broadly.

Belonging is not only important to these Jewish summer camps financially (after all, many of them provide at least a few stipends to those who cannot afford to attend), but belonging functions ideologically as well. Rose theorizes what it means to be Jewish outside of a commitment to the State of Israel—if belonging to this group called "Jewish" is possible when one rejects the centrality of a Jewish state to Jewish identity. Like Freud, Rose is deeply skeptical of what happens when people cohere into a group. She writes that "people en masse are only inspired to an extreme" (223) and that what binds people together is a commitment to things that make them feel good about themselves, that affirms the notion that even when we're acting as individuals, that we are a part of a group, and that "whatever we do we are cut and thrust above the rest" (228). This understanding of belonging to a group is central to the operation of the summer camp and it is apparent in camp cheers, competition, and spirit that re-affirm that

Figure 6. "Kissing Rock." Video still from *Gabey and Mike: A Jewish Summer Camp Love Story* (2016) by Alexis Mitchell and Stephanie Markowitz. (Director of Photography: Ava Berkofsky)

everyone within this environment is a part of something larger than themselves, and whatever they are a part of is the absolute best and most important thing that exists.

In our film *Gabey and Mike: A Jewish Summer Camp Love Story* (see Figure 6), this sentiment is made apparent toward the end of the film. Through a series of chapters that focus on the burgeoning love/lust of the characters of Gabey and Mike, we are also introduced to the space of the summer camp through a voiceover narration provided by Stephanie and me, performing nostalgia about the memories we each have of Jewish summer camp. We speak about the kinds of fashion that were popularized within the camp environment, the kinds of crushes and/or heartbreak we experienced every summer, the intensity of cliques, color-war, bullying, and camp musicals, and at the end of the film, we recount the last night of camp, where kids stand around a giant fire pit and cry for hours and hours because of how much they will miss each other once returning home from their summer away (even though the majority of them live within twenty miles of one another in the city). What is made apparent, through the use of camp and irony throughout the film, is that the level of joy, and/or campy exuberance for each of these activities, is heavily produced through a form of mob-mentality that makes campers believe that they are somehow missing something if they are not part of a clique, wearing the right pajamas, or crying just as much as every other camper on the last night of camp. While Stephanie recounts her experience of watching everyone cry at the fire pit on the last night of camp while we see images of boys and girls gripping each other, and crying on one another's shoulders from summer camps in the nineties, I break the awkwardness of these dramatic sobs by explaining that I used to force myself to cry, out of a fear of not belonging.

The camp Kyle attended has been written about in a number of online articles dealing with sex and the summer camp. The current Executive Director of the camp is an expert in gender inclusion and teen health education, and contrary to Kyle's experience at camp, where sexuality was not really spoken about but just "known," this director has recently brought explicit programming to the camp's schedule, leading optional sessions where "campers can discuss relationships, and can delve into the physical and emotional components of safe sex" (Feldman). Though the camp deals with sexuality and inclusion of sexual difference openly, they boast a policy called "HAKWACO," an acronym for "hugging and kissing with all clothes on." As Shire points out in her playful article "Hooking Up at Summer Camp," however, "while camp directors are none too pleased to find campers getting handsy by the lake, they are quick to advertise the fact that the seeds of marriage are often planted at camp." The pride of group bonding and sexual exploration and openness cannot be separated from the importance of marriage and child-rearing as Jewish mitzvot (commandments). Though these mitzvot have historically been the role of heterosexual reproduction, the openness toward queer sexualities is subsumed within the same overall goal of perpetuating the Jewish "bond"—the energy produced through the excitement of childhood lust and burgeoning sexuality is the precise energy that is channeled into what summer camps refer to as "team-building," but what is also transformed into the type of "nation-building" that is present in the case of Birthright, which Freud, Rose, and others warn us about.

Discussing his experiences at Jewish summer camp, Kyle highlighted an aspect of the camp he thought was particularly interesting—and imagined it to be unique to the camp itself. Every year, he said, the camp paid for a small number of Israelis to come work at the camp as counselors:

> So we had Israel day and we would eat Israeli food and we would have seminars with Israeli staff and they would tell us about life in Israel and life in kibbutz, and life in the army. And I remember, I'm surprised

they did really, but we did a drill, they showed us what life was like in the army if you're training, you have to run and drop and run, it was intense. (Lasky)

I asked Kyle what he thought was the most compelling about this relationship with the Israelis that the camp forged for them. He said:

It was the only time I really learned about the kibbutz and I thought that was really cool. I thought, I'm going to go live on a kibbutz when I'm older . . . well the person who was telling us about it was a lesbian and her name was Yael and her girlfriend was also there and her name was Ronit and they were both really hot. Ha! Like hippies, like really hippie, and so that's what drew me to that. I thought all kibbutz were full of hot lesbian, Israeli women. (Lasky)

This comment makes obvious the work of sexuality and desire in the space of summer camp, and the ways in which that work is exploited for, in this instance, forging a solidified and memorable relationship to the state of Israel: by positioning young, desirable Israelis as a stand-in for the state. The slippage here between desire for a person and the nation is an easy one, and though it can be viewed as harmless and unintentional on behalf of camp directors and staff, the way sexuality is used as a tool to mobilize a sense of togetherness in these spaces is impossible to ignore. By promoting an accepting and open environment full of drag performances and camp plays, the camp can use sexuality and love, in whatever forms it expresses itself, as a way of tightening and perpetuating the bond between Jewish people. By creating an environment where everyone is meant to feel welcome not because of, but through their desires, Jewish summer camps can do the ideological work of nation-building, providing a focused outcome for the Eros produced throughout the space.

Notes on Church Camp

D. Gilson

I wish none of this had ever happened.
Sometimes I thank God that it did.

—GARRARD CONLEY

The ultimate Camp statement:
it's good because it's awful.

—SUSAN SONTAG

What do you get when you cross a penis and a potato? Adam asks as we dip our mushy tater tots into ketchup, *A dicktater.* We erupt in laughter. We laugh because his joke transgresses. Adam is our counselor, a freshman at Central Bible College on a soccer scholarship. We are seventh grade boys going into eighth, thirteen going on fourteen, and Adam is a boy becoming a man, becoming what we want to be. This joke transgresses because Adam said *penis*, and *dick*, and later in our cabin, he will pull down his soccer shorts to moon us, and for years I will remember the tautness of his ass, two cheeks lightly dusted in blonde hair, and for years I will remain envious. This is all transgressive because this is church camp.

The Assemblies of God has run Crosspointe, a decidedly evangelical and specifically Spirit-filled camp on the north shore of Lake of the Ozarks, since the late 1940s. As a teen, I spent a week there every summer. A week of swimming and obstacle courses, of crushes and bad cafeteria food and nightly church services, which, because we were Pentecostal, went late into the night if the Spirit stirred us.

In his first letter to the Corinthians, the apostle Paul glosses glossolalia: *For if you have the ability to speak in tongues, you will be talking only to God, since people won't be able to understand you. You will be speaking by the power of the Spirit.*[1]

The Assemblies of God—the largest charismatic denomination in Christiandom—holds sixteen Fundamentals of Truth. Most of these are fairly nondescript, typical of evangelical Protestantism more broadly, ranging from belief in the deity of Jesus Christ to belief in his impending second coming. What distinguishes charismatics from other evangelicals, however, is a belief in Pentecost today.

According to the denomination's website,[2] Assemblies of God parishioners believe that "Baptism in the Holy Spirit is a Special Experience Following Salvation that empowers believers for witnessing and effective service, just as it did in New Testament times," and that "The Initial Physical Evidence of the Baptism in the Holy Spirit is 'Speaking in Tongues,' as experienced on the Day of Pentecost and referenced throughout Acts and the Epistles." This essay circles around one week at camp: the week I was baptized in the Holy Spirit, evidenced by speaking in tongues, and the week I was also baptized a sexual deviant, a queer boy, a faggot-in-the-making. Though my days in the church are squarely in the past, I set out here to explore how the campy performance of Pentecostal code continues to inform my queer aesthetic, scholarship, and everyday life.

Yes, I spoke in tongues for the first time at that church camp on the shore of Lake of the Ozarks. A bona fide, code-speaking Pentecostal, I would turn fourteen two months later. But at that camp, too, I learned another code. Not boy code, per say, but *a code of boys*.

Put simply: Scholarship on glossolalia leaves me wanting. Perhaps this is because invariably, as anthropologist William J. Samarin argues, "psychopathological explanations oversimplify religious glossolalia" (121).[3] If we surmise that the majority of scholars, myself included, are some form of secular (atheist, agnostic, humanist), then writing about a religious phenomenon from childhood is especially difficult; this is perhaps especially true of speaking in tongues, which even though I know it was never this simple, I want to paint now as both hysterical and fake. But perhaps the self splits—my current queer atheist self, my former Pentecostal self—only to be brought back in some productive marriage of seeming, but also deceptively complementary, opposites.

Or, as Michael Warner beautifully imagines, "For us who once were found and now are lost—and we are legion—our other lives pose some curious problems." He goes on to ask, "Is there no relation at all between our once and present selves, or only a negative one? Is there some buried continuity, or some powerful vestige?" (216). Warner's use of *vestige* in the latter question is especially potent to me now. *Vestige*, according to the *OED*: "A mark, trace, or visible sign *of* something which no longer exists or is present . . . [but] which remains after the destruction or disappearance of the main portion." What vestiges of my young queerness informed by adolescent faith, and what vestiges of that (no longer present?) faith informed—nay, continue to inform—my queerness?

Many might argue that I was *born* queer[4] and *became* Pentecostal, surmising that queerness is a natural state of being, while evangelical faiths require a conversion experience. Though this is perhaps true on the one, obvious hand, I would argue I no more chose my Pentecostalism than I did my eventual, out-and-proud queerness. Which is to say, by my lower-class whiteness in the Missouri Ozarks, I was born into a faith that eventually and merely required an (in my case, anticlimactic) affirmation of that faith. If my family had been wealthier, we would have been Presbyterians, Lutherans, or perhaps Baptists; but because we were white trash—my siblings were raised by our mother in a literal trailer park, and it wasn't until our mother married my father and I was born that the family moved into a house with a foundation—we were white America's lowest. Thus, we were perfect candidates for charismatic citizenry; as Harold Bloom argues, "respectability in any case is hardly likely to descend upon Pentecostals" (185). And perhaps we were the lowest of the low in white America because our denomination, the Assemblies of God, was a white Christianity in blackface.

As with all faiths, the origins of contemporary Pentecostalism[5] are readily disputable, though many trace these simultaneously shallow and deep roots back to a 1906 revival held at the Azusa Street Mission in Los Angeles. Led by a charming, fire-and-brimstone African-American preacher, William Seymour, the revival at Azusa was a decidedly Black affair where, we are told, the Holy Spirit descended and baptized the masses, evidenced by them speaking in tongues of fire. According to Harold Bloom,

> By the autumn of 1906, the Azusa speaking with tongues had begun
> to spread around the nation, and thence around all the world. After a
> meeting in Hot Springs, Arkansas, in April 1914, the Pentecostals
> soon founded the Assemblies of God, the dominant white group in the
> rapidly segregating movement. African-American Pentecostalism has

never ceased, and it remains an irony of the American Religion that
the authentic founder of our Pentecostalism was William Seymour,
who did what his [white] teacher Parham could not do. The Assemblies
of God, to the best of my knowledge, does not honor Seymour, but
without him they would not exist. (184)

Here, the white taking up of Black forms is a truly American story; our
nation was built, both literally and figuratively, on such conditions, so why
would this not extend to the building of American faiths, too? But if the
turn to religion is a turn to identification with the Other (the Christ, the
beyond-this-world, or, for most in the Assemblies of God, the non-white),
what might the potential of such an appropriative performance be? Eric
Lott argues that such an "art of [white] impersonation is built on a contradiction. Appreciation, deference, spectatorship, and emulation compete
with inhabitation, aggression, usurpation, and vampirism" (198), but he
admits that this blackface may, indeed, point to a surprisingly pure sense of,
albeit complicated, desire.[6] And it is from such a wellspring of desire that
queer potential boils over and begins to speak in tongues.

Weekly at Crosspointe, attendees elect a royal court of king, queen, prince,
and princess. Looking back, the whole process seems dubious, not only
absolutely adolescent, but also antithetical to American Christianity,
which, even though I no longer practice a faith, I have always understood
to centralize equality for its adherents. Nevertheless, each cabin was
charged with nominating a camper to compete for the court. The summer
I was almost 14, my cabin nominated me.

    First, a panel of camp administrators asked each of us a bizarre cadre of
questions. *What is your favorite bible verse? If you could have dinner with any
person, dead or alive, who would it be? What do you look for in an ideal mate?*
And finally, *Have you been baptized in the Holy Spirit?* From these interviews,
three boys became finalists for camp king, and three for camp prince, to be
chosen in a general election. I became a finalist for prince.

    Which would have been enough—more than enough—except for the
reason I could not be considered for king: the last interview question. I had
never been baptized in the Holy Spirit. I had never spoken in tongues. I
would never become king of Crosspointe Bible Camp because at that point,
my membership in our Pentecostal faith was second-rate at best. The day
after the interview I delivered a self-deprecating campaign speech to the
entire camp; it was a hit, I was elected camp prince, and I should have been

ecstatic. Sitting back down with the rest of my cabin for evening services in the giant amphitheater, a tacky silver crown of plastic atop my sunburnt head, Nathan hooked my thumb with his pointer finger. *It's okay,* he whispered, *you're going to get filled with Holy Spirit tonight. I just know it.* He knew I was mad. Nathan let his hook linger, fishing itself further into the palm of my hand. I let him.

Tongue-speakers speak in a tongue of ecstasy, and ecstasy is a code of many codes. Describing early twentieth-century charismatics, the historian Robert Mapes Anderson explains how "the Pentecostals have been ideal workers and citizens in every respect except for their cultivation of ecstasy" (239). If the Assembly of God Pentecostals were white trash brethren of the Black tongue-speakers, loosely connected by a smaller, yet important denomination known as the Holiness Church, then these whites, too, shared with their African-American brethren a demeaning image of hard-working, yet sexually unruly, folklore. We all spoke in codes of ecstasy, an astaticism of spirituality closely twinned with sexuality, a twinning, it is clear to me now, that could never be undone. And though like Warner I refuse to call the Pentecostal experience orgasmic—as it does both orgasms and Pentecostalism a disservice—the metaphor does have some saliency.

Undoubtedly, the best literature of Pentecostal ecstasy has been Black. From Zora Neale Hurston to the more contemporary ZZ Packer, tongue-speakers appear in Black writing far more often, and far more favorably, than they ever do in white writing. Without question, the most famous literary Pentecostal, however, is James Baldwin, who converted at 14, roughly the same age I was that summer at church camp, but under very different circumstances. Though the queer Baldwin would eventually reject both God and church, as a young man he was what I was: a zealot baptized in the Holy Spirit, speaking in tongues and learning a code that served him the rest of his queer literary life. At age 14, Baldwin was filled with the Holy Spirit and quickly became a preacher, drawing large crowds to Fireside Pentecostal Assembly. By 17, Baldwin became disillusioned with the church, though surely, like many of his characters—especially John Grimes, the protagonist of *Go Tell It on a Mountain*—he continued to use that specifically charismatic code to bring fire to his writing. Of his days in the church and their influence, Baldwin would later explain it "was like being in the theatre; I was behind the scenes and knew how the illusion was worked" (37). But what most without a background in such a faith might misunderstand: illusion still holds some truth, even if that truth is that one has convinced oneself of the existence of the nonexistent.

Did I really believe I was speaking in tongues? friends will ask me now, and I will laugh, *No. Maybe. Yes. I don't know.* In short: It's complicated.

In a poem observing a lover speaking in tongues at a Pentecostal service, Traci Brimhall better describes the truth of the matter: "What keeps her here, tied to this life? What weakness? / What strength? The answer pulses on her tongue. / The answer is trembling, unspeakable" (71). Which is also to say: The answer is split in half, is half-truth, is knowable, and yet. The nightly service following the ceremony where the royal court was crowned fell on Wednesday, three nights into our week here so campers unfamiliar with the Pentecostal mores would have enough time to accustom themselves to a service specifically for those seeking baptism in the Holy Spirit. It was my night, I knew it, and Nathan prophesied it as we awkwardly held hands, or hooked fingers, or began.

I do not remember the sermon that night, but can surmise it was some watered-down soliloquy on Acts 2, the singular chapter on which the Assemblies of God has built so much of its theology. *When the day of Pentecost came,* our 1998 version might have read, *the campers were sweaty in the Ozarks humidity, singing a roller coaster of worship songs that pitched and quieted, pitched and quieted, as the Holy Spirit filled them in waves.* In opposition to mainline Protestantism, altar calls in charismatic Christianity can meander for hours. Though by the late 1990s, Assemblies of God parishioners were, for the most part, not handling snakes or flailing wildly in the aisles of backwater churches,[7] we were still seeking the Holy Spirit, spending hours at the altar crying and eventually, it was hoped, speaking in a language unknown. We called this our prayer language, the tongues of angels, Shekinah glory; other evangelicals called this heresy, blasphemy, sacrilege; most of the world called it fake, dumb, or hysteria. Even now, I am not sure who is correct.

Eventually I made my way down to the altar. Nathan and our counselor Adam flanked me; with their hands on my shoulders, Nathan and Adam prayed over me in their own prayer languages, asking, surely, that I, too, would become one of them: spirit-filled, Christ to a broken world. Were we not, however, the broken world itself, regardless of how Christ fit into our lives, or didn't? As they prayed, I knew I couldn't make it look too easy. I wailed out to God—*Fill me with your sweet Spirit, dear Jesus, please, I beg of you,* etc., etc.—and cried as I had seen the others cry. Thirty minutes later, maybe 45, I began to speak in tongues.

If glossolalia here, as an act of decidedly American Pentecostalism, is also an act of white trashiness, then might it be married to a performance of camp when spoken through the tongue of the queer? I rely heavily on Susan Sontag's infamous, but too-often misunderstood, essay, "Notes on 'Camp,'" to begin plainly: Camp "is *one* way of seeing the world . . . a quality discoverable in objects and the behavior of persons" (277). Sontag moves onward to theorize camp as a purposeful redemption of trash into artistic treasure; this is especially true of those producers whose identities we group under the ornery label Other: queers, non whites, and women. I am not exaggerating when I claim I wanted to speak in tongues; but because I think the act was somewhere between a hysterical fiction and a hysterical fiction that alluded me with an active truth—the need to belong, as a human, and the need to perform, as a queer—I must read the act itself, the actual tongue speaking, as an artistic act of exaggeration.

My own tongue speaking embarrasses me still. Every former Pentecostal can tell you that each Spirit-filled adherent develops their own, most-often ridiculous, prayer language, nearly as original as one's DNA. Mine? A bastardized utterance of my poor French accented by random phrases from the Japanese cartoons I'd taken to watching on our family's satellite dish. I am embarrassed to admit this, yes, but thankfully Sontag intervenes because "Camp responds particularly to the markedly attenuated and to the strongly exaggerated" (279). My tongue speaking, in true queer fashion, was nothing if not a performance in camp exaggeration. The remainder of Sontag's landmark essay centers upon her bifurcation of some camp as naïve (pure) and some as deliberate; her eighteenth thesis reads: "One must distinguish between naïve and deliberate Camp. Pure Camp is always naïve. Camp which knows itself to be Camp ('camping') is usually less satisfying" (282). In this way, it is hard to think of my time in Pentecostalism as camp, insofar as while I was faithful, my heart, as evangelicals are fond of saying, was actually *in* it; but after my conversion to queer atheism, my first instinct was less naïve, was to redeem what I had done through laughter, parody, purposeful redemption. Eventually Sontag wonders, "Perhaps, though, it is not so much a question of the unintended effect versus the conscious intention, as of the delicate relation between parody and self-parody in Camp" (282). Huh.

Je m'appelle je m'appelle urusee c'est la sugee bien, I'd pray over and over, the one chain I remember now, 16 years later, *my name is my name is shut up it is awesome good*.[8] And the act was good, or God was good, depending on who you asked. Near the end of her "Notes," Sontag concludes, "Camp taste nourishes itself on the love that has gone into certain objects and personal styles" (292). At the time I believed it was the perfected love of the Holy Family—God the Father, God the Son, and now God the Holy Spirit—that nourished me. Closing my eyes and thinking back, however, seeing Nathan and Adam weeping alongside me, hugging me close, whispering their own prayer languages in my ears, their teenage breath hot on my neck, I realize it was camp and it was love, but it wasn't God's love nourishing me.

If we are to believe the biblical account, when those gathered in Jerusalem for Pentecost were filled with the Holy Spirit, it sounded very different than the prayer language my friends and I in the Assemblies of God spoke. According to Luke in the Book of Acts,

> Now there were staying in Jerusalem God-fearing Jews from every nation under heaven. When they heard this sound, a crowd came together in bewilderment, because each one heard their own language being spoken. Utterly amazed, they asked: "Aren't all these who are speaking Galileans? Then how is it that each of us hears them in our native language? Parthians, Medes and Elamites; residents of Mesopotamia, Judea and Cappadocia, Pontusand Asia, Phrygia and Pamphylia, Egypt and the parts of Libya near Cyrene; visitors from Rome (both Jews and converts to Judaism); Cretans and Arabs—we hear them declaring the wonders of God in our own tongues!" Amazed and perplexed, they asked one another, "What does this mean?"[9]

What it meant, of course, is that they could understand each other despite language barriers, a most practical gift God was bestowing upon them. For the most part, contemporary glossolalia resembles such practicality in no way whatsoever. My holy gibberish was as unintelligible to my friends as my friends' prayer language was to me, and that was the point. That is what made it, somehow, real. We at once sequestered ourselves linguistically while performatively joining a collective. And how queer it is to think about that now. Luke later writes of these people breaking bread in their homes and eating together "with glad and sincere hearts." Which if we stop to think about it, is something both Christians and queers do; however, each group may differ in after-dinner activities.

Though I was now Spirit-filled, we could not leave the service immediately. Adam stayed until the wee hours of the morning, sometime around three, but now that I was blessed, or chosen, or elect, Nathan and I stammered back to our seats, feigned interest in the loop of worship music for a few requisite minutes, and made our escape.

Wednesday night services were special for another reason. With camp staff occupied at the altar, praying over the swarm of teenagers seeking baptism in the Holy Spirit, the rest of Crosspointe lay unsupervised. Cut through with swaths of Missouri oaks, with rocky, shallow creeks and bluffs overlooking the colossal Lake of the Ozarks, the area was a virtual playground, brimming with spots for campers to dodge the gaze of their counselors. It must have been about midnight when Nathan and I made our way to the western-most dock of the camp's lakefront. The waxing moon was straight overhead; shadows danced off the kayaks moored there. As we made our way down the dock, I grabbed Nathan's hand. We ran to the end, jumped into the water fully clothed, and came up gasping for air, but laughing. Nathan hooked my leg with his, grabbed my hair, and planted his open mouth upon my open mouth. This was my first kiss, unexpected, on a night now with two baptisms.

Such an essay would be amiss to not point out: Christianity has a long tradition of going into the wilderness—of camping—with a gusto of camp. In Genesis, Cain takes his brother Abel into the forest, only to murder him in cold blood. When God asks Cain, "Where is your brother Abel?" Cain sasses, "Am I my brother's keeper?" And though this story has always struck me as odd—Isn't God omniscient? Does he need to ask Cain what happened?—it is not unlike a scene from one of the films Sontag places in the canon of camp. In my crushes at church camp, it strikes me now, I was not unlike Bette Davis in *All About Eve*.

In perhaps the most famous sequence from the film, Davis floats seamlessly through a cocktail party she is hosting. Going from being compared to a hysterical Macbeth, to greeting a man in French who doesn't interest her but from whom she accepts a drink, to finally ending up cornered with a man she purposefully did not invite to the party, all in the span of less than a minute, Davis neither misses a beat, nor drops her cigarette, all in heels and a corseted cocktail dress. Camp at church camp for a queer boy like me was something analogous: My guard could never be down. I had to float seamlessly from speaking in tongues at the nightly service to sucking Nathan's cock down on the dock.

And, importantly, back again. What followed Nathan and me from the dock was a deep-seated shame that is not unique to queer sex generally, but is unique, I think, to queer sex within the evangelical tradition. Every night we vowed never to touch each other again, and every next night we did. For years. And for years at church camp we spent hours praying for God to take away our desire for each other, though never admitting this aloud—a prayer language provided by the Holy Spirit hides, thankfully, the specificity of sins. And for years we fell away from our recommitments almost nightly, in a pattern of ecstasy, orgasm, shame, redemption that perhaps screwed up my sexuality for years to come, some would say, or perhaps gave me a knack for the theatrical, for the aesthetically queer, for the mode of camp itself, which Sontag argues is "the sensibility of failed seriousness, of the theatricalization of experience" (287).

"Camp refuses," she adds, "both the harmonies of traditional serious-ness, and the risks of fully identifying with extreme states of feeling" (287). Here Sontag seems to theorize camp as similar to, or perhaps the parallel of, a popular Christian-ism: We were called to be in, but not of, this world. But for the queer teen at church camp, a lot of campy fun could be had in this world, on Satan's playground, like sneaking into the woods at night. Or during swim time, palming the small of Nathan's back just below the water line. Or in the showers, feeling Nathan's foot glide across mine as he walked to his own showerhead. In this way, both camp as mode and camp as place are simultaneously subtle and theatrical, naïve and self-aware, both Christ-like, Spirit-filled, and queer as hell.

The writer of Matthew explains we must be vigilant, always going to the wilderness to prepare as Christian men. "Make ready the way of the Lord," he yells, "make his paths straight!" We tried. But as Bette Davis tells her party guests in *All About Eve*, "Fasten your seat belts. It's going to be a bumpy night."

Though I suppose I disagree with Sontag's seventh thesis: "All Camp objects, and persons, contain a large element of artifice. Nothing in nature can be campy." Or better said, I agree with her first proclamation—camp as bursting with artifice—but I think she overlooks the camp Americans have long brought to the wilderness,[10] and in the twentieth century specifi-cally, the camp we have brought to camp.

After all, what is natural about taking a group of suburban teenage boys to the wilderness, to cabins with roaches and no hot water, to nightly bonfires replete with stories connecting us to the bona fide Native Ameri-can within? In this way, evangelical church camps are no different than sleep-away camps of all stripes, from elite New England camps on pictur-esque lakes, to survival training in the Arizona mountains for those teens deemed "troubled." All these camps share "a large element of artifice." But considering the focus on spiritual warfare, itself an idea of complete artifice, Christian camps do centralize a type of camp unavailable to their secular brethren.

An object lesson in the artifice of camp at camp: the obstacle course. Deemed necessary for team building—*Though one may be overpowered, two can defend themselves. A cord of three strands is not quickly broken*[11]—every summer Adam or another counselor assured me the obstacle course would be fun. I was a fat, un-athletic, queer boy with a love for *The Golden Girls*; the obstacle course was never fun, but was, in hindsight, a lesson in artifice. One obstacle in particular illustrates this sacred artificiality: The Great Wall.

We are told we are missionaries on the Mongolian border. We are told our objective: smuggle Bibles into Red China, a land, we already know from our suburban church experience, where Christianity is outlawed, but craved, and delicious sweet-n-sour chicken awaits us. What stands between us and the salvation of the largest people group on Earth is The Great Wall. What stands literally before us now is a fifteen-foot wall of two-by-fours. I do not trust it, narrative or construction, but the obstacle is not optional. Our team develops a strategy. Push the lightest member of our Bible brigade to the top of the wall. Push the next member, whom the first will reach down and help up. Repeat, repeat, repeat. As the heaviest missionary, I was saved for last. All my teammates atop the wall reached down as I jumped up from the bottom. They grasped my arms but, despite their numbers, could not pull me up. I flailed against the wall like a dying fish brought to the beach and left there.[12] Eventually, I fell from their grasp, landing in the mud below with a thud. My teammates laughed and laughed but the good news was not lost: their Bibles made it to China, while mine remained on this side of the Wall, muddy in Mongolia.

Kathryn Bond Stockton suggests that "one finds it hard to see how *gay* for teenage boys isn't still a landmine, even at this moment, that they have to mind in their teen world" (50). Hours ago, being baptized in the Holy Spirit lacked detonation because the performance was one, at least in part, which I controlled. When Nathan kissed me, it is cliché but true, fire erupted in my mouth as his was my first gay kiss, my first landmine, as Stockton imagines. And my religion was hell-bent on obliterating such landmines for its young men.

This is not an essay about conversion therapy, or my brief foray therein, for many of those already exist.[13] No, what I want to approach is a vortex of queer sex and Pentecostalism in tandem, landmine upon landmine upon landmine, a detonation that produces some type of fruitful marriage between seeming opposites. If the origins of American Pentecostalism in the early twentieth century produce a fraught but meaningful relationship between Black charismatic faiths and white, then might my queerness now, I wonder, grow by looking back to the codes I learned at camp?

"Camp rests on innocence," Sontag explains, which "means Camp discloses innocence, but also, when it can, corrupts it" (283). What followed was a cycle of innocence corrupted and made pure again and again corrupted that held Nathan and me for years. A cycle of kisses, then praying in tongues, handjobs, then redemption, blowjobs, then, *We can never do this again. It's wrong.* This cruising through sin and redemption and sin again begs an important question Valerie Traub and David Halperin ask, "Can we do things with shame that we cannot do with pride?" (4). And of course, Nathan and I would do it all again, on Friday nights in our basements or in the bathroom at our favorite coffee shop, the Mudhouse. But mostly, on docks late at night. At church camp each summer on Lake of the Ozarks, at the public fishing dock near the Springfield Power Plant, at the cabin his father, our church's pastor,[14] owned on Table Rock Lake, forty-five minutes south of our hometown where we'd drive summer nights after we got our driver's licenses, our sixteenth birthdays just a week apart. Nathan and I were friends, but friends on opposite peripheries of a circle of friends because we had to distance ourselves. Traub and Halperin call this "the mutual hostility and self-imposed isolation of the shamed" (4). And this was the code: We shared a queerness that neither of us wanted. Proximity put us in danger. Distance and nonchalance were our salvation. It was the pattern of heat and cold, fire and ice, that would become the basis of my dating and sexual life as a gay adult, a pattern that continues to this day.

The code I learned in Pentecostalism was one of exclusive inclusion: that once one gained membership in the club, it was not only hard to lose it, but that the membership also came with a community unparalleled in love and enthusiasm.[15] No matter how bad at sports I was, the athletes in my youth group became my brothers; no matter how little they read, I hung out with them every night. Queerness works best, I argue, in a similar fashion. When I meet another gay man and we camp it up, we are connected, no matter the differences of our lives. No matter if he is a stockbroker and I am a writer, or if he is Black and I am white, or if he is rich and I am poor. Though all these differences *do* matter, they cease to be barriers when queerness performs camp, when we share cocksucking and exaggeration and storytelling, all things I learned through the code of my church at its summer camp.

When I return to the Ozarks now, I occasionally run into Nathan at the grocery store or a coffee shop. He is married with three children and pastors the church in which we grew up. Many in the church would say I—the queer atheist—have lost my way. Many of my queer brethren would look at Nathan and say something similar. *Oh honey, once a cocksucker, always a cocksucker.* I'm not so sure anyone is right here. If I was born a Pentecostal and left the faith, couldn't Nathan have been queer and abandoned this queerness? Could we each carry a piece of what we forsook into our adult lives? Could a bit of our teenage queer Pentecostalism still linger?

I think back often to that dock at church camp where much of this began. Fondly, but a fondness always wrought with a slight sadness that such a nostalgia necessitates. I write this from a dock not so unlike the one at camp, where a university's rowing team practices and people bring their dogs to swim. Sontag is open beside me: "Camp taste supervenes upon good taste as a daring and witty hedonism" (291), and it is this campy pursuit of pleasure that both my Pentecostalism and queerness, at times in turn, at times in tandem, have taught me most. My feet in the water, I look west as the last light vanishes beyond a hill of pines on the opposite shore. I think of Nathan, his wet head resting in the crook of my neck, however briefly, before he went back to pray for forgiveness.

NOTES

1. 1 Corinthians 14:2, New Living Translation.
2. At the time of this writing, ag.org features a diptych banner, its left side a vague scene of women in bright blue dresses carrying baskets atop their heads, presumably somewhere in Africa, its right side a vague scene of white college students laughing on a grassy quad, presumably somewhere in southern California. This is a typical aesthetic I saw, and perhaps participated in producing, throughout my time in the denomination: a fetishization of third-world, poverty-stricken "savages" in need of saving alongside the mythical, good-looking, young white parishioner having fun *and* saving the world. That charismatics (or at least more mainstream charismatic Pentecostals like most Assembly of God parishioners) place such an emphasis on being fit, hot vessels for Christ is perhaps surprising, especially given common tropes of smaller groups of "unfashionable" holy rollers. For a glimpse into this phenomenon, see *This American Life's* "Tell Me I'm Fat," episode 589, act four,

which focuses on the ideal body fat requirement Oral Roberts University placed on its students during the mid- to late twentieth century. However, this might not be exactly fair; as Harold Bloom argues, "Pentecostalism flourishes much more abroad than in the United States, because shamanism is more universally accepted in Asia, Africa, and Latin America than it is here. Yet Pentecostalism had to begin here, because its extreme supernaturalism had to be a reaction against a triumphant naturalism, against a society where power was enshrined in an abundant materialism" (188).

3. Or as Douglas Field, in his beautiful essay on James Baldwin and Pentecostalism, similarly asks, "In a critical era that is dominated—at least in Baldwin studies—on areas such as gender, masculinity and sexuality, might it be that the sophistication of cultural studies is ill-equipped or simply unable to grapple with the religious?" (438).

4. Not to reject Lady Gaga and most mainstream gay rights activists' idea that I was "born this way," but . . . okay, I do reject that in favor of a queer theoretical bent (for actual queer lives) that queerness is what we choose, mold, and re-mold over a lifetime.

5. Many American forms of Christianity, including the Shakers and Mormons, have practiced "speaking in tongues" at certain points in their history, though eventually abandoning the practice. Glossolalia for charismatic Pentecostals, however, seems to be the point of their entire history.

6. Such an appropriation becomes even more complicated when connected with queer sexual desire, which I argue, in line with Harold Bloom and Michael Warner, is a type of religious ecstasy. To this end, Richard Dyer explores his own sexual desire for non-white men, which mirrors the white Pentecostal's desire for Black Pentecostalism: "The sexualisation of my feeling for some non-white men has undoubtedly lent intensity and poignancy to my awareness of race, but I do believe that it is an eroticisation of a much wider feeling, expressed not least in friendships . . . It is the felt connection between gays and ethnic minorities that is important here, as much as romantic and sexual encounters with non-white men" (6).

7. In fact, the church I attended as a teenager, James River Assembly of God just south of Springfield, Missouri, was far from a backwater congregation, antithetical to much of the cultural imagery we have of Pentecostals. James River was part of the mega church movement that proliferated throughout the 1990s, and continues today. Currently, the church has two campus locations and over 12,000 congregants; its main campus houses a state-of-the-art fitness center, two bookstores, and a Starbucks. Though not the focus of this essay, the burgeoning mega church as cultural text continues to amuse, intrigue, and infuriate me.

8. This was my teenage cleverness, an inarticulate repeating of *Je m'appelle je m'appelle* when one of the biggest hits on the radio was Eminem's "My Name Is," a white trash anthem with its repetition of "My name is, my name is" known by nearly everyone under the age of thirty.

9. Acts 2:5–12, New International Version.

10. Sontag's camp is inherently urban: "Camp is esoteric—something of a private code, a badge of identity even, among small urban cliques." And this seems to me one of the biggest missteps in her argument overall, a necessitation of camp as urban. And though I do not have space here to fully explore this, I will at least allow that in Sontag's defense that at the midcentury, the two biggest purveyors of camp in her estimation—Jews and homosexuals—were more highly concentrated in American urban centers.

11. Ecclesiastes 4:12, New International Version.

12. Earning me the nickname "Flounder," which stuck through high school and probably had some contribution to an obsession with my weight that continues into the present.

13. See, for example: Garrard Conley's *Boy Erased* (New York: Penguin, 2016); Alex Cooper's *Saving Alex: When I Was Fifteen I Told My Mormon Parents I Was Gay, and That's When My Nightmare Began* (New York: Harper, 2016); and K. Tyler Christensen's article "'First, Do No Harm': California's S.B. 1172 and My Experience with Sexual Orientation Change Efforts," *Huffington Post* (2013).

14. Again I am a cliché. I remember driving to this lake house in Nathan's Jeep and singing to him, "The only one who could ever reach me, was the son of a preacher man." Yes, he was the preacher's son, I the deacon's, and of course how could we not be fucking?

15. As cheesy as this sounds, it has been true to my life. And though secular academia has provided me my closest friends now, that passionate community as a whole has been absent from my life, save for my time in the church.

Queer at Camp

A Selected Assemblage of Resistance and Hope

Mark Lipton

1. Dear mum & dad: I hate camp. Please come and get me. I hate everyone. Love m.

2. My summer camp stories refuse any attempts at Edenic bliss. What am I doing here? First, this camp sucks; and foremost, camp is not home. Despite my certainty that camp existed long before the invention of home—that firelight among our early hominid ancestors—as a child I recall craving home, clinging to anything resembling home. There was no home. There was no family. My experiences of summer camp contained a collection of colonized settler children and young adults accessing the Canadian landscape: subjects sent far from home to a residential camp, like school, where dominant ideological worldviews of imperial and colonial realities were received and inculcated. There was no Indigeneity; there may have been survival skills training—I can swim; there was respect for nature and earth within the domains of an authority. In my story, however, my suspicion of all things camp results from a lived distrust of nature. My body refused nature; my biopower and biopolitics refute nature within an urban habitus and with a body that should not be alive: Asthma, Allergies, AIDS, Ankylosing Spondylitis . . . Want to learn about the letter B? As a

result, my camp stories reinforce a sexually violent, white male supremacist, aggressively yet innocently entertaining his colonial and imperial futures. There are no others, no Others, no resisting or resistance. This camp sucks.

I can only exist outside the parameters of this camp, this civilization; I am rendered invisible, disappeared, and deterritorialized. Without question, the camp of my past is wound up in complicated balls of tangled yarns where my queer sensibilities, my Jewish identities, and my psychophilosophical perspectives on the world collide. The knots must be cut with sharp precision in order to hold with clarity the multiplicities of my camp worldviews.

In *Homo Sacer: Sovereign Power and Bare Life*, Giorgio Agamben writes about camp as "the pure, absolute, and impassable biopolitical space (insofar as it is founded solely on the state of exception)," and this *camp* space/place, Agamben continues, "will appear as the hidden paradigm of the political space of modernity, whose metamorphoses and disguises we will have to learn to recognize" (78). In the assemblage of stories that follow, I reveal and unmask the various configurations of my camp. In the country, in the bush, on the streets, and in the club, camp abounds and proliferates across multiple domains and orders. An assemblage of this kind functions as the most valuable means by which metamorphoses and disguises become socially relevant and politically meaningful.

3. As Susan Sontag's "Notes on 'Camp'" entered its fiftieth year, I began to share some of my musings, both political and apolitical, on my nature, value, and uses of camp as a creative and symbolic tool for navigating my world. As I near my fiftieth year, I contribute to this conversation provoking further engagement, as camp lies deep in my heart. This assemblage begins to unravel these balls of yarn and unknot that which is tangled.

4. The contested objects of camp worldviews are constituted by historical, cultural, political, psychological, and discursive practices (Lefebvre). Deleuze and Guattari's notion of "assemblage" helps me characterize and understand how camp, its content and affect, manifests into discursive figures (*A Thousand Plateaus*). As a discursive practice, "camp" is a metaphor with multiple associations and past histories. The metaphor of camp implies transience (whether real or imaginary) while keeping in mind the partial and situated nature of particular symbols, texts, contexts, and meanings. Mobilizing insights from queer and feminist discourses on the relations between camp, queer, and affect, I provide part theory, part memoir, and part performance around which I orient a series of attachments, impressions, and emotions. I am working through my challenges of camp

as a contested subject and object, but also cultivating my own past, my own memory, and applying a psychoanalytic gaze to my multiple associations and past histories. These histories, these memories, however, remain "rituals of power" (following Foucault), selecting what is important, falsely constructing a continuous narrative into the ruptures and contradictions of my life. Following Judith (Jack) Halberstam, I "advocate for certain forms of erasure over memory" (*Failure* 15) because I refuse to tidy up my disorderly histories and am suspect of my own subjugated knowledge.

5. Working within the problematic of what Sara Ahmed terms the "cultural politics of emotion" (2004), or Ann Cvetkovich calls "public feelings" (2008), I condense "past histories of association" and "generate effects" (Ahmed 13). Like Cvetkovich:

> I am also questioning professional norms that demand success, productivity, and a seamless public persona. I find myself working in this idiom in part as another experiment in form and as an ongoing engagement with questions of confession, self-display, and coming out, first inspired by feminism's sense of the personal as political and bolstered by queer theory's work in making new knowledges possible. (463)

Following José Esteban Muñoz's process of "disidentification," I gaze as an outsider reconfiguring how my worldviews negotiate with mainstream camp cultures—not by aligning with or against exclusionary camp works but rather by transforming these works for my own cultural purposes. My camp perspectives are "disidentified," both as survival tactics and activist performances of my world and myself.

My disidentifications, then, take up ontological, epistemological, and social issues as well as political and cultural dimensions of human life (Deleuze and Guattari 1987). Much of the discourse, it seems, is centrally concerned with difference, power, and a multiplicity of texts. But I see this discourse as insufficient. As queer theory is declared dead by the likes of Michael Warner (2012) and Jeff Nunokawa (2007), lonely by Michael Cobb (2007), and starved by Lauren Berlant (2007), it seems the stories and metaphors of camp are overwhelmingly a "flat discourse" (Puar 152). Insights from reverse discourse do not apply here. If assemblage writing can be read "as righting" (de Leeuw) my assemblage/writing emerges from a framework suggested by Eyal Weizman's concept of "the politics of verticality" (2002).

6. Verticality implies a vectorial movement and flow, like blood pumping through arteries. The movement of blood never exactly follows a single

coherent logic or path. Upon closer inspection, the complex interactions among blood vessels reveal how issues like pliability, viscosity, and blood velocity all create a flow of blood vessels bouncing against the walls of human arterial channels, this way and that, often at different rates. The range of factors that impact my politics of camp include the emotional labor and physical weight created by each story. Like my blood and my body, my version of camp is affected by everything I do—when and how I eat and drink, the way I move about my house, my experience of physical strain as I stare into a screen. Jasbir Puar's assemblage/writing foregrounds movement between material and symbolic, real and imagined bodies, boundaries, and borders; similarly my spaces of—and for—camp are rendered visible like "networks of contact and control, of circuits that cut through" (154). Muñoz does more for me within this context; his disidentifications influence my pursuits within decolonized liberation theologies. In *Disidentifications*, he argues that queers of color are left out of representation in a space "colonized by the logics of white normativity" (xii). Disidentification is his way of responding to dominant ideologies. He presented a strategy that neither assimilates nor opposes, but helps me examine ways to negotiate power. With camp, my negotiations are like niche geometry. As I apply these approaches to assemblage/writing I present each new flow as a number, like in Sontag's original essay. The numbers are related for me, but more important, different readers might be drawn to some flows of discourse over others. In short, this assemblage is an attempt to capture the polysemic value of camp. My musings about camp are read in dialogue with (and for) Muñoz's "queer utopia" as I collect my memories and stories to consider links between camp and sexual awareness, different formulations of radical consciousness, and varying forms of anticolonial refusal, resistance, and struggle.

7. I play with and politicize camp; engage my own camp sensibilities; examine camp from the darkness and in the light; to camp my thinking about camp for my aging mind, self, and society. What should our queer camp look like in today's world, the twenty-first century? Might camp today, its affect, its seriousness, and its gravity mean, as Halberstam suggests in *The Queer Art of Failure*, "missing out on the chance to be frivolous, promiscuous, and irrelevant" (6)? I would hate that; I love cruising the archives and libraries, which began inadvertently as looking for sex. Now, I work like/with Melissa Adler's *Cruising the Library: Perversities in the Organization of Knowledge*, actively seeking out Halberstam's "visionary insights and flights of fancy" (Halberstam 6) as methodological rigor. My

promiscuous methods (can methods be slutty?) follow Halberstam into the library, "to lose one's way, and indeed to be prepared to lose more than one's way" (6). Promiscuous scholars unite!

8. Lisa Duggan and José Esteban Muñoz (2009) suggest a dialectical formation between hope and hopelessness. They call for a "critical modality of hope"; there is "a political necessity of engaging feelings of hopelessness that do not simply lead to complacency" (275). The wars are not over; *ergo* twenty-first-century camp must be political. All non-normative identities claim a named or nameless queerness. The camp of days past fails to function as a weapon. Fifty years ago, Sontag skimmed the surface of resistance.

"The whole point of Camp is to dethrone the serious" (Sontag). Herein lies camp's inherent political nature. By setting up "more complex" relations, camp engages a politics of disparity, difference, and différance. Political camp, on first glance, seems to reduce the meanings and values of all that is at stake, yet, I argue, any challenges to social order for social justice can hurl camp discourse into actual political change. Look to The NAMES Project Foundation, The AIDS Memorial Quilt as bio-politically explicit camp justice. Queer social collectives, those participating in a camp logic, recognize both an affinity toward—and membership with—the collective camp meaning makers, and an acceptance of this individual and collective work as part of a political practice. Camp is representative of the matrix of socioeconomic relations that determines the conditions within which queer identities and biopolitics are conferred, accepted, and recognized as part of any democratic social project. Collective action is the modality of hope most likely to impact policy. Talking is one thing; walking the walk gets things done.

9. Showgirls! Frivolity abounds. I now look at the receptions, deceptions, intentions, and attention of camp as signifying practice. The film *Showgirls*, for many, is late-Capitalism's camp classic (Verhoeven 1995). However, I cannot claim MGM's *Showgirls* as camp. As a text, it does not adhere to my understanding of queer sensibility. Some claim, like Ara Osterweil (2003), the film *Showgirls* is a camp artifact. Osterweil, who describes herself as a "missionary of bad taste," finds camp, hears camp, or smells camp—mostly demonstrated by affective responses, her U.C. Berkeley students' interpretive readings, and subsequently, the larger interpretive communities that stick to (or stick it to) camp sensibility. The film itself, with its seven shining Razzie awards . . . well, you got me there. I don't see pure camp or naïve camp. The film lost nearly $25 million at the box office. Perhaps that is why MGM, in 2003, tried to cash in on these camp-oriented, queer positive,

interpretive communities by rereleasing and redistributing *Showgirls*. Is this the same territory marked out by Susan Sontag when she pronounced "the ultimate camp statement" is that "it's good because it's awful" (292)? So bad it's good; so good it's bad? I don't think so. Sontag must be wrong.

Critical efforts to reclaim *Showgirls* as a pop classic abound—most recently in Toronto, with film critic Adam Nayman's work *It Doesn't Suck: Showgirls*. Nayman invokes Sontag, claiming how the "theatricalizing of a hyper-feminine person" functions as a form of "feminist camp" (90). Golly gee, in the name of Sontag, what is going on? Does anyone really see feminism or camp in Elizabeth Berkley's portrayal of Nomi, the small town girl who hitches her way to Vegas; a destiny for dancing; practicing for the pole; pushing her way to the top of the sex-glam, topless *Goddess* show; Queen of the Cheetah Club; a rags to riches radical? For Jeffrey Sconce in the "Showgirls: Roundtable," the film is reclaimed as "a long-lost Edenic text of bliss" (Lippit 45). What the fuck? For the love of Sontag, let me be clear. Here is my opinion of the film: *Showgirls* sucks. It may be the worst movie I have ever seen. It should be shot. It should be locked in a vault, buried in the ground, and covered with rocks. *Showgirls* sucks. I prefer Magic Mike's non-stop erotic cabaret. At least the rooster caws and crows; cocks brag and trumpet and my desire for some leghorn ignites, with heat and passion.

But as camp missionary Ara Osterweil points out, the possibilities for camp are always ready to abound. Thus I look to one of the film's interpretive communities: UCB Theatre—better known as *The Upright Citizen's Brigade*—and its camp rendition called "Showgirls. The Best Movie Ever Made. Ever!" Created and written by Jackie Clarke and John Flynn, "Showgirls. The Best Movie Ever Made. Ever!" takes us inside the film, heralding its feminist ideals and its responsible portrayal of minorities and sex workers.

It's a regular Thursday night, 9 PM in New York City. Peter and I are headed to UCB's theatre. We have great seats for "Showgirls. The Best Movie Ever Made. Ever!" (spoken with emphasis, accentuating a heavy Long Island, New York inflection). As we enter the space, I am transported to the Cheetah Club, Nomi's star-world. Peter gets us drinks and I hear Peaches' remix of the glam rock song "Gay Bar" repeating in the background. God I love Peaches. Slut-walking, queer-talking Peaches; trans-around-the-world Peaches. They call her Peaches. Any questions of normative gender roles are instantly contested and challenged. Camp is in the air. The camp missionary was right. I sensed camp. *Ergo*, who cares if my assessment of camp is intentional or mine alone. Reception is deception; intention cannot direct attention. It's up to you friends. You get to decide. You.

10. For me, camp is a celebration, elevation, and worship of my difference, of my deviance, of my queerness. Once upon a time, in a land just like this one, a camp sensibility helped queer men like me navigate through the secret labyrinth where our desires and our culture were incongruous, at war. This was a very dangerous world. They could fire us from our jobs. They could print our names in the newspaper. We could be arrested! We have been bullied. We have been bashed. Bullying began in elementary school. Fag. Sister. Feller; bashing was (and still is) a real fear, like that time in Boston's Back Bay, making out with my much-older boyfriend in his truck, only to be ambushed by a pack of teenaged boys; baseball bats; one attacker had a hammer and began smashing the truck's windows; black eyes; broken bones; Brian, Adrien, Richard, and my trophy Kevin, Oh! The shit we got into back then. Secrets and lies; shame and fear; painful solitude, loneliness, and isolation. Victim. Victim. Victim. Hey, did you hear? It Gets Better (*It Gets Better Project*, 2010). Back in the day, we didn't have *Savage Love*; we didn't have *YouTube* campaigns; I didn't have any support. I learned a set of secret signs, secret codes—both verbal and non-verbal—to aid and relieve my erratic navigation through the world. Camp was one of those codes. Gaydar in the bookstore; cruising parks at night; coming out to my girls; feeling my way around in the dark, in the backroom, bathroom, boys will be boys.

The articulate John Wolf explains how camp is a sense-making, world-making practice operating at the level of internal subversion rather than external revolt (295). Because of this internal subversion, the material forms of camp often pass unmarked and unnoticed, "especially if viewers are not on the lookout" (295). Are you paying attention? Are you listening? Hark, what sound doth camp make? Here, listen. Do you hear it? What Richard Dyer explains as that sour "knife edge between camp and hurt, a key register of gay culture" (178). Camp is gay men poking fun of ourselves, at ourselves as we fail to perform, to be manly or masculine. As Dyer concludes his remarks about Judy Garland:

> We feel that sense in the intangible and ineffable—the warmth of the voice, the wryness of the humour, the edgy vigor of the stance—but they mean a lot because they are made *expressive* of what it has been to be gay in the past half century. (191)

The acoustic ecology of camp registers, these expressive sounds, these ways of uttering language are another of the secret codes for navigating the lived experiences of queerness, while having the safe patriarchal position to retreat.

11. This retreat, it seems to me, is what marks camp as important and meaningful. Camp is a containment of sorts—a means of containing the subject's response to oppression. Camp logics respond to fear: of a failure to pass, of discovery, oppression, death, and continuing the history of victimization without revolt. Camp utterances, those registers of dour circumstances, sound to me like ecstatic reclamations usually saved for more, or more purely aesthetic, experiences. The aesthetic, whether an actual object or not, offers agency and empowerment to our displaced identities looking for justice. These elements of my queer sensibility are, as Wolf suggests, "a weapon to combat those (very real) legal and social injustices that continue to exist" (294). The war is not over folks. Annie, get your gun.

12. Camp—its actual meanings and signification, vacillates and dithers, like a drunk NYU student on Waverly Street, according to the discipline or decade you're working in or from. (That's a joke. I'm old). We may not have been placed in the same camp; or gone to camp at the same time. An extensive literature review will confuse those readers soliciting a clear definition.

Thank god for Wikipedia. Seriously, I'm going to cite Wikipedia: "Camp is a social, cultural, and aesthetic style and sensibility based on deliberate and self-acknowledged theatricality." (The references here are to Babuscio [1993, 20], Feil [2005, 478], Morrill [1994, 110], Shugart & Waggoner [2008, 33], and Van Leer [1995, 60].) Wow. Someone wrote an essay for college. The upshot here refers to Susan Sontag's popularized conceptualization in 1964. People love Susan Sontag. For many years, I loved Susan. Sontag's "Notes on 'Camp'" opens the door; American consciousness learns a new word. Pop Camp! Thanks Susan. You're so cool.

Nick Salvato critiques Sontag's flip definition of camp—"failed seriousness"—as missing the tone of camp and its impact on its audience. He narrows the scope and province of the term by explaining its usefulness in two ways: (1) camp must be "understood as a practice that calls attention to the constructedness and performativity of gender and sexuality; and (2) camp must echo some preexisting text, trope, or set of codes in this negotiation of gender and sexuality" (636). Salvato emphasizes the affective dimension of camp—namely its ambivalent attitude toward source material, the subject, the object. "Camp requires of its deployer a simultaneous identification with and disavowal of the object of its contemplation" (636). So definitions are ambiguous, ambitious, or enigmatic.

Put denotation aside and let's try to agree on a shared understanding. In *Notes on Camp/Anti-Camp* (2012), Bruce LaBruce supports some of Sontag's suppositions. LaBruce writes, "Sontag rightly points out that camp is a certain mode of aestheticism," its essence found in "its love of the unnatural, of artifice and exaggeration," and "its esoteric nature, amounting to a private code or a secretly shared badge of identity." However, LaBruce's somber analysis points to the rise of gay conservatism, a growing tendency toward conservative camp: "For what are Sarah Palin, Newt Gingrich, Bill O'Reilly, Donald Trump and Herman Cain other than conservative camp icons enacting a kind of reactionary burlesque on the American political stage?" ("Notes on Camp"). Video killed the radio star. LaBruce leaves me feeling unhopeful.

13. Like LaBruce, scholarly opinion seems to regard the fall of camp or the death of camp—maybe it was the AIDS epidemic, or today's conspicuousness of queer identities (see Harris 1997; Flinn 1995; Finch 1986; Booth 1983). I remember overhearing some fabulous lesbians at P.S. 122 one night in the mid 90s: "Fran Leibowitz says camp is dead." When I was coming of age in New York City, these debates were as hot then as they seem to be today. Literature on camp positions it as an artifact of oppression-era queer history. Thinkers like Andrew Ross describe how camp emerged as a pre-Stonewall survivalist strategy for resisting oppressive dominate culture. Stonewall + 50 years = cold or boring camp, dead camp, the death of camp. Bye-bye.

But wait. It can't be. Have you met my friends Brian? Richard? Chris? Kenny Kenny? Camp cannot be dead! Scholars like Wolf and Osterweil resist this death of camp. For Wolf believes camp, as a queer sense-making practice and decoding strategy, is vital for subverting dominant gender roles, heteronormative practices, and hegemonic institutions ("Resurrecting Camp"). Could it be? Is camp as relevant today as ever? Does homonormativity get in our way?

Remember folks, we may not be living in a country where being queer is against the law, but those days are not so far back in our history to be erased and forgotten. The International Lesbian, Gay, Bisexual, Trans and Intersex Association (ILGA), lists 78 countries with criminal laws against sexual activity by lesbian, gay, bisexual, transgender, or intersex people. And that's a slight understatement; it's more like 81.

Please don't forget that today we still live in an era where sex, gender, and sexuality are under close surveillance, where us queers are subject to reckless policing, where marriage equality is an argument, and where "religious freedom" laws passed in Indiana (April 26, 2015) make it seem legal to discriminate against us. Look to the State of Kansas, where lawmakers (March 23, 2016) are targeting transgender students with what the *Advocate* is calling the "Dangerous Bathroom Bill." This bill allows students the right to sue their school for up to $2,500 if they witness any transgender students using the "wrong" bathroom.

Laws and legislation like this are just plain ugly, mean-spirited, and intended for harm. But remember, people: "Religious freedom" laws are on the books in twenty U.S. states. Brian, Richard, Chris, Kenny Kenny, why aren't you here now? I need you! We need you! More now than ever!

14. For Wolf (2013) and Flinn (1995), camp sensibilities must persist— of course they may be "transformed and renegotiated" (Wolf 288). If "camp is not dead," as Wolf writes, we may have buried it alive (288). I'm not so sure. Shouldn't we let the dead rest in peace? Must we try to raise the dead? By insisting on camp's currency, don't we run the risk of promoting zombie camp? Zombie camp. Now I like that. In fact, I prefer zombies over Bruce LaBruce's Anti-Camp. Perhaps his version of conservative camp should be rezoned for these monsters: See Sarah Palin, Rush Limbaugh, Ted Cruz, and Donald Trump as queer camp zombies. Necro-biopolitics are alive. Who or what is the figure of Trump, with the wry smile and really, really bad hair? My camp world is coming for you, coming at you. You are Trumped. Is this hope or hopelessness? The light of hope requires a journey into the imaginary—a queer never-never land.

15. By today's standards, I think Sontag is fucked. I'd like to say she's dead wrong, but I don't think I should keep cussing. Sontag reduces and essentializes the link between camp and us queers. She writes: "While it's not true that Camp taste is homosexual taste, there is no doubt a peculiar affinity and overlap . . . not all homosexuals have Camp taste. But homosexuals, by and large, constitute the vanguard—and the most articulate audience—of Camp" (64). For Sontag, "life is theatre" (107), *ergo* camp *as* a self-conscious, meta-textual, ambivalent, incongruous, transformational, excessive, and expressively styled dramatic and theatrical form.

Camp is resistance, survival, subversion, and critique. Is that what Sontag means? Does your terrific pathetic life resist tears, sorrow, and pain through laughter? Oh Susan, come out and reveal the true meaning of your words; come out wherever you are. Susan, it's time for you to defend your antidisciplinary camp project. Come on Susan: I OUT you, queering you and your subject.

16. Peter and I lived on 24th Street between 9th and 10th Avenues in London Terrace, New York. I would often climb to the building's rooftop to look south at downtown, the World Trade Center, Chelsea, and the

Village, look west at the sun setting across the Hudson River. Reading in
that solitude was such a joy! To the west, one rooftop terrace over, was the
penthouse of Susan Sontag. I would see her. Frequently. Black coat. Scarf
over her head. Susan looking out at the same world as me. Of course, in the
building directly south of Susan's—where I would go to swim—lived
Annie Leibovitz. Annie lived in the south tower penthouse; Susan in the
north. What a great arrangement. What luxury. Camp excess. How bourgeois. Peter and I shared a studio apartment, with a (rotten) dog. I would
often find them looking out at—or for—each other. Soon, I was stalking
Susan. I wanted to be reading her work knowing where she was standing,
imagining what she was thinking. Joy.

Walking home from the Center on 13th Street after one of the ACT
UP meetings, I was riled up. What do you mean Susan Sontag isn't out?
Jay, Michael, Daniel, my political friends were teaching me how to get
angry. Come out Susan. I invited them up to my rooftop to spy on the
lovers. Come out Susan. She didn't come out that day. Daniel, camp sensibility in tow, recites from memory Rosalind Russell's precise dialogue
from the film *Auntie Mame* (DaCosta 1958); I can see him now in pantomime: Daniel/Mame is on the phone with Mr. Babcock from the Knicker-
bocker Bank. She's been dodging him for days:

> Well, hello, Mr. Babcock. How nice to hear your voice at long last. I
> too am looking forward with anticipation to meeting you. The little
> lad is fine. He can't wait to meet you. (Hurry, my tray, darling! Auntie
> needs fuel.) Do drop over anytime, Mr. Babcock. In how many min-
> utes? Yes, 57th Street is right in my neck of the woods. Spitting
> distance?

The camera captures Russell's dour expression, and she says, "How vivid."
I lived spitting distance from Susan Sontag. How vivid. We all started spitting off the roof. Look Susan, it's raining. Thanks camp.

17. In the name of my own difference, I spit on camp.[1] I spit on Sontag.
On queers. On queer nation. I spit on ACT UP and its working groups. I
spit on the human immunodeficiency virus. I spit on this disease. I spit on
AIDS. I spit on camp. Spit on Sontag for letting me live my deviance. Spit
on Deviance. On Disease. On Disorder. Sontag isn't the radical we need
for today. Restore queers to themselves. Rip inferiority from our brains.
Spit on the trap of equality. And on all manifestation of patriarchal culture.
Spit. I spit on camp, in all its manifestations. Spit. I spit on camp and how
it follows me around.

18. The term "assemblage" comes from Deleuze and Guattari's thinking that questions the "presumed organicity of the body" (Puar 193) and to articulate how biopolitics fuse image with information, body with affect, representation with regulation. John Phillips clarifies Deleuze and Guattari's model of assemblage as referring to "the connection between a state of affairs and the statements we can make about it" (Phillips 108). The philosophical concept of assemblage highlights my poststructural framework of subjectivity, emphasizing how identities get mapped onto particular bodies in particular contexts through (relatively stable) discursive arrangements and relations of power (Foucault 1982). The positioning of camp (and identity for that matter) within these discursive fields enables and constrains what can be stated and enacted. Recognizing how my identity is both performative and relational, presentational and discursive, cyborg and goddess, my expressive enunciations are interpretations that contain a possibility to both recite and rewrite those very discourses that authorize and politicize me (Butler 1993).

When camp sensibilities and camp logics are understood as camp/assemblages, multiple iterations emerge. First, as has been addressed, camp as queer, drag, carnival, hyperbole, and satire. But there are other iterations that must not be forgotten and that skate over the discursive subject of Sontag's camp yet remain inside historical, political, and social networks of meaning and action governed by asymmetrical relations of power. Charlie Hailey breaks camp, or decamps Sontag in *Campsite: Architectures of Duration and Place*. He explains, "[T]he multiplicity of camps forms an open network, within which the nomadic subject makes connections through repeated but differential operations. The camp is the site of nomadic experimentation where thinking and making, arriving and departing meet" (29). His vectorial (yet selective and acute) methods frame "camp thought," and his rhizomatic exercises frame "camp construction" (29), such that he posits camp as both "subject matter" and "method" (36). This distinguishing of camp as method becomes a heuristic device for place-making.

19. For instance, camp is a place and space for extracurricular or cocurricular activities, like "summer camp." My parents sent me away to summer camp at the age of seven. For the next eight years, during two summer months, I partook in the conditioning of my body and identity through activities within colonial contexts and frameworks. In this context, I was a failure. Always Other; always abject; everyone knew my displacement and difference—or so I felt.

Following my socio-symbolic constellation, other iterations of camp consider, by design, the construction of a place-bound physical dwelling or a shelter, such as a "death camp," "refugee camp," or "concentration camp." As in, not all of my family were able to escape the horrors of World War II; many died in Nazi concentration camps. I acknowledge that running my sense of the abject and Otherness of summer camp alongside Nazi concentration camps and other death camps is a deliberate move to elucidate how camp as a material, spatial, mobile, and metaphorical concept always invokes exaggerated identities. Camp, whether subject or method, can be—must be—a restructured affective response to time and place. Where are we? Where am I? How can I find my way home? "Through travel and inhabitation, the nomad circumscribes and inscribes the construction of *home*, which then becomes bell hooks's place of discovery—a ground made productively unstable by traveling in place" (Hailey 240–41). Any alternative discourse realities implicated in camp methods and metaphors give way to tricky and fuzzy identificatory practices that are discursively produced yet subjectively experienced.

20. Perhaps the most compelling camp metaphor relying on an alternative discourse is the example of Camp X-Ray. This camp was a temporary detention facility at Guantanamo Bay, so called because temporary camps were named sequentially following the NATO phonetic alphabet. Camp X-Ray. Number twenty-four. The first twenty detainees arrived at Guantanamo on January 11, 2002. Controversies abound; camp controversies. Are today's citizens familiar with the questionable legal status of detainees? Do the varying and unreliable government processes for trying each case challenge you? Scare you? Break you? Bring you to your knees? The names of detainees are obfuscated. I can recall maybe one or two . . . How about you? It's chilly at camp today. Time to forget. Time to move on.

Does anyone still want to go to camp? Do young queers want to be "set apart"? "Set apart" is a general translation of Giorgio Agamben's *Homo Sacer*. Camp is both sacrosanct and damned; camp violates that which is inviolate. Achille Mbembe applies Agamben's ontological distinctions with the term "necropolitics." Simply, necropolitics considers the uses of power, whether social or political, that dictate how some humans may live and how some must die. This is intense and serious ideology; camp politicizes human bodies, reducing and removing ontology and biology in place of power (and oft-forgotten religion). Puar applies affect as a site of bodily creative discombobulation and resistance, an approach for increasing monitoring and modulation. She foregrounds "questions of affect as bodily capacity not only in relation to forms of living and dying, but also to debility and disability" (163). *Terrorist Assemblages* is Puar's rapprochement of Foucauldian biopolitics and Mbembe's necropolitical critique. Named "bionecro collaboration," Puar's critique conceptually acknowledges biopower's direct link to death, while remaining bound to life. Life and breath; death and taxes; partisan or apolitical; in or out; life or death; conceptual duplicities such as these symbolic discursive ideologies mimic a zero-sum politics. For *me* to count in today's democratic world, as a queer citizen, something has to give; someone has to go; my inclusion requires an Other's displacement; one-for-one; or one-for-many (or so it seems).

In this case, the Othering is set in motion by me, my queer camp activisms and actions, and my values for justice, human, and civil rights. In my reach for equality, visibility, and recognition, I participate in democratic social relations. As Camp X-Ray suggests, the costs of social inclusion embrace ongoing oppressions, in this case through rampant racism and Islamophobia. Did anyone really trust that social change was somehow set apart from Faustian bargaining? Camp logic shows how there will always be winners and losers. Utopian futurity. Sorry Folks. Queers belong, sure. Born this way, baby. We two are one. But someone, *out* there, has to pay.

21. *This is Camp X-Ray* is the name of Jai Redman's 2003 installation, created with the support of the Ultimate Holding Company art collective. Ultimate Holding Company describes itself as "a group of creative pioneers and provocateurs operating at the junction of contemporary visual art, engaged design practice, and social activism." As a collective, they are concerned with processes of collaborative production and creation, with social solidarity, and with the role of artists in creating sustainable communities of practice. Here is twenty-first-century camp and its artistic sensibility.

This is Camp X-Ray was a full-scale replica of part of the United States military Guantanamo Bay detainment camp. The installation showed guards and prisoners in cells and interrogation rooms. Known interrogation techniques were demonstrated. Constructed in Manchester, England, the installation was operational for eight days in the cold of October in 2003. David Schaffer describes his experience:

> The watchtower guard demanded to see my ID, and for a second I
> thought I'd been caught trespassing on a military installation. When I
> asked him what he'd have done if I had no identification, he casually
> said: *I'd shoot you!* . . . I had naively expected a guide to greet me and
> take me on a tour of the installation . . . instead, more like the reception you would get in Guantanamo Bay, there was no welcome—I was

just met by a razor wire-topped perimeter surrounding the football pitch-sized camp. *Some people have even asked if the camp is actually a genuine prison.* (BBC Manchester, 2003)

Camp art imitates camp life. Imagine the frivolity of this installation; the cost was only partially covered by Arts Council England. Envision the theatrics, the failed seriousness, over the big panopticonic top. This is my "critical modality of hope"; I read twenty-first-century camp in this installation. The work makes and marks a deadly serious act and political position about the harsh conditions of the genuine, actual camp in Cuba. The politics are undeniable. All the racism and xenophobia contained within prison camps are politic extensions of the horrors and homophobia of Nazi concentration camps. Camp has legs.

The year 2003 was also the year Susan Sontag was *Regarding the Pain of Others*, writing how "it seems exploitative to look at harrowing photographs of other people's pain in an art gallery" (9). The site of *This Is Camp X-Ray* subverts her gallery spaces, as the camp is installed on what BBC reporter describes as a "wasteland" surrounded by day-to-day urban living (Schaffer 2003). I read Redman's installation and the work of Ultimate Holding Company as a queer, camp sensibility for today's world. Camp is creative, immersive, and political.

22. Approximately 750,000 Palestinians were displaced from their homes in 1948. Victimization, poverty, and passivity are stereotypes of these people, as they move from city to camp, from citizen to refugee, from a home-center to the periphery of the world. They fled to neighboring countries—Jordan, Syria, Lebanon, and to the parts of Mandate Palestine that became the West Bank and the Gaza Strip. Today, there must be almost five million refugees. In fact, according to the United Nations Relief and Works Agency for Palestine Refugees (UNRWA) there are 5,869,733 registered people living across fifty-eight refugee camps in the area ("UNRWA in Figures 2017"). The Palestinian refugee community constitutes one of the largest and certainly the longest-lasting refugee populations in the world. The plots of land on which these refugees camp are either state land or, more commonly, leased by the host government from local landowners. In other words, refugees do not own the land on which their shelters are built. They have a right to live there, to use the land for residence—as *home*. Few question the socioeconomic conditions in these refugee camps: poor, large numbers, over-crowding, and inadequate infrastructure as in limited water, power, roads, septic systems, and sewers. Here is camp without affluence.

23. In 2012, at the Dheisheh refugee camp in Bethlehem, two artist/activists introduced an experimental educational and project-based program called "Campus in Camps." Sandi Hilal and Alessandro Petti's experiment began as a two-year program of Al Quds University, with the support of Al-Quds Bard, and hosted by the Phoenix Center. "Campus in Camps" engages young participants in programs dealing with new forms of visual and cultural representation of refugees and their camps after more than sixty years of displacement. Hilal and Petti write in their artist statement how the initiative stems from the realization that refugee camps in the West Bank are in a process of transformation:

> Despite adverse political and social conditions Palestinian refugee camps have developed a relatively autonomous and independent social and political space: no longer a simple recipient of humanitarian intervention but rather as an active political subject. The camp becomes a site of social invention and suggests new political and spatial configurations. (qtd. in Kuoni and Haines 118)

Camp as state of exception; refugees re-invent social and political practices to improve their everyday life and alleviate suffering without normalizing the political exceptional condition of the camp itself. The participants of these programs are not passive students but active agents who do things, make spaces, intervene in concrete ways in their communities—and in doing so, take charge of reimagining what it means to live as a refugee and to live at camp. Camp is home. "Campus in Camps" helps refugees enable a libertarian world, an environment of civil dignity, where education and life are decolonized and reinstated within codes of cultural practice that support local culture—all the while resisting the interests of Israeli and Palestinian struggles for political power. Is this an anti-political politics? How queer. The subversions of camp logic through camp methods employed in "Campus in Camps" reveal the matrix of socioeconomic relations that determines the conditions within which refugee identities and biopolitics are conferred, accepted, and recognized as part of any social project.

24. I don't challenge David Fernbach's assertion about the "frivolity of camp" (206) hiding the meaninglessness queers feel—inside. I won't deny Richard Dyer's indication that queer (and for Dyer, he speaks about gay men, but still, queer) interest in cultural affairs and artistic sensitivity informed camp sensibilities whereby parodies of "femininity" suppress traditional, "normal" masculinity—at least prior to gay liberation in the early seventies. I embrace Jack Babuscio's portrayal of camp as "a creative

energy" reflecting an alternative if not subversive consciousness that resists mainstream values; camp is "a heightened awareness of certain human complications" (*Gays and Film* 40), which is a result of our social oppression. Ultimately, I follow dear Christopher Isherwood's assertion when he confesses that camp, as a sensibility, is "terribly hard to define" (125–26). What was Sontag thinking? Public intellectual influenced by populist audiences?

Though many identify camp culture as non-political, both Babuscio and Dyer inspire the political significance of camp; it lays bare the false, superficial, and constructed nature of gender and non-conforming gender identities thereby discovering a way "of poking fun at the whole cosmology of restrictive sex roles and sexual identifications which our society uses to oppress its women and repress its men" (Dyer, *Gays and Film*, 67–68). Restrictive cosmologies assume binary logics for both material and psychic discursive strategies and worlds; sense is not the result of the Aristotelian worldview but a holistic and synesthetic bodily reaction (or response) to external stimuli. State systems of biopower preclude any holistic system of meaning, further limiting human sense perceptors as the tools for worldmaking.

25. What Sontag and some others miss when considering the function and intention of camp is its implicit and, especially, its explicit political value. Camp is explicitly political. Not just because I say so. Because camp provides agency for change.

Andy Medhurst describes, "trying to define camp is like attempting to sit in a corner of a circular room" (154). Any and all definitions of camp are always and impossibly inadequate:

> The problem with camp is that it is primarily an experiential rather than an analytical discourse. Camp is a set of attitudes, a gallery of snapshots, an inventory of postures, a *modus vivendi*, a shop-full of frocks, an arch of eyebrows, a great big pink butterfly that just won't be pinned down. Camp is primarily an adjective, occasionally a verb, but never anything as prosaic, as earth-bound, as a noun. (Medhurst 155)

Distinctions between camp and Camp and/or "camp" are meaningless to me. All camp notions are complicated presentations of ecstatic responses; pre-Sontag, these responses were usually reserved for aesthetic worlds. Today, camp reclaims the ecstatic as agency for breaking down walls or codes or whatever needs corruption in order to achieve release from oppression. Let my people go! I hear violins as Smokey sings, "'cause love like ours is never, ever free; you pay some agony for the ecstasy" (Robinson). Oh, the agony! Oh, the ecstasy!

26. For Sontag and me, our camp involves "a new, more complex relation to the *serious*. One can be serious about the frivolous, frivolous about the serious" (288). I argue how this complex inversion invites an inherent political nature to camp logic. My queer identity, defined as an oppositional lifestyle by that dominant Other/Order, was viewed medically as gender inversion. Michel Foucault's "reverse discourse" (*Discipline & Punish* 43) demonstrates how queer legitimacy began to speak on its own behalf, often in the same vocabulary using the same categories by which my queer was "medically disqualified" (49). The gendered-suppression of camp produced an inversion of masculine behavior leading to a performance of femininity that, according to Lynn Segal, involves a positive aesthetics sensibility: "A sense of beauty and a sense of pain" (145).

Similarly, Jack Babuscio explains how camp reflects "a heightened awareness of certain human complications of feeling that spring from the fact of social oppression" (*Gays and Film* 40). Camp is having it both ways; this doubleness—or to use Sontag's morally weighted word "duplicity," is a function of camp. But I insist Sontag is wrong in her discourse. Duplicity denotes the double-dealing of deceitfulness. Camp is not deceitful. Sontag's writing, sadly, was subject to her time. This might explain why she missed out on the active, political queerness of this serious topic.

NOTE

1. Inspired by the feminist writing of Carla Lonzi (*Let's Spit on Hegel*, 1976).

The Camping Ground "Down Under"

Queer Interpretations of the Australian Summer Holiday

Paul Venzo

Outside the weather is blistering, while inside air-conditioned shop assistants patiently bauble plastic pine trees and fill window displays with tinsel, rotund effigies of Santa, and faux-fur reindeer sleighing through polystyrene snow.

Within days the exodus from city to coast will begin.

People say they are "going down" to the beach, as if it were a place inherently southern, a place literally down under. SUVs are packed to their metallic gills with all the necessities of summer camping life, and soon they clog the narrow streets leading toward beachfront holiday parks. The small towns of the eastern seaboard swell, pregnant with out-of-towners.

Some dreadlocked skeg[1] dressed in ratty board shorts and a singlet that barely covers his sunburnt chest is trying to hitch a ride. His cardboard sign, written in pathetically cross-hatched pen, simply states "BEACH."

A kid, dripping ice cream down the flanks of a shiny four-wheel-drive, pleads with her parents to take the hitch-hiking surfer on board. They don't flinch, and mum inches the shark-nosed car inches forward toward its destination.

Charlie Hailey's *Camps: A Guide to 21st-Century Space* describes many different forms of camps and camping, and points to the political, cultural, and even economic complexities that are often part and parcel of the various iterations of outdoor living, both temporary and permanent. And yet, when I turned to this text to see how camping is manifest, experienced and theorized in my own backyard—Australia—I found a single brief entry that noted our shameful record of incarcerating asylum seekers in detention camps both on and off shore (260–61). While this is undeniably salient to any discussion of camping as a mechanism of surveillance and control, it inspired me to think about other forms of camping in Australia, far from the dominant imaginary of the global north.

For many Australians, camps and camping are synonymous with an end-of-year pilgrimage from the metropolitan centers to peripheral, regional communities and environments, particularly those located along our vast coastline. Many thousands of campers in tents, caravans (trailers), and mobile homes travel to such places during the vacation period of Christmas, the New Year, and school holidays, culminating with Australia's national holiday on January 26. With this form of camping in mind, I am interested in how my local caravan park[2] functions as an articulation of queer space and queer time, within the context of Australian history and culture generally. This chapter is therefore structured by my personal experiences with beachside holiday parks in my hometown of southwest Victoria.

I happen to live only a few hundred meters from such a site, and so I have had the opportunity to observe this phenomenon at close range. Over many years, I have observed this environment as a kind of self-contained, cultural geography: a place where different versions of Australian middle-class identity are performed. Here I will use this knowledge to compose a series of vignettes. These short bursts of creative writing record my experiences and observations, and act as a springboard for discussing how geography, history, gender, sexuality, ethnicity, and class intersect in the environment under study. My aim is to investigate how, for many young Australians, the beachside family holiday is a kind of "suspended animation" between school and home, childhood and adulthood.

Moe Meyer, writing in *The Politics and Poetics of Camp*, suggests that the term "queer" is useful whenever we wish to investigate those instances in which subjectivity is revealed as "performative, improvisational, discontinuous, and processually constituted by repetitive and stylised acts" (2). Along these lines, I argue that young people on summer holiday near my home find themselves in a physical and socio-cultural terrain in which various modes of queerness flourish, both in the aesthetic qualities of the camping ground and in the activities that take place there.

Newly arrived campers peg out their territory in sandy plots, across which sun-bleached grass spreads itself thinly. Tents are unfurled and hoisted, circus-like, while caravans have roofs popped and annexes affixed, and bored children loll about, unimpressed by the various tasks assigned to them.

For the first few hours at least, each camping site is self-contained, even private, as if the forty-acre block has been shrunken, and transferred from suburbia. By evening, life begins to spill out across its borders. Conversations drift into the night air. Bikes are left—wheels still spinning—at the edge of the bitumen road that runs the length of the park. Sand is trudged from beach to tent to shower block to kiosk and back again.

The smell of barbecue is ubiquitous. Men, pot-bellied with middle age, poke at charring sausages with metal tongs.

At a table nearby, two women happily ignore each other over a bottle of white wine. One is playing with the kids' Jenga, and as the building blocks topple she mutters under her breath: "Bugger."

Judith (Jack) Halberstam argues that "'Queer space' refers to the place-making practices within postmodernism in which queer people engage and it also describes the new understandings of space enabled by the production of queer counterpublics" (6). On a basic level, this means that queer space can therefore be understood as those environments—physical, digital, architectural, social—where queer people gather and interact. This could mean a website, a community event, a sex venue, a nightclub or café, for example. However, extending this definition further, the concept of queer space might also refer to environments that, on the surface of things, appear as bastions of heteronormative life—such as the shopping center, the church, the family home—but that, when examined closely, reveal more complex and queer associations between identity space and place.

Most architecture responds to the activities and values of the cultures that inhabit them. For example, the family home, in western societies, tends to be broken up into shared living and dining spaces, spaces for the car and outdoor entertaining, a master bedroom where mum and dad sleep, and smaller, separate bedrooms for their children. In this manner, the ordinary, middle-class home is designed for a particular kind of social subset—a heterosexual couple and their children—who perform family life in specific ways. These are people who get married (and often, divorced), have kids, go to work, study, play, and eventually reproduce into other, similar social groupings. While there are, of course, plenty of queer folks who inhabit this very kind of social and physical architecture in various ways, the prevalence of these kinds of spaces tells us something about the dominant way of living in places like Australia, and the way this shapes our perception of what is desirable, "normal."

However, the holiday park provides possibilities for re-examining and rethinking how everyday life operates. For example, western suburbia tends to feature the clear demarcation of households. Contemporary housing developments, in Australia at least, involve the use of high fences, buildings built to the edge of plots, as well as architecture that does not look over neighbors' yards or living spaces. Conversely, the holiday park / camping ground blurs boundaries between one household and another. While allotments are demarcated by loose boundaries of turf, caravans, tents, and the general equipment required for camping tends to involve the overlapping of domestic life. Indeed, the small, confined spaces dedicated to sleeping accommodation mean that domestic activities such as cooking and watching television, listening to music, eating, and so on are more likely to take place outdoors, within earshot and eyesight of other campers. Washing of clothes and the activities of the bathroom are similarly housed in communal spaces such as toilet, shower, and laundry blocks.

The communal nature of such a space means that despite attempts by people to try and colonize their own little patch of family turf, life in the holiday park has a tendency to spill out across the borders of each plot. This high-density form of accommodation and its communal facilities mean that people from different places and ethnicities, if not social strata, find themselves in close proximity. So, while on one hand this space is a microcosm of family life it must, through sheer necessity, be conducted more publicly and communally than might otherwise be the case when living at home in urban and suburban areas. In an online article in the *Australian Geographic*, charting the popularity of camping across several decades, it is suggested that while camping:

> everyone is always on view. It's a popular pastime to wander along the lines looking into other people's camps and acknowledge particularly elegant or ingenious set-ups. The only fences here are the web of guy ropes dripping with beach towels. Camping is a communal activity, where conversations are struck up over site barbecues. (Ginis)

The camping grounds / holiday parks described in this chapter simultaneously mirror and disrupt the architectures of domestic space by replicating many of its features but layering them with the requirements of communality. If you were to view such a space from above you would see that it is broken up into "suburbs": spaces where people stay in tents, others where there are caravans, plots for longer-term residents, each with their own facilities block that might include a laundry, showers, toilets, barbeques, and so forth. Often these zones are in formation around a central administration building, which itself often includes a small shop and perhaps a café or restaurant. While fences may be absent in the camping ground, zones are often broken up by hedges and roads with various signs, signaling how one should behave in this space: Drive slowly, go that way for the beach, no littering, and so on.

The holiday park reveals the uncanny nature of domestic life: how it is structured, how it operates, and the various identities and roles that become attached to such a space. In the Australian publication *Born in a Tent*, Bill Garner observes that, with camping, "We get away from one sort of home only to go to the trouble of creating another . . . Camping concentrates our attention on things we otherwise take for granted. The most ordinary routines and actions become subject to consultation, choice and decision" (19–20). Watching families try to make dinner using a single burner gas stove, or wash dishes in a lukewarm bucket of water, or play board games (while simultaneously checking social media on a smartphone) one could be forgiven for thinking that camping is a kind of play-acting at real life, much like children might play with tea sets and toy ovens. This is a kind of miniaturization of daily life, but the essence of this kind of temporality is the way in which everyday activities are defamiliarized. In essence, the camping I observe draws attention to the routines of daily life and renders them uncanny.

The strange, uncanny quality of the "home away from home" is exemplified by the degree to which campers may go to replicate the luxuries of domestic life. The holiday park is a kind of impromptu city where people set up mobile, temporary homes decked out with many of the conveniences we associate with middle-class life: such as fridges, Wi-Fi, flat screen televisions, and cooking stations. SUVs, laptops, mobile phones, surfboards, and wetsuits are ubiquitous. And yet such conspicuous displays of wealth fit unevenly with the perception (somewhat erroneous considering the costs involved in contemporary forms of camping) that this is an inexpensive kind of holiday, one that involves roughing it by sleeping on uncomfortable blow-up mattresses and, for many campers, trudging back and forth to the bathroom, meters away down the road.

It is not my intention to fully investigate the double-meaning of the word "camp," prone as this term is to ongoing debates within cultural theory about what exactly being or doing camp might mean (Bergman, Cleto). However, I do want to acknowledge that the idea of aesthetics and sensibility—notions that are common to much of the discourse of camp/campiness—has relevance here. Susan Sontag, in her oft-quoted essay

"Notes on 'Camp,'" argues that "All camp objects, and persons, contain a large degree of artifice. Nothing in nature can be campy . . . Rural camp is still man-made, and most campy objects are urban" (279). However, it is worth noting, in particular, that the seaside holiday park represents a faux or even phony kind of urban *realism*: an environment that, because of its ersatz recreation of everyday life, renders objects and persons as both/either camp/queer.

If, as Sontag would have it, camp relies on a certain form of extravagance and exaggeration, then the holiday park—a specific mode of "camp" camp—might go some way to underlining this idea. Where else is it commonplace, even desirable, to eat lunch in public wearing fluorescent Speedos (bathing suit) or a bikini? In what other environment would bright white strips of zinc across your nose be de rigueur, except perhaps on the cricket pitches of India or Pakistan or South Africa? In this age of mobile technology, how can games such as totem tennis and quoits be considered a good use of one's time, even feats of graceful athleticism? And what of tables groaning under the weight of brightly colored plastic crockery full of food rich in fat, salt, and sugar, all ready to be smothered in blood-red tomato sauce (ketchup)?

At this point of the evening the park is alive with the clanking sounds of cutlery and the scrape of plates. The sounds of dinner bash against the noise from flat-screen televisions blaring out game shows and sports broadcasts.

It is as if I'm riding through an outdoor white goods sale: there are fridges, toaster-ovens, stereo systems, and blinking mobile wifi units, while—in all their analogue glory—waxy surfboards lie abandoned on the grass.

I pull up short when a half-hearted fight between two boys erupts in front of me. An older girl steps in to pull the boys apart.

"Stop it, dickheads!" she yells, a fistful of T-shirt in each hand, pushing them apart.

The evening has washed in on a low tide. The sun sets reluctantly, throwing out its pink-orange arms in a rather melodramatic farewell.

The carnival that sits snug against the dunes already is whirred up into a frenzy of lights and bells and over-loud dance music. Youngsters bash about in dodgem cars and bring themselves to the brink of vomiting on rides whose names invariably end in "tron."

Kids ensure the dental work of the future by eating fairy floss,[3] cobwebbed about bamboo sticks.

Two police swagger through the crowds, their batons hula-swaying against their hips. One of them stops for a free shot at the shooting gallery and misses wide.

*The "carni folk" watch on, glassy-eyed with the boring predictability of it all.
Their pockets are full of loose change. Their minds are full of education schools
didn't provide.*

*Some yobo[4] lets off a contraband firecracker. Its dragon flare shoots up over-
head, in the direction of the beach. The two cops glance at each other—a "we'll
have to pretend to give a shit" look—and head off towards what is now a
pathetic, red fizz dripping down the shirtfront of darkness.*

While it is tempting to think of the camp ground as a predominantly
physical architecture that reveals the kitsch and exaggerated qualities of
the paraphernalia of everyday life, in the context of the Australian summer, the kind of camping I describe in the vignettes is also an instance of
the embodiment and practice of queer time.

Halberstam argues that queer time is a concept that describes "those
specific models of temporality that emerge within postmodernism once
one leaves the temporal frames of bourgeois reproduction and family, longevity, risk/safety, and inheritance" (6). In this sense, queer time might be
thought of as disrupting, challenging, or re-imagining the way many of us
structure daily life, framed by routines of work, child-rearing, and commitments to family, and in conformity to social norms around recreation,
shopping, education, and so on.

Time spent camping, in the context of the beachside holiday described
in this chapter, is not so much a case of being outside the temporal frames
nominated by Halberstam, but rather simultaneously being in and re-
imagining/reconfiguring them. The summer holiday spent at the beach
simultaneously mirrors ordinary, domestic family time and reorders it,
bridging the gap between everyday activities and the pursuit of relaxation
and pleasure.

Whereas family life as composed within the home tends to proceed with
monotonous regularity, the temporal dynamics of camping are different.
For example, traditional modes of work and education are temporarily
suspended, even absent, and the daily activities described above become
subservient to modes of recreation and social interaction. Being outdoors,
swimming, late dinners, lingering conversation, eating, watching movies,
and so on tend to impact on the kind of "reproductive" family time Halberstam notes as heteronormative.

For those of us in the southern hemisphere, time spent on summer holidays by the beach also straddles the transitional moments between one
year and the next. For many in Australia, this includes the celebration of
Christmas and the New Year. Moreover, the period of the summer holidays is a kind of cultural in-between time, in which we symbolically mark

out the end of one period of life and the start of another. For example, for young people it signifies the end of one school year and the beginning of the next, so that the summer holiday can be thought of as an integral part of becoming older, and the journey towards adulthood. In this sense, time spent camping is akin to a kind of temporary adolescence, whereby time is not marked out by labor or the routines of adult life, but rather is a transitional, in-between, and even ludic time, where play, rest, and socialization take precedence.

"I got an iPhone 6."
"Bullshit! Did not!"
"Did too. Mum said I could have it for Christmas and me birthday."
"Lucky fucka. I got a wetsuit. Not much use when we get home."
"They don't go off, idiot. Ya can always use it again next year."
Checking his phone.
"Jess is here."
"Where?"
"There, dick-brain."
A girl approaches, her thumb swiping across the screen of her cell-phone.
"Hey. What's up?"
"You here too?"
"No shit, Sherlock."
"Yez wanna get somethin' ta eat? Tommo and I are gunna get some chips."
"Nah, already had lunch. Gunna go to the beach. Your brother here?"
"Why? You got the hots for him?"
"Whatever. God you're disgusting."
"They real?"
One of the boys points at her Ray-Bans.
"Course they're real."
"D'ya see the fight last night? It was awesome," says the other guy.
"Who was it? Those Lebbos I bet."[5]
"Nah, some Skips got fired up over a chick."[6]
"Fuckin' Neanderthals. Hey, let's get outta the sun."
"I gotta go piss first."
"Too much info mate!"
The ping of a phone.
"It's your brother, he's lookin' for you."

Here I have suggested that my experience of contemporary camping culture is a mechanism through which I have come to see the queer potential of such an environment. As a homosexual man, educated in the post-structuralist era of 1990s higher education, I am tuned into reading seemingly straight environments through a queer lens, sifting through what I see, hear, and experience for signs of subversion, for any hint of a challenge to heteronormative ways of thinking and being. Part of this is the mobilization of the kind of camp "sensibility" I have mentioned previously. As a participant in/observer of such a site, it is the way various forms of masculinity are articulated in the holiday park that immediately captures my attention. I am interested, therefore, in the intersection of masculinity, outdoor living, and the Australian context as means to uncover the queer potential I feel whenever I enter such a space.

In the Australian context, camping was traditionally identified with the establishment of agriculture, prospecting, the construction of major infra-structure, droving, and anthropology. These kinds of camps were typically male-dominated. Indeed, many of the early representations of camping in Australia are paintings and photographs of groups of white European men living together in the Australian bush (Garner 73–76, 82–83, 104–5, 116). One of these (14–15) is a photograph titled "Men relaxing in bush camp," dated to 1900–1910. Six men of various ages are depicted in various states of relaxation around the entrance to a large canvas tent. Two of the men are petting dogs resting on their laps. To their right, a man squats in front of a pail, washing a piece of clothing. On the opposite side, a man smoking a pipe has one hand on his counterpart's head, as he scrapes a cutthroat razor across his mate's upturned cheek. The activities of this scene are repeated in many other images and illustrations in Bill Garner's book on the history of camping in Australia; for example, the drawings on page 121 depict men—in various states of undress—shaving each other, washing, cooking, and sewing.

Certainly, these scenes of domestic camp life seem to subvert the tradi-tional gender roles we might otherwise associate with this era. Moreover, this close, physical, same-sex environment lent itself to homoeroticism, and there is historical evidence to suggest that sexual relationships and activities between men living in such intimate proximity was, if not well-publicized, certainly known to exist in these spaces (French 39–42). While these images and ideas come to us across a century of cultural change and development, to what extent might these early representations of Anglo-Saxon men camping in the bush inform contemporary experiences, when transferred to the more organized yet no less intimate setting of a beach-side holiday park?

While the history of camping in Australia is predominantly focused on the activities of white Australians of colonial origin,[7] in the contemporary era it has been taken up with gusto by a range of different ethnic communities from within Australia's multicultural population. White, middle-class folk are now joined by second and third generation members of ethnic communities with ancestral roots in Europe, Asia, and the Middle East. In the post-war period, European migrant communities established themselves in the (predominantly western) peripheral suburbia of capital cities such as Sydney and Melbourne.[8] This meant relatively easy access by car to smaller coastal communities nearby. The capacity of such groups to partake in long, beachside holidays may also be read as a sign of the economic success enjoyed by migrants and their children (and, indeed, *their* children) arriving in the second wave of mass migration to Australia in the latter half of the twentieth century.

For a particularly noticeable group of boys and young men, the multiculturalism of the holiday park has led to a version of masculinity that blends the more traditional aesthetic of the laconic Australian surfer with a more curated form of euro-styling. They use the camping ground to display their gym-trained bodies, show off highly groomed skin and hair, play soccer bare-chested, and mill about the camping ground canteen in groups. Crotch-hugging swimming costumes (Speedos), singlets, shorts, and thongs (flip-flops) are their favored attire, and they "work" this uniform to its extreme, especially in order to maximize the spectacle of their bodies and offer it as a site of consumption for onlookers, and each other. Adidas has particular brand significance here: its logo stamped on everything from backsides to bum-bags (fanny packs). In the morning they work out in makeshift gyms, doing chin-ups and sit-ups on playground equipment, or pounding the boardwalks as they simultaneously train and tan. In the evening they sit about smoking, flipping through social media posts and gambling for small stakes over cards.

Flirtation with girls occurs with a kind of extravagant heterosexuality that is enacted through body-display, over-exaggerated claims of sexual bravado, and play-fighting. These lads are effortlessly affectionate with other guys. Indeed, they stand out by their willingness to touch and flirt with their male counterparts, as if their charisma and machismo are born of their belonging to and closeness with a group of other young men who enact similar peacock-like behavior.

I am interested in these behaviors not because they invoke cultural or ethnic stereotypes or Otherness, but rather because of the ways in which they confidently inhabit this space and perform a particular version of masculinity within it. From diverse ethnic and cultural backgrounds, these lads complicate the idea of a standardized or normative way of enacting and embodying young Australian masculinity. Moreover, their interpretation of sexual and gender identity updates the homoerotic aesthetic/sensibility I have described previously as a feature of outdoor living in the colonial period.

At this hour, in the dunes, teenage boys and girls have drifted into couples.

These have been formed over the past days by furtive glances, brief conversations over melting ice cream outside the campground kiosk, and the sharing of illicit ciggies in the post-surf arbors of scrubby tea-tree.

The peacockery of the boys has fan-tailed to a state of almost perpetual semi-nakedness. The girls don't bother to hide their interest or express their ambivalence. Any coyness, from either side, has dried up like the grass beneath their dirty toes.

But this one's different: He's walking the edge of the tide like it's a slackline.

This afternoon, wandering back from the beach, he saw something. He wasn't perving, he tells himself. He couldn't not look was all. He had taken a shortcut that snakes behind the trailers and tents. Beside a large, army-green tent he had paused, immobilized by a low, primal sound coming from its interior.

Through a mesh-covered window he could see a young man—just a year or two older—lying naked on a camp bed, one hand clasped around a mobile phone.

Their eyes met, just for a second or two. Neither spoke, but the guy inside the tent mouthed, silently: "Happy New Year."

The camping ground/holiday park reveals the body in ways unacceptable in other areas, spaces, and times of ordinary life. The clothed body, so often symbolically decorated in line with the activities of capitalist society—think of the city and the ubiquity of business attire—is replaced by the body as a sign of leisure and relaxation, still associated with brands and the economics of recreation, but somehow outside of the framework of daily labor. For adolescents especially, the camping ground is a site in which the semi-naked body—even in its liminal state—is celebrated as its own kind of "work in progress." Here, pubescent and post-pubescent bodies are uncovered, revealing the transitional nature of adolescent, teenage years. This kind of body is always already queer, insofar as it is in flux, unstable and unpredictable. The bodies of young people are growing, changing, and still in the process of discovering and applying sexual and gender identity to the self: They are *becoming* bodies, infused with the potential of conformity/non-conformity to hetero-normative ideals.

The close proximity of family units in the holiday park means that various forms of contact, particularly between young campers, are almost guaranteed. Indeed, the camping ground can be conceived as having a certain carnivalesque quality, in which this time out of time, home away from home, allows for lingering social interactions, changes to the work/

leisure balance, and the display of bodies, not to mention the pleasures and perils of sex and sexual display.

In considering the idea that the camping ground is an erotic/sexual space, I am struck by the recollection of a local truism: that many young people lose their virginity in the nearby holiday park over summer. While this sort of claim may seem apocryphal, the fact that it circulates as an idea suggests the broader notion of the camping ground as sexual/erotic, especially for young people. From my own observations of sexual display noted previously, the holiday park may be understood as a site where young people begin to enact and embody sexual identities, outside of the surveillance of the home, school, and other institutional environments.

In the preceding vignette, I describe a chance encounter just before New Year celebrations begin: a period of "calm before the storm" in which expectation is building, and yet is not quite realized. It is a period outside the schedules of study, work, and organized leisure activities (Halberstam 6), a liminal time/space that echoes the liminal qualities of the adolescent body as it comes to sexual awareness and maturity. New Year celebrations inevitably draw large crowds to the seafront, where the holiday park and a fair ground (carnival) are located. Alcohol, music, fireworks, and the blend of local and visiting young people infuse this moment/environment with a heightened social, even erotic, potential. The approaching end/beginning of another year functions as a kind of crescendo, the apex moment of the holiday season. Moreover, the happenstance encounter between two young men described earlier underscores my broader aim to defamiliarize the camping/caravan park and reimagine it, revealing aspects that traditionally remain unseen, unspoken, and unrepresented in writing about camp/camping.

However, we should not assume that this always occurs in heterosexual or normative terms. In fact, the liminal space/time represented in the vignettes accompanying this writing are designed to give expression to the potential of this environment to be understood as a queer environment and, therefore, one that engenders queer behaviors and experiences. In *Camp Grounds: Style and Homosexuality*, David Bergman attempts to reinforce the connection between homosexuality, the aesthetics of and cultural practices associated with, camp. The essays in *Camp Grounds* point to various fields—for example, literature, music, performance, sex—in which gay people create, embody, and enact camp-ness. As my observations suggest, the holiday park at the center of my discussion can be understood as both a terrain in which heteronormative life is queered, as well as a site that is historically and culturally synonymous with homosocial, perhaps even homosexual, aesthetics and practices.

The vignettes that are interspersed throughout this chapter function as a kind of queer imaginary, through which my own aesthetic and cultural "sensibility" hones in on those aspects of outdoor living that both "show up" and challenge heteronormativity. As any good carnival does, this environment is a temporal and spatial intervention into conceptions of domestic, everyday life, in which the ordinary and mundane are revealed as sites of instability, liminality, desire, playfulness, and disorder. For me, the primary actors on this stage are young people, for it is they that truly claim this space and make it their own.

The days have reached a peak-intensity of heat, the summer has baked into the earth, into skin, into our late-eaten food, into the bricks of the house. At night, the air conditioner asthmatically exhales our cool dreams.

I walk out, barefoot, to the letterbox. Catalogues for school shoes and exercise books and backpacks have appeared.

From the front veranda I look out towards the beach. I can see patches of grass have appeared among the tents and caravans, straw-pale from lack of rain and sun. People are packing up: go a few hundred meters to the highway and the road will be choked with cars, their bronze-faced owners grinding gears back towards life in the city.

Sand will spill out on clean carpet. Showers will run long. Skin will be slathered in moisturizer. Supermarkets will be raided for food that needs a fan-forced oven. School fees will be rounded up and paid, and bits of school uniform appraised—"will this old thing go another year?"

Probably not.

Next door's gate squeals on its hinges. Ange and her friend Stacey appear, like sleek black seals in their wetsuits. Each carries a surfboard, too big to fit comfortably under their arms.

"Hey!"
"G'day. Off to the beach?" I ask, redundantly.
"Yep. Touros are goin'. More space on the break for us."[9]
"Have fun."
"See ya."
I can hear the gentle clank of leg ropes as they make their way down the lane.

NOTES

1. Skeg: surfer.

2. In the Australian context, a caravan park is the term used to describe an area/business that caters to campers in tents, motor-homes, caravans (trailers), and so on.

3. Fairy floss: cotton candy/candy floss.

4. Yobo: lout, buffoon.

5. Lebbos: Lebanese.

6. Skips: Aussies. Skippy was a famous Australian television character (a kangaroo).

7. The history of white settlement in Australia is a complicated one, shifting across time and interpretation from the concept of *terra nullius* (a "nowhere and nothing" space, ripe for colonization) to more recent discourses pertaining to Indigenous land rights and traditional custodianship. Almost ironically, in the quest to colonize Australia, white Europeans often borrowed from the Indigenous tradition of outdoor living, learning how to exist in the bush by constructing temporary shelters and hunting for "bush tucker." However, in the case of white settlement, such activities did not necessarily lead to a harmonious integration of people into the natural environment. In many cases, the result was the subjugation and control of natural resources and the eventual expansion of western culture and urbanization.

8. Such groups have an ancestral connection to camps, but of a very different kind. The National Archives of Australia contains information about the migrant "reception and training centres," traditionally referred to as migrant camps, located in rural areas of Victoria, New South Wales, Queensland, and Western Australia. My own father spent his first weeks in Australia in such a place, as an Italian migrant to Australia in 1963. Despite the vast majority of Australians living in urban communities along the eastern seaboard, it is interesting to note that it was in rural environments that migrants were first introduced to Australian culture.

9. Touros: tourists. Break: surf break, where the waves break as the result of a reef or sandbar.

PART II

Camp Stories

Camping with Walt Disney's *Paul Bunyan*
An Essay Short

Tammy L. Mielke and Andrew Trevarrow

The relationship status of queer people and the Walt Disney Company is complicated. That's the takeaway from Sean Griffin's *Tinker Belles and Evil Queens: Walt Disney from the Inside Out* (2000). On the one hand, as Griffin shows, queer people and especially gay men are among Disney's most devoted fans as well as personnel, and in the 1930s "Mickey Mouse" even functioned as code for gay. At the same time, the company has "promoted a specific version of gender, sexuality, and the body—'naturalizing' the heterosexual patriarchal family structure and replacing sex with romance" (49). Disneyphiles have thus needed to poach queer meaning from ostensibly straight productions, especially in the decades before same-sex desire became more legitimized legally and culturally. Griffin traces the history of such poaching alongside Disney's various borrowings from drag and Camp culture. He revisits some of his formative experiences viewing Disney films, emphasizing the appeal of their theatricality and playfulness. "Looking back," he writes, "I could see how Disney's films had at times created a space for me during adolescence to (secretly) express my budding sexual orientation" (xi). Griffin also detects a camp sensibility in the feature films *The Little Mermaid* and especially *Aladdin*, thanks in part to the involvement of animator Andreas Deja and producer Howard Ashman (142–45).

Inspired by Griffin, we stage a queer and Camp-friendly reading of Disney's 1958 animated short *Paul Bunyan*. Directed by Les Clark, one of Disney's "Nine Old Men" core animators, *Paul Bunyan* was nominated for Best Animated Short in 1959 (but lost to Warner Bros. Cartoon's *Knighty Knight Bugs*). We see in this popular but unexamined short the same tensions between a masculinist, putatively heterosexual agenda and a queer and proto-Campy sensibility, one building on the North American tall tale of Paul Bunyan. The story of Paul Bunyan has a long history, but each version includes the same elements: A giant boy from the east coast becomes a logger and ends up clearing the land from the east to the west coast, creating some of the geographical landmarks in the northern United States. Paul associates with various lumberjack camps but tends to move on once he's established his powers or outlived his usefulness. Camp and camp meet in Disney's interpretation of the tale, which runs a cool seventeen minutes and is punctuated with song. The queer and Camp elements of Disney's film aren't simply the result of Disney's own complicated relationship with queer possibility but also emerge from the broader history of the Bunyan tale. This particular tale, with its exaggeration and hyperbole, its male homosociality and cross-species bonding, and its camp setting, seems queer-friendly at the least. We propose that Disney's *Paul Bunyan* works as a camp/Camp short, inviting queer identification with the outsized lumberjack and his outlandish story. Ours is an essay short, in turn.

A Queer Child Among Men

In *Out of the Northwoods: The Many Lives of Paul Bunyan*, Michael Edmonds notes that the Bunyan stories circulated for decades before finding their way to print. The first stories of our extraordinary lumberjack seem to have first circulated in the logging camps of Michigan, Minnesota, and Wisconsin in the late nineteenth century. The tale was ostensibly popularized by logger and amateur artist William B. Laughead in a series of pamphlets for the Red River Lumber Company, leading to more retellings and adaptations across assorted media. In 1922, Laughead expanded his initial two pamphlets, *Introducing Mr. Paul Bunyan of Westwood, California* (1914) and *Tales About Paul Bunyan* (1916), into *The Marvelous Exploits of Paul Bunyan*, which found wide circulation. There's no single source text; the tale is folkloric in its multiple origins and ongoing permutations. There are many versions for children. The authenticity of the tale as "folklore" is debated, with some arguing it qualifies instead as "fakelore," a literary invention masquerading as folklore. We're not worried about this distinction; if anything, the tale's possible status as fakelore underscores its Camp associations. Beyond print and screen iterations, there are statues of Paul Bunyan in old logging towns, and the name Paul Bunyan graces all sorts of cultural sites (bowling alleys, bike trails, restaurants, a broadcasting network, a petting zoo).

Disney's *Paul Bunyan* frames the tall tale as part of our collective history, opening with a shot of a library shelf and with this voiceover narrative: "These are books about America. Its history, its geography, and its heroes. But it takes a big book like this one to tell the story of American folklore, the tall tales about men doing big things in a big country." We see a shot of a book with exactly that title, as the narrator shares a list of those men, such as John Henry, Pecos Bill, and "the one who towered above all of them, Paul Bunyan." Disney situates Bunyan's "birth" in Maine and tracks his progress from east and west and always just south of the Canadian border (bringing up ongoing questions about whether the tall tale is an American appropriation of a Canadian figure). At the end of the short, Paul winds up in the Pacific Northwest, where he loses—just barely—a logging competition against a salesman with a steam saw. The film ends with Bunyan and his famous ox companion dejectedly heading north, beyond Canada and into the great white north, where we are told he works and plays until this day. The story of Paul Bunyan thus retells the American story of conquering the frontier, and doing it the hard and manly way, before industrial logging equipment made the job easier. Ever the nostalgic mythmaker, Walt Disney himself told a newspaper columnist in 1948 that figures like Paul Bunyan were "heroes made in our likeness . . . [and] as good a reflection of our national traits as any history can offer." He went on to note that the "mighty" men of American myth such as Bunyan "were just exaggerated portraits of the normal, busy, indomitable, toiling man of their day. And they are worth looking at . . . to re-educate our minds and our children's minds to the lusty new world of America" (Walt Disney, quoted in Hedda Hopper, *Chicago Tribune*, May 9, 1948). Historian Adam Tomczik writes that the logger camp was "a final bastion of the traditional [i.e. gender-segregated] workplace in America," one exemplifying "a discourse of masculinity in a rural setting" (697). The Paul Bunyan tale more generally glorifies that discourse of rural, old-fashioned masculinity, as does the Disney version.

Paul Bunyan shifts a number of story elements from other iterations of the tale. One major change Disney brings to the tradition: Paul gets a childhood, and a queer one at that. The short is narrated by three men who interact with Paul across certain stages in his life. Kyle McNabb, a lumberjack by trade and Paul's first "father," notes that he "should have known something unusual was going to happen that night" because a "southeaster" was blowing in. Our story begins with Baby Paul arriving in the mode of Moses, floating into the community. This narrative is punctuated with phrases that underscore the oddity of the event: "an odd-looking craft on the beach," "never saw anything like it!," "a baby—and it was a whopper!" Paul does not fit in the community in the way a regular child might. His large form makes that impossible.

Instead of being raised by a single family, Paul is adopted by the entire community. Although he has no father and no mother, the entire village works together to meet his needs: A sewing bee and a knitting circle provide his wardrobe, for example. When he goes to school, he is too large to fit into the schoolhouse, so he takes his lessons outside. When he dives into the local swimming hole, he nearly empties it of water, but the other kids laugh and use him as a diving platform. And, later, Christmas is held in the square "on account of Paul. He was too large to fit into a house." The characterization of Paul's childhood and growth establishes him as different from—but still accepted by—his community, even before he becomes the legendary lumberjack.

It isn't only the women of the village who nurture and care for Paul. McNabb explains that everyone pitches in to meet Paul's needs, at which point the short cuts to a scene of women spinning yarn and knitting socks for Paul. A traditional scenario, at first glance—but notably, this is one of the very few in which women appear, and even here, two men feed the yarn to the two women knitting a sock for Paul as the camera pans from right to left, from the spinning wheels to the large knitting needles. The following scene shows the men lifting the giant baby bottle to the top of the cradle, using a crane. We might surmise that heavy lifting is typically men's work, so no surprise here. But as the bottle is given to baby Paul, it is men who place the nipple in Paul's mouth. The bending of traditional gender roles continues in the short as McNabb leads the singing to put Paul to sleep at night. By depicting Paul as surrounded by males, Clark and Disney perhaps set the expectation for viewers that Paul's happiness depends on men.

Such play with gender roles continues into Paul's school days. His female teacher shrieks a high-pitched "Eek!" when Paul lifts the schoolhouse roof to show her the math sum he has completed. She is the only voiced female character within the film, and is exaggeratedly feminine in dress and behavior. It is the only moment in which Paul is seen in the company of a woman. The moment passes and once school is out, Paul returns to a male-only community.

Because of his size, Paul is positioned between childhood and adulthood. He is more than a boy, and even more than a man. When he joins his classmates at the swimming hole, for instance, he's too big to fit, and the boys flee when he approaches. Sings the boys' chorus: "Although he loved to swim, what a time he had, what a problem me oh my/when his front was in the water, his back was high and dry." We see Paul, having landed in the swimming hole, on his hands and knees shaking the water from his hair. The other boys then join him and one asks, "How about a dive, Paul?" Paul scoops him from the water and Paul's index finger becomes the springboard for all the boys. He reclines in the swimming hole as the boys climb up his forearm and onto his shoulders, jumping off his head as well as his index finger. This scene of play is homosocial and homoerotic.

The villagers present young Paul with a double-bladed axe. The axe, gifted him by McNabb in the guise of Santa, is so heavy that it takes four men to drag it out. Paul immediately runs from the town square with his axe and begins to chop down trees with one swing. McNabb tells us, "Paul took to cuttin' timber like a duck takes to water." As he grows, he becomes so prolific at chopping trees that the "sawmills had enough lumber to last a lifetime" and the town rapidly expands thanks to enlarged farmland. But because he's so good at chopping down the frontier, Paul runs out of room and has to leave. He leaves a note of goodbye saying that he's headed out West where there are "lots of trees and plenty of room." In her work on the queer child, Kathryn Bond Stockton posits that queer childhood involves the feeling of being closed in:

> One can remember desperately feeling there was simply nowhere to grow. What would become of the child one feared oneself to be? For adults, then, who from a young age felt they were attracted to others in wrong ways, the notion of a gay child—however conceptually problematic—may be a throwback to a frightening, heightened sense of growing toward a question mark. Or growing up in a haze. Or hanging in suspense—even wishing time would stop, or just twist sideways, so that one wouldn't have to advance to new or further scenes of trouble. (3)

While Paul does not despair about the future, he is closed in around others—other humans, at least. Nowhere in the Disney short does he follow a traditional path of marriage and children; rather, to borrow from Stockton, he "grows sideways" rather than "up" (in a sense, he is born already grown up, and then some). And while embraced by the community, he is destined to leave it, too large for human civilization and human company. Only once does the film show Paul in the same frame as the other loggers, who are grouped together and wave at him as they sing of his accomplishments. We might say that Paul grows sideways into legend, or that legend makes space for sideways growth. *Paul Bunyan* makes space for the queer child, even if it also suggests a decidedly queer future for that child. Queer viewers—children or not—may well identify with Paul and his experiences of inclusion and exclusion.

I Got You Babe (Oxing Around)

That's not to say that Paul doesn't grow or change, only that his growth or change isn't conventional, even in this context. His voice deepens, and more critically, he forges a bond with a queer companion, a blue ox that he names Babe. Here another of Stockton's observations about the queer child applies, that said child identifies with and even "grows by" animals (she is building on Deleuze's "interval of animal"). Up to this point, Paul has never encountered a creature like him. We might speculate with Stockton that the ox "is a vehicle for the child's strangeness" (90) as well as a partner in such. Paul saves Babe, who is frozen in the snow. There's not much normal about Babe; he is a pet but a wild ox; he is blue; his size is proportionate to Paul's.

Paul and Babe's adventures seem eroticized. Their first meeting begins with an upside-down, frozen Babe, who seems to be dead. Paul pats Babe's face and, off screen, turns Babe into an upright position, sliding him over a fire. Babe thaws out, opens his eyes, and smiles, as the fire turns to steam underneath his body and Babe lets out a sigh/groan. The narrator at this point notes that Babe was "mighty grateful for being rescued." The camera frames a close-up of the head and shoulders of both Paul and Babe, face to face. Babe shakes his head, bats first his ears and then his eyes in a flirtatious manner, and proceeds to lick Paul from lower neck to chin in one long tongue movement. "They hit it right off and became *real* pals," the narrator continues. The subtle, seemingly innocent play between Paul and Babe continues throughout the short.

Griffin notes that sexuality is almost hilariously "suppressed"—that is, expressed symbolically—in postwar Disney productions, especially in the studio's theatrical animated features (38). Disney had ventured into more explicit territory earlier, but the studio suffered a backlash, and "1950 saw a full-scale return to the fairy-tale format that audiences wanted from

Disney . . . Sexual imagery was again submerged into images of patriarchal heterosexual romance—dancing, walking in the moonlight and a chaste kiss in a wedding carriage" (Griffin 41). Hence the covert, queer, proto-Campy thematics of Disney films ever since.

Consider, for instance, the scene in *Paul Bunyan* in which man and ox wake up together having created a number of monuments, many suggestively phallic, such as Pike's Peak, animated as standing alone (not in a mountain range) and erect. Babe wakes the sleeping Paul by using his tail to playfully punch Paul in the face. This action is followed by a face lick (as in their first meeting). The narrator calls their interaction "roughhousing" and explains that it results in the creation of the Grand Tetons. Babe butts Paul from behind and into the logger's groin. Paul throws Babe, bending the ox's horns, which Babe quickly straightens. In the voiceover, the audience is informed that all this "ox play" makes Paul and Babe "just a little bit dirty." Paul and Babe's next job is making a crooked river straight. The short ends with Paul and Babe "up in Alaska" where they are still "oxing" around. The animation cels for the action of Paul and Babe in Alaska show the same man-ox play involved in the creation of the Grand Tetons. Paul and Babe end the film together, and we are told "they are mighty happy" because "there is lots of room up there, ya know?" They never lose their bond: This interval of animal is forever.

In Short

Paul's queerness—his outsized abilities, his bond with Babe the blue ox, his singular lifestyle—aren't incidental to Disney's take on the tall tale but rather constitutive of it. Tall tales in general abound with exceptional characters with unusual abilities or powers engaged in impossible tasks. The tall tale is a queer genre at heart. It has Camp elements, in the sense that camp involves exaggeration and hyperbole, in Sontag's classic formulation "a mode of seduction which employs flamboyant mannerisms susceptible to double interpretations" (281). "The whole point of camp," she notes, "is to dethrone the serious" (288). She also remarks that Camp "is good *because it is awful.*" Norris W. Yates likewise stresses the extravagance of the tall tale, in which details become more and more fantastic to the point of the preposterous, akin to Camp's "dethroning of the serious" by way of "realistic" mimicry and detail accumulation. *Paul Bunyan* was made just as Disney was moving to "become an educator and moral guide for America's youth," according to Disney critic Steven Watts (334). It exploits the theatricality and queerness of the tall tale and tells the story of a decidedly unconventional hero and his odd companion, all the while safely appealing to classic and nostalgic themes of rugged masculinity and frontier wrangling. It does not offer social critique except indirectly, if at all, which brings it closer to some definitions of Camp. At the least, *Paul Bunyan* is suggestively if not definitively Camp, and some six years before Sontag's famous notes on such.

Illegal Citizen

The Japanese-American Internment Camp in Soon-Teck Oh's *Tondemonai—Never Happen!*

Ana M. Jimenez-Moreno

Camp emerges as an unlikely defense strategy in one of America's most bleak spaces, the Japanese-American internment camp. Written by one of the most famous Asian-American actors[1] in the 1970s and staged by the East West Players,[2] Soon-Teck Oh's play *Tondemonai—Never Happen!* (1970)[3] dramatizes the assault on civil liberties that took place between 1942 and 1946 when Americans of Japanese descent were "relocated" through a widely supported presidential order. Oh uses the physical and psychological space of the internment camp to foreground male gay and bisexual bonds. Camp[4] comes out in the play as the means to defend "American" national identity *and* the possibility of queer affect. The two-act drama of *Tondemonai* revolves around Koji Murayama's trauma of being doubly pathologized by the State[5] and his community as Japanese/American[6] and gay. The play also includes his family's experience of the Tule Lake internment camp. *Tondemonai* is a phenomenological study of queerness that mobilizes Camp aesthetics to undermine how the main character is politically reduced to a single victimized identity. These markers of identification—Japanese, Kibei, gay, bisexual—implode in the internment camp.

My essay looks at the queer intersection of Camp as a performance of political sedition. The early reviews of the play show us a public too ready to fetishize the Asian-American male gay protagonists as exotic while falling virtually silent on the political and aesthetic elements of Oh's play. By analyzing the invisibility of Camp in critical discourse and through Sara Ahmed's theorization of orientation, we will see how queer camp in *Tondemonai* becomes a formative space for the development of a civic identity.

Reading Queerness

The play's literary effect of displacing us, the audience, in time and space mimics the way Japanese-Americans were displaced from their ethnic roots and their civil rights during their internment in the 1940s. Oh's frequent shifts, ten major temporal and spatial relocations, are an example of how the form as much as the content of *Tondemonai* carries Oh's political message. The prefatory note of the play explains:

> This is a story of a young man who is "suddenly" told that he is free after a decade of confinement.
> The story unfolds in his mind, hence FLASH FORWARD is as important as FLASH BACK in telling this tale of an injustice by a majority to a law abiding individual.[7]

It is precisely this queered time and space that contemporaneous reviewers of the play most resisted but that most powerfully and violently conveyed the distress Japanese-Americans felt as their civic rights evaporated in the harsh desert sun.

Looking back at this play from our time, Greg Robinson applauds *Tondemonai* for presciently dealing with Japanese-American attitudes toward internment and Asian-American perspectives on queer identities. When *Tondemonai* premiered, however, most reviewers were as puzzled by the pacing of the play as they were enthralled by the representation of Otherness onstage. In 1970, the *Los Angeles Times* reviewer Margaret Hardford claimed that despite the play's laudable attention to the plight of Asian-Americans during World War II, it "would have been less confusing if he [Oh] had chosen a simpler format" (6). This is echoed by Darby Summers in *The Advocate*: "The play, a strange one and most difficult to follow, is told in small flashback segments" (12). Summers further asserts that "The work is an Oriental mood piece as inscrutable as the Far East itself" (12). Overall, the reviewers explain away the play's aesthetic nuances through stereotyped understandings of Asian-American representation. It is not that Koji (or Oh) is unable to weave together his experiences into a presentable whole, but that the links between past and present, reality and fantasy, citizen and alien, camp and jail are prioritized. The connective tissue between events expresses a non-linear but also non-cyclical understanding of time. This associative and highly experiential model of time points us towards a phenomenological understanding of the world. The reviewers ignore the form and fixate on the content, thereby disregarding the indictment leveled on the U.S. government and the Japanese-American community for their silence on internment.

It is easy to pathologize Koji based on his experiences. Cathy Caruth explains that the traumatic "event is not assimilated or experienced fully at the time, but only belatedly [. . .] To be traumatized is precisely to be possessed by an image or event" (4). Though this would, at first, seem to fit Koji's inchoate psychic world, this passively defined act of possession of the subject by the abject/object does not explain Koji's active Camp behavior. Koji refuses to be a victim without agency by playing up the very real and harmful power dynamics between him and those who seek to be institutional gatekeepers.

My essay treats Camp as an aesthetic, rather than a "sensibility," as Susan Sontag famously calls it in "Notes on 'Camp'" (275). Fabio Cleto's powerful theorization of Camp as a queer aesthetic illuminates my own reading of this pioneering work of drama, even though I take it to different ends. Cleto states that "as an object of camp decoding, the actor exists only through its in(de)finite performing roles, the ideal sum of which correspond to his own performative 'identity' [. . .] Camp thus presupposes a *collective, ritual and performative existence*" (25; emphasis original). Therefore, one has to take seriously the satirical and serious, female and male, political and ahistorical facets of Camp performance. But beyond that, our participation in the performance by our encoding and decoding of the actor also makes Camp function. The two nodes of his definition, community and subject, are both raised and razed through the process of identifying Camp as queer. And while the "collective" that Cleto mentions is not conventionally civic or institutional, I would invite us to see it as both. My essay takes Koji and his lover's claim to institutionality seriously, without skepticism that mistreats a call for inclusion as vapid nationalism.

Sontag's 1964 "Notes on 'Camp'" was for many years the definitive document on this subject in the second half of the twentieth century. Camp's connection to queer culture has been debated among scholars[8] as much as Camp's ability to be political.[9] Sontag cites Wilde and leaves a few clues about Camp's ties to male homosexuality. However, she largely "sanitizes" Camp by eliminating the way in which it emerges from "the production of queer social visibility" (Meyer 7, 5). Richard Dyer and Jack Babuscio campaigned to undo Sontag's erasure of queer culture from Camp. Writing in 1977, Dyer desperately claims that "Camp is the one thing that expresses and confirms being a gay man" (11). Babuscio, focusing on film, treats what we may call the phenomenology of queer film. Camp triangulates the relationship between the medium, the subject, and the queer aspects of both. For him, Camp in film is a "heightened state of awareness of certain human complications of feeling that spring from the fact of social oppression" (40). Babuscio's queer phenomenology involves both the affective and political sides of being a gay man. Though they do not explain how features of Camp would become so seamlessly gobbled up by mainstream Hollywood,[10] Dyer and Babuscio do rightly defend Camp as a (male) queer act of subversion.

Citizenship in Theory

Tondemonai reflects, or rather refracts, the lived reality of many Japanese-Americans in the 1940s. On February 19, 1942, President Franklin D. Roosevelt signed Executive Order 9066 sending around 110,000 Japanese-Americans—regardless of their citizenship status—to ten distant internment camps.[11] These spaces conform to what Giorgio Agamben defined as camp, namely all instances of suspended law and denaturalization (42). Although Japanese-Americans were citizens, they were not considered to be "really" loyal to America. For many white Americans, Pearl Harbor provided "evidence" that these foreign citizens needed even more constant supervision. As Emily Roxworthy explains, Japanese-American "persecution was staged—over and over again for the more than three years of the Pacific War" (6). When the government started to conduct raids, the Japanese-American victim, the FBI agent, and the reporter seemed to be recreating scenes from popular media where Asian-Americans were largely portrayed as criminals (Roxworthy 94). Whether silence expressed their resistance, desperation, or shock, it could only be interpreted by the media and the State as a testament to their guilt. Speaking out went against the restraint and decorum Japanese-Americans felt they needed in order to be read as civilized by the State authority and the public. Oh zooms in on one family's experience of American fascism and uses the protagonist to voice his rejection of being a criminalized group and of the forms of internalized racism many had come to accept.

In *Tondemonai*, the space of the camp stretches far past the wire fences to include homes—that become bunkers—and hospitals—that become jails. Fred, Koji's partner, points out that Koji's apartment "is like a shelter designed to perfection. It's under the ground, as tight as a box. You can shut the out-side out completely if you want to—like a jail is" (Oh 3). The apartment that Fred describes is both a space of safety ("shelter") but also, eerily, a space of forcible containment ("jail"). The internment camp is an instance of what Charlie Hailey, building on Agamben, terms "strategic camps of control" that "seek to hold areas by force" (240). The U.S. military and government held control of Japanese-Americans by wresting civil rights from them. The play's multi-purpose space does have to do with the lean budget the East West Players had in 1970, but it also reflects the dual nature of the homeland Japanese-Americans belonged to.

Koji's apartment works on different levels. On one hand, the apartment where Koji and Fred's sexual encounter takes place stages Koji's recuperation from government persecution. On the other hand, that space works as Koji's unconscious trying to come to grips with the jail (within the internment camp) that requisitions and punishes Asian-American identity. The jail within Tule Lake (a highly guarded Japanese-American internment camp)—like Koji's bathroom where he keeps a type of negative shrine to his oppressor—is perhaps the only space that is not represented onstage. As Hailey posits, "camp spaces endure," and though they seem to index the transitory nature of the issue or conflict that they are trying to contain, they become permanent stations of remembrance for wider systematic conflicts (3).

Tondemonai follows Koji from Manzaner to Tule Lake, a camp for "disloyal" Japanese-Americans. The Tule Lake Japanese-American internment camp in which Oh sets the play was indeed more segregated than similar facilities because it purportedly housed subversive nationals. This status was determined by a "loyalty questionnaire" offered by the government. Koji and his mother, Ume,[12] refuse to answer the form "correctly." For those who did not answer Questions 27 and 28 to the satisfaction of the government, Tule Lake and deportation to Japan were the two options left open. Koji, like other Japanese-Americans, was dissatisfied with the form of the questions. It asked them to "forswear" any previous (criminal) allegiances, as if the government assumed that Japanese-American internees had been disloyal to the U.S. government at some point in the past (Roxworthy 64–65). Tule Lake is the place where Koji met Fred's tender and unnamed lookalike, and where he spent the majority of the war. Lastly,

Koji's apartment is a recreation of those conditions in Tule Lake that gave rise to his need to protect himself psychologically. Koji accesses Camp aesthetics to resist the scripted performance he is forced to enact in these State-controlled areas.

Camp is how Koji, a Japanese-American guilty until proven innocent, mediates his queer and Japanese-American identities. Koji understands that he has no access to patriotism because to "act right" as a Japanese-American is to be disloyal to the United States (Roxworthy 140). Koji's dilemma reflects the real-life difficulties Japanese-Americans had before and after the war when dealing with their status as citizens, if not residents, in the United States.[13] In an act of reversal, Oh denies most Americans physical representation in the play. During Koji's interrogation about his and his family's loyalty to the United States, the questioner's voice is never heard, nor is he represented onstage. In lieu of an actual body, the stage directions inform us that "The lights on KOJI become almost blindingly brighter" (Oh 21). The Anglo-American interrogator is associated with the light of a Foucauldian inquisitor. In his defense, and to show his displeasure, Koji quotes, at length and with verve, an eminent American[14] who idealizes the United States as a reserved political space in which one has the freedom to dissent:

> KOJI: Let me tell you, loyalty is not an oath of allegiance, not a flag waving, not a fervid verbal declaration [. . .] Instead of answering your questions, I would like to quote an American who I think is much more articulate than myself. He said loyalty is not conformity [. . .] Pardon me? Oh, you would like to hear what I have to say. This genuine American said, loyalty is a tradition, an ideal, and a principle. [. . .] This eminent American said, "Loyalty is the flower of the traditions of freedom, equality, tolerance; the tradition of higher law, of experimentation, cooperation." [. . .] "Loyalty is a realization that America was born of revolt, flourished on dissent—became great through experimentation." (Oh 21)

This all transpires as "The Star Spangled Banner" plays on a piano in the background, as (presumably) non-diegetic music. Ultimately, Koji's answer to the interrogation is, "Shit—yes, shit!" (Oh 21). Instead of interpreting Koji's final statement as a repudiation of the credentialed American's theorizations about loyalty, seemingly coded as Anglo-American in the context of the speech, I invite us to read toward a recuperation of the institutions passionately endorsed by Koji throughout the speech. Loyalty as a tradition, and therefore as an adhesion to institutionalized thought, versus loyalty to a government, is what Koji advocates as a means to protect his queer identity and citizenship status. Koji's vision is of a productively struggling representative democratic system. His refusal to comply with the rules, his histrionic performance in front of those who can incarcerate him, is Camp. Koji is not allowed by his interrogators to *be* an American, but he will not exoticize Japanese-American stoicism and therefore turns to Camp.

In *Tondemonai*, the minority subject develops as a political agent before the queer body is situated in a political framework. However, both modalities are expressed through experimental features that pay close attention to the specificity of the dramatic element (the interrogation) and therefore to a certain extent minimizing the boundaries between spaces (i.e., stage as setting). Sara Ahmed's work on queer phenomenology[15] helps us understand how Koji manages to orient himself toward a space that seems, at first glance, inhospitable for a queer man, let alone a Kibei man, to thrive. The branch of phenomenology from which Ahmed's theory develops salvages agency for the subject without ignoring the substantive doubts postmodern scholars had about the subject's ability to act autonomously. Her concept of orientation allows us to see and describe Koji's movement toward, not away, from institutionality.

Bodies, Ahmed contends, are shaped by phenomenological interactions with spaces. Her study of how social relations emerge from both being oriented toward and being embodied in a certain space guides my investigation of how the space of the Japanese-American internment camp is at the forefront of negotiations between the agent and the State. Ahmed further argues that queerness disrupts and reorders those relations by not following the accepted paths, thereby precipitating a politics of disorientation that puts other objects within reach. Koji orients his queer desire and national-racial identity toward the internment camp. He does not seek to possess or write over the experience, nor does he accept the historical account and erasure of the event. By mobilizing Camp and experimentalist techniques, Oh describes a subjectivity that is fragmented, but not powerless.

Tondemonai broke new ground due to its queer content and style in the 1970s but also because it is one of the first plays to treat Japanese-American internment. It was only until the 1981–82 season that the East West Players—the same company that staged Oh's play—produced "Breaking the Silence Series," also known as "The Internment Camp Series." The company was emblematic of an age when the "drastically changing landscape of American theatre—with the revival of ethnic theatre in America, the growth of region theatre companies, and the social political climate of the nation—provided a space for a new and unique force amalgamated in the EWP [East West Players]" (Kurahashi 3). In 1968, Oh submitted his play to the first script contest organized by the East West Players. Oh's *Tondemonai* intersected with the East West Players when they were just beginning to form their identity and repertoire. Esther Kim Lee laments the fact that "Internment camp theatre has been dismissed and even forgotten mainly because of its controversial emphasis on assimilation and accommodation" (20). Critics like Lee argue that plays dealing with Japanese-American internment have only considered that to reclaim American citizenship means to forgo certain cultural markers of difference. *Tondemonai* is a play with Camp characters that, through their performance, complicate and nuance queer, Asian-American, male identity.

Citizen at Camp

Camp has aesthetic and political valences in *Tondemonai*. The campy aspect of the play mostly comes out through Cherry Williams, Koji's Japanese landlady. She is married to an African-American wounded Vietnam War veteran who only speaks through a gong in the play (Oh 47). The way she speaks, her gestures, and her playful manner with "Ko-chan" (a diminutive for Koji) mark her as a Camp diva[16] and as perpetuating a gross stereotype. In the middle of Koji and Michael Takeno's argument, Cherry runs in having "decked herself up most ridiculously—the heaviest make-up; flowery Japanese hair-do; and a red flower patterned gaudy Japanese kimono" (Oh 43). Michael was once Koji's Nisei (first-generation) friend but their experiences in the internment camp drove them apart. In the present time of the play, Michael asks Koji to claim evacuation money—remuneration by the government for the financial losses suffered by the Japanese-American community. Koji, who was an aspiring pianist at the time of his internment, interprets Michael's insistence as a sign of his former friend's guilt for (potentially) ordering other Nisei to break Koji's fingers. Cherry superimposes a melodramatic story about her imaginary child being in a burning building over the two men's argument. Koji cancels out the importance vested in the figure of the child.[17] He tells her to "F your child" (Oh 43). When Cherry mock protests, "Why you F a child!" Koji returns grotesquely, "I'd do it even to ducks" (Oh 43). With Cherry, Koji plays up Michael's tacit connection between homosexuality and pathology: "You damn stupid pervert [. . .] Do you know what they call your kind of self-righteous consciousness? Hypochondria" (Oh 42–43). This is an instance of what Cleto terms "deliberate camp" whereby the camping subject "debunks its seriousness" through self-representation, through "artificiality that passes for natural, [through] queering straightness, and as such necessitates an external perception that travesties the object of perception" (25). In order to protect themselves from the political, ideological, and medical charges enmeshed in Michael's accusation of perversion, Koji and Cherry push this image of subjecthood to its breaking point. Michael explains Koji's homosexuality, which he embraced only after internment, and feeling of victimhood, as a product of Koji's "fantastic imagination," a psychosomatic by-product (Oh 43). Koji's choice of potential sexual partners (child, duck) emphasizes his "perversion" while at the same time unveiling it as a performance.

Koji and Cherry's Camp conversation figuratively pushes Michael out of the door. Recall Sontag's gloss of Camp as frivolity, the celebration of the overwrought and histrionic, of what she calls "failed seriousness" (283). The doubly staged camp performance put on by Cherry and Koji (one, in front of an audience, and two, in front of Michael) represents a specifically queer form of political mobilization. It is not just a passive seeing or cultural transgression, though these are efficacious in their own right, but a catalyst for action. In some cases, these productions force the War Relocation Officers to shed their false mask of civility and treat the internment camp as a prison, and in other cases it forces unwanted, hypocritical characters to leave the stage. Once their common enemy exits, Koji and Cherry adopt an exaggerated, polished register. Now, when Koji notices Cherry's outfit he says, "I like it. It is so obscenely ridiculous. It is a *masterful fantasia*" (Oh 44; emphasis added). Koji outs Camp as political because Cherry's representation of a Japanese woman in front of a Japanese audience (Michael and Koji, but also the mostly Asian-American audience of the East West Players) is strategic. By participating in a stereotype of Japanese femininity, as exotic and dramatic, she breaks the stereotype. By taking the performance to its extreme, Cherry unearths it as *only* "a masterful fantasia" that cannot be equated with the person that is Cherry. Instead of perpetuating the stereotypes of Asians as histrionic by nature, Japanese women as exotic, and homosexual men as pathological, the recourse to these Camp clichés delegitimizes them as acceptable representations of the Other.

The dispute over money as reparation between Michael and Koji is really about their disagreement over how to represent themselves as citizens. Michael has a Western name, and he is one of the leaders of JACL (Japanese-American Citizen League), an organization meant to assimilate the Japanese-American community into the State. Koji retains his

Japanese-derived name and cleans up horse dung seven days a week (Oh 10). To not assimilate is to not proceed up the social ladder. In what we might take as the "present time" of the play, Michael goes to see Koji to try to convince him to take the evacuation claim money. Koji reads this as a bribe to forget the violence incited by Michael and those who wanted Japanese-American bodies to conform to an ideal of citizenship. Koji tells Michael that he will take the money only if Michael manages to straighten out his fingers. While Koji might be evoking the straight/ queer word play, it is more likely that he is referring to the life as a professional pianist, husband, and father that he lost when Michael decided to direct violence toward his fellow Japanese-American inmate. Twice Koji suggests that if he should cure him, he will donate the money to Michael's "youth organization."[18] The conversation that ensues between Michael and Koji emphasizes how the internment camp, meant to subordinate subversive Japanese-American bodies by white men, became a place to subject one's people to self-effacing violence.

Koji points out how (ethnic) particularity is criminalized in a series of Camp maneuvers meant to frustrate the neat boundaries between subject and object:

> MICHAEL: Why don't you try to lead a decent, normal life?
> KOJI: I can't; I've castrated myself.
> MICHAEL: That's against the law.
> KOJI: Is it?
> MICHAEL: Who operated on you?
> KOJI: You.
> MICHAEL: A desperate subterfuge of excuse for being a homosexual.
> KOJI: Why do I need an excuse?
> MICHAEL: Because it is illegal. [. . .] Does your conscience bother you?
> KOJI: Be careful. You might bite your tongue. The word should be quite
> a mouthful for you. (Oh 42–43)[19]

Koji equally tags Michael as a hypocrite and as queer. Figuratively, Michael's mouth is full of Koji's castrated member. Is Koji self-castrated because of the way effeminate homosexuality was persecuted? Did Michael castrate his friend because of his homosexuality or because of his refusal to be a Japanese-American of good standing? Roxworthy documents the violent rift between Japanese-educated Kibei and assimilationist Nisei that historically occurred inside and outside of the internment camp (135). Michael and Koji represent two opposing ideas of how Japanese-American citizenship should be claimed. Koji's failure to assimilate what Michael thinks of as the right form of citizenship highlights Cleto's argument that Camp "as a 'style' of performance doesn't exclude [. . .] it presupposes an element of perception, an encoding and decoding of the self and the world as stage, and of failure of intentions" (26). In his attempts, Koji encodes queerness and a Japanese-American experience into the heart of American citizenship. His mode of manifesting this is through Camp, which enables him to debunk Michael's idea of citizenship based on a meritocratic system that benefits only docile and erasable bodies. Koji, oriented toward the internment camp and Camp, turns what Michael thinks of as an excuse on its head.

Koji's relationship to his Caucasian wife, Jane, continues to treat the problem of castration even while the power and gender dynamics in this couple are different. Deeply in love with Koji, Jane joins him at the Manzaner camp, virtually defying and denying her citizenship status. Jane not only "dresses up" as a Japanese bride but withstands the harsh disapproval of Koji's mother, Ume. Ume questions her son, "Why this American girl? Don't you find her somewhat peculiar in the Japanese garment?" (Oh 36). Ume asserts that Jane cannot be expected to put on a costume and be treated as Japanese —just as they, perhaps, with all their acculturation, will not be treated as American. Jane's utopic vision goes much further than dressing up to erase difference:

> Mrs. Murayama, no, Mother, you are only seeing the visibles. You are refusing to see the invisible barrier which will become a yoke on every Japanese-American's neck. Mother, after a few generations of this sort of inter-marriage there will be no gaps where anyone can build any kind of fence. (Oh 36)

Jane's metaphors call attention to their imprisonment, and to the policies, politics, and mentalities behind the fences constructed between peoples. In Jane's (dystopic?) future there will be no recourse to discrimination, but at the same time her vision is totalitarian. Even though Koji loves Jane, he cannot comply with her theory which, in part, penalizes particular ethnicities and demands compulsive inter-marriage. To express this, Koji elicits the tactics behind Camp, exaggeration, to undermine Jane's logic: "There will be no Japs, no Chinks, no Kikes, no Nig—" (Oh 36). Notice that there is no reference to Anglo-Americans because, Koji argues through this racist rant, it is assumed they are neutral bodies. The effect of the racial slurs does not faze his mother who simply asks, "Is that why you want to marry this

American girl?" to which her son promptly answers, "No" (Oh 36). He does not want to marry Jane for the ideals of a compulsory multiculturalism borne of assimilation and coercion.

Jane's cross-cultural embodiment as well as her idealistic vision come into conflict with Koji's queerness and precarious political subjecthood. In order to find some sense of home within the camp, Koji invites Jane to play at being a heteronormative husband and wife. Slowly through their farce, Jane divulges that she was gang raped, or at the very least hints that there was a sexual encounter between her and some officers—"I only saw the hideous grins" (Oh 51). The following passage is a great example of what Andrew Ross defined as camp—"an explicit commentary on feats of *survival* in a world dominated by the taste, interests, and definitions of others" (144; emphasis original). As the conversation goes on, Jane reveals that she had reasons for being with the officer(s):

> I could have endured any humiliation if only you were not so—damp [. . .] You were wallowing in that sweet pain of being wronged, yet you let yourself be fed and protected by Americans. [. . .] I began to loathe everything about you, your indecisive apologetic smile, furtive glances [. . .] it got to the point that your mere presence was nauseating. I craved for something natural, light, warm without being wet. [. . .] I threw myself at the sergeant. (Oh 51)[20]

After Jane discloses her disdain of what she understands as Koji's feminized behavior, she admits that she lost their child and with it, the utopic vision of an amalgamated future. Jane reads Koji as a victim, for she cannot read heroism if it is not heteronormative, coded white, and able-bodied. Jane's values of multiculturalism and ethnic pride are not objectively harmful, but the way that she goes about imposing them is destructive. Koji's survival tactics reveal a closeted queer community within the ranks of the soldiers through the missing object of the "furtive glance." Jane does not see how Koji's Camp performance as a desirable victim secured him practical material benefits and how he outed the queer system. Koji's Camp space and queer time dismantle the progressivist, assimilationist, and totalitarian visions of Michael (a Japanese-American friend), Jane (white ex-fiancée), and the State.

Koji's other major love interest in the play, Fred, helps to create and resolve some of the tensions brought up by Jane and Michael's politics. The stage directions establish a connection between Jane's and Fred's struggling ideas of citizenship: "KOJI has turned away from her [Jane], and does not see her leaving, FRED comes to the door. KOJI turns around and finds FRED instead of JANE" (Oh 51). The continuity of the action juxtaposed with the shift in time signals to the audience that while Fred is replacing Jane in the scene, the tensions of sexuality, race, and citizenship continue to be at the forefront of the discussion. In Koji and Fred's present, Koji adapts Jane's previous confessionary mode. When Fred tells him that Cherry Williams informed him that Koji was once married, Koji responds, "That's right, and I just discovered I killed her" (Oh 52). In Koji's version of the story, he recounts how Jane came back to their room distraught, and that he suspected it was the "big sergeant" who raped her (Oh 53). In this version, he assaults the sergeant and receives a "life-time imprisonment" that gets curtailed to ten years (Oh 53). It is Baby Sergeant York's face that Fred sees clipped to Koji's bathroom wall, a shrine to rancor and humiliation in a space devoted to excrement (Oh 7). At this point, Fred functions as a substitute for the deceased Jane. It is only now that Koji can explain that by giving into her model of the rebellious hero, he was punished by the State and she lost her life.

Although Fred, like Koji, is an embodiment of multiculturalism, he deals in a different set of idealisms than Jane. In the first segment of the play, Fred tries to broach the distance between him and Koji—not wanting the relationship to be a purely physical one—by urging the protagonist to ask him a question about his identity. Fred explains that he is indeed Chinese, "A third generation thoroughbred. You might ask, then, why Fred Chung instead of Chiang Kai-shek, Mao Tse-tung, or some kind of a name which would be more suitable for a thoroughbred like me" (Oh 6). Fred highlights the hybridity of his name as well as his "breeding," mobilizing Camp exaggeration to undermine these very concepts. Fred's name does not reinforce identity through the aspiration towards purity. He has integrated two cultures in a way that Jane's utopic vision does not. When Fred asks for Koji's name, the issue of how ethnicity impacts citizenship arises:

FRED: Japanese?
KOJI: No.
FRED: American-Japanese.
KOJI: American by *jus soli*. (Oh 6; emphasis original)

The unstated portion behind Fred's "simple" question, "Japanese?" is "Are you, by heritage, Japanese?" Koji's response addresses his citizenship status more than his biological heritage. Fred believes he has found the politically correct answer when he declares, "American-Japanese" period. Koji thwarts him again, correcting Fred's assumptions with "American by jus soli," meaning, American by "right of the soil," commonly referred to as

birthright citizenship: the right of anyone born in the territory of a state
to nationality or citizenship (Vincent 80). Koji demands to be read as a full
citizen, not one whose hyphenated status also forecloses full civic rights.
The feeling of displacement caused by the play's constant jumping in time
and space mimics the way Japanese-Americans were jostled between different types of subjects under (and outside) law. The literary mobilizes the
political message of an identity that does not, in effect, patrol the borders
between different kinds of citizenship. Koji repossesses camp as a space
and enables Camp as an aesthetic that reconciles, on his terms, the dispari-
ties between Japanese, American, citizen, alien, gay, and bisexual statuses
that were put in relief during internment.

Near the end of the play, we approach the best articulation of Koji's
argument for the institution of citizenship. Fred returns to Koji's apartment after being offended by Koji's standoffishness. Instead of a romantic
reunion, Koji and Fred enter into the politics of a queer man entering the
armed forces. Fred comes to the conclusion that: "I think in any country
they would have shot you and me without a question for what you did and
for what I have done. But this country is different" (Oh 57). Instead of
reading this statement as naïve or willful negligence, I see Fred's use of
"country" as part of the tradition that Koji evokes during his interrogation,
namely that of a volatile representative democracy. While homosexuality
was still criminalized in 1970, Fred, as a refraction of Koji's consciousness,
still posits that the country could protect the lives of its queer citizens. The
romance arc that Koji would like to rehabilitate is interrupted by Fred's
essentialisms: "You are a Jap who loves a Chinese boy" (Oh 56). It is possible that Fred is echoing a quote earlier in the play that has been historically attributed to West Coast Zone military commander General John
DeWitt (qtd. in Roxworthy 108): "A Jap is a Jap. April 13th, 1943" (Oh 19).
In this context, Fred participates in the same kind of strategic Camp that
Koji mobilized during his interrogation. Fred's mutation of General
DeWitt's tautological statement opens up the possibilities of how a (Kibei,
queer, American) "Jap" can *be* in relation to others.

Oh's play attends to the tensions in Asian-American queer identities,
and to the way in which they are not resolved. Formally, the irresolution
comes from the experimentalist aesthetics that make it difficult to establish a straight timeframe. But the tensions are also not settled by simple
economic reparation, by recapitulating one identity over the Other, or by
the love plot. The irresolution of the romance between Koji and his suit-
ors signals the persistence of unrest between queer and civic identities.

The last time that we see Koji and Fred together, they have established a relationship, but one in which Fred no longer needs to try to love Koji and Koji has not learned to love without resentment (Oh 60). Fred enlists in the army and is about to embark to war. After he exits Koji's life for the last time, Koji asserts that he will not wait for Fred's return despite the thin promise that was made between them. The act of love, waiting, would be a burden on them both: "You, yourself said I couldn't live my lost life through you, and you were right. We won't need each other; you won't need me, and I don't think *my need is for you*" (Oh 61; emphasis added). In a strange way, however, Koji's act of renunciation is an act of love, for he is not going to use Fred as some avatar for his ten years of confinement. The love plot cannot mend the wrongs inflicted on the Japanese-American community, but it can bear witness to a reconciliation between different kinds of American identities.

In the final stage shift, Koji wakes up to kindly Bernard, a nurse at a mental institution. There is evidence that the Koji-Bernard scene is the culmination of the protagonist's stress under Fred's leave-taking. It could also function as a coda, taking us to a time before Koji was grounded by Fred. In either case, the actions between the two male characters make visible the different ethics of care that Bernard represents as the ideal of an institution like this and the empty service that the facility doles out. Someone on the intercom asks Bernard to get Room "K-127" ready, basically to move Koji out of the ward (Oh 65). In contrast to this impersonal announcement, Bernard expresses the mixed emotions he feels seeing Koji go: happy because he is well but sad because he will miss the other's company (Oh 65). Koji literalizes the emotional coldness of being evacuated from the institution by pantomime: "BERNARD stops[,] sensing that something is happening with Koji, who has opened his trunk and starts to put on clothes over the clothes he already has on. He begins to tremble" (Oh 67). Koji literalizes the cold reception that he now finds at this particular institution. We do not know if Bernard will pathologize this emotionally sad Camp performance. The stage directions are neutral due to their lack of adjectives. However, the ending is optimistic and key to the resolution in another section of the ending. *Tondemonai* leaves us with a new queer family in place of the one lost and shattered by the effects of U.S. government policy. Bernard recounts to his patient that he was surprised that Williams, Cherry's husband, claims Koji as his son and that Cherry takes such good care of him even though they are not related by blood. Williams follows Camp protocol, asking Bernard to look at his (non-existent) knees.

When Bernard admits that he sees "Absolutely nothing," William responds: "You poor thing. No wonder you don't see Koji is my son" (Oh 65). The Camp family portrait is taken: a disabled veteran, a histrionic woman, and a distraught Kibei man make an interesting family, one that recuperates agency through establishing non-biological paternity, exploding stereotypes, and reclaiming citizenship.

The internment camp, as a space where Camp is possible, becomes Koji's means to escape the bifurcating logic of American fascism. Although usually not represented in media, Oh makes a point of highlighting the intra-Asian frictions represented between Koji and his Chinese-American lover Fred. These two characters seek to reconcile queer and Asian-American identities into a citizen. The space of the camp, which seemed to represent a state of exception to legal protection of difference, proves to be a fertile area from which to negotiate the terms of protection, if not representation, in front of the State. While the State blanketed certain kinds of differences, *Tondemonai* recuperates difference without fetishizing it. The hostility between Koji, Michael, and Jane stems from their status as Kibei, Nisei, and Anglo-American, as well as the erasure of their civil liberties. Oh's Camp internment camp play seeks to resolve issues of inter- and intra-ethnic tensions by claiming a space for non-pathologized difference and a non-sectarian concept of citizenship.

NOTES

1. Oh is best known, however, for voicing the father, Fa Zhou, in Disney's *Mulan*.

2. The East West Players is "the nation's oldest and arguably most prestigious Asian-American theatre company" (Kurahashi xi).

3. Hereafter referred to as *Tondemonai*. Interestingly, the missing "it," or the subject of the "happen," is not present, indicating the silence imposed on and by Japanese-Americans in relation to their experience of the internment camp.

4. I will refer to the aesthetic of Camp with a capital *C*, and camp as a space with a lowercase *c*.

5. The State, as in the United States government, as an institution.

6. Koji is a "Kibei," meaning a Japanese-American educated in Japan.

7. It is unclear from the reviews if the epigraph ever made its way onstage.

8. Cleto's reader includes many of these foundational essays, mostly in Sections II and V.

9. McMahon argues that Camp cannot be political because the style overtakes the content (89).

10. Ross explains the phenomenon by stating that "the technical rationality of capitalism had found ways of administrating and exploiting the liberalization of attitudes towards sexual pleasure" (144).

11. On December 21, 2006, George W. Bush signed HR-1492, directing the government to preserve some of the former Japanese-American internments as heritage sites.

12. Interestingly, her name means "dream" in Japanese, and this play is indeed a dream or nightmare.

13. Even the Japanese-American Citizens League (JACL), Michael's group, was historically believed to be a pro-Japanese project hidden under the guise of "Americanization" by the FBI (Roxworthy 71).

14. Most likely referring to Henry Steele Commager, a historian who helped define modern liberalism. See Wilsey 144 for quote.

15. Though Ahmed's and Babuscio's queer phenomenologies have a lot in common, Ahmed's phenomenological subject is active, whereas Babuscio's is receptive.

16. For a fascinating account of historical men in drag and onstage in Tule Lake, see Roxworthy's account of Yukio Shimoda, a Nisei man who performed as Carmen Miranda to an audience made up mostly of War Relocation Authority officers at Tule Lake (154–56).

17. Lee Edelman *avant la lettre*.

18. The reason that Koji does not use the acronym "JACL" could be that he wants to emphasize the parallels between the Nazi youth group and the fascist tendencies in this literary representation of JACL.

19. Summers, from *The Advocate*, reports that the translation for *Tondemonai* was "emasculation" (12).

20. Her rant against Koji also sounds like something that contemporary (to Oh) Japanese-American men and women were leveling on their parents for not protesting their unfair treatment.

Why Angela Won't Go Swimming

Sleepaway Camp, Slasher Films, and Summer Camp Horrors

Chris McGee

In the early 1980s, American horror films had a fleeting fascination with summer camps. *Friday the 13th* (1980), owing some debt to the box office success of camp comedies such as *Meatballs* (1979) and *Little Darlings* (1980), was among the first of a series of so-called slasher or splatter films set at summer camps. Slasher films were memorable for their gory violence, grisly make-up, and technical effects, as well as their endlessly repeatable plot. Carol Clover describes this plot as "a psychokiller who slashes to death a string of mostly female victims, one by one, until he is subdued or killed, usually by the one girl who has survived" (21). Vera Dika notes of slashers how important it is that "the entire action takes place in a single setting," a setting that, in order for the killer to so easily dispatch this younger group, is "exclusionary, separating the young community from the rest of society" (93). It is easy to see why slasher films were so attracted to the summer camp, which had a lot to offer as a setting. The isolation and darkness naturally afforded by the locale made for plenty of opportunities for sexual transgressions and for places to hide. The secluded and vulnerable groups with little access to help made for easy victims. And the clash of civilization and backwoods threats were practically written into the set. Just as important, summer camps were also immediately recognizable as an American place, as an idealized space where death and mayhem were even that much more shocking. Slasher films were "positioned," Dika continues, "in a middle-class American community," which "fosters a degree of likeness to that of the viewing audience" (93). They occur in a place "that is simultaneously everywhere and nowhere, but yet distinctly American" (93). In many of the other more notable slashers of the time, the plot unfolded in high schools, college campuses, sorority houses, and even trains. The first and perhaps most famous of the slashers, *Halloween* (1978), found its version of terror in suburban neighborhoods and middle-class homes. Films like *Friday the 13th*, *The Burning* (1981), and *Sleepaway Camp* (1983), meanwhile, emphasized the survival narratives that could only come from feeling helpless in the woods.

The cult favorite *Sleepaway Camp* (1983) is one of the most bizarre and infamous entries in this canon, arriving just as the wave of summer camp slashers was dying down. It is a film that tells both a literal queer story and an odder, deeper, queerer, more complex story in its subtext. As the film opens, two young children, Angela and Peter, witness their father's death while boating on a public lake. Eventually we learn that Angela and Peter's father is gay, and another man who was boating with them is actually his lover. Eight years later, Angela is sent off to Camp Arawak with her cousin Ricky, though she has become exceedingly shy and reluctant to talk, a fact that causes her to be relentlessly bullied. The bulk of the film sees each of Angela's bullies violently murdered by a figure that appears to be her overly protective and hotheaded cousin Ricky, although the killer is always obscured. Angela is discovered in the closing minutes with the severed head of a boy who has been pursuing her and the truly shocking ending reveals that Angela is actually a boy, Peter from the film's opening, raised to be a girl by her disturbed aunt who always wanted a daughter. It is, we are stunned to discover, Peter/Angela that has been that elusive murdering figure all along.

As Timothy Shary has argued, "The true consistency in virtually all teen horror films remains their concentration on youthful fears of being different, becoming sexual and confronting adult responsibilities, fears that the horror film is ideally suited to examine" (56). *Sleepaway Camp* makes a great deal out of these very fears by repeatedly returning to the anxieties attached to gender and sexuality that occur at summer camp, precisely by attending to anything that would expose Angela's awful secret. The film is filled with activities (dances, races, volleyball, swimming, baseball) that threaten to expose the main character Angela's physical attributes in some form or another, either because she would have to strip or because she might act like a boy. In the simplest ways, *Sleepaway Camp* works its way through many of the standard beats of summer camp films, as bodies have changed, expectations of gender are clearer, and romantic interests blossom. In a brief scene midway through the film, a group of boys badger a group of girls to strip on a beach and go skinny-dipping. In another much longer sequence a group of boys play softball and a clearly nerdy boy makes a key play. One of the camp counselors is a body builder who is often seen lifting weights in the background, wearing shirts that advertise local gyms. Bodies are a constant concern in *Sleepaway Camp*. Yet as a horror text the film also has a vested interest in making these same standard tropes of teen comedies as unsettling as possible, and much of this anxiety comes from Angela's awkwardness. The most popular girl at Camp Arawak and one of its worst bullies is a girl named Judy, who has grown breasts and hips in the year between summers. She is especially frustrated that Angela doesn't participate in sports, or talk, and in one scene she confronts her while other girls giggle:

> Hey Angela, how come you never take showers when the rest of us do?
> You queer or something? I know what it is, you haven't reached puberty
> yet. I bet you don't even have your period. She takes showers when no
> one can see she has no hair down below.

Unlike the *Friday the 13th* films and other slasher films that feature promiscuous teens, exploitative nudity, and obligatory sex (even those with a passing familiarity with the genre knows that skinny dipping is a constant theme in summer camp movies), *Sleepaway Camp* spends little time on sex. Rather, it attends to these common conventions with a decidedly different sort of emphasis, and precisely because the gender of the main character, and in turn killer, is so fraught.

Sleepaway Camp is very hard to pin down ideologically. Prior to the final revelation and excluding the slasher conventions, the plot has the appearance of a more straightforward budding teen romance, as a boy named Paul consistently pursues Angela in ways that aren't out of keeping in a film like *Little Darlings*. If *Sleepaway Camp* were not so clearly a horror film, it might be a story of Paul finally pulling Angela out of her shell, turning her from shy girl to someone who feels natural at camp. And yet the revelation of Angela as a trans figure, not to mention the queerness of her father, are presented as absolute shocks to the audience. It is truly difficult to see the film as anything other than homophobic in the ways Angela is traumatized by her gay father or transphobic in the way her body is revealed at the end of the film. Indeed, *Sleepaway Camp* features one of the most famous final images in all of the slasher canon: its main character, Angela/Peter, standing nude, covered in blood, a knife in one hand and severed head by her feet, screaming as the camera tracks out to highlight the shocking discovery of her penis. The film presents Angela's body as a subject of revulsion and horror. As the camera pulls back, Angela screams, the soundtrack crescendos, and the screen turns to shocking green. As Harry M. Benshoff notes In *Monsters in the Closet: Homosexuality and the Horror Film*, "Since the demands of the classical Hollywood narrative system usually insist on a heterosexual romance within the stories they construct, the monster is traditionally figured as a force that attempts to block that romance" (4). In terms of her confusing body and as an obstacle to romance, Angela is just such a monster.

Barbara Creed argues that "the central ideological project of the popular horror film . . . brings about a confrontation with the abject (the corpse, bodily wastes, the monstrous-feminine) in order to eject the abject and redraw the boundaries between the human and the nonhuman" (46). Creed suggests that "the horror film works to separate out the symbolic order from all that threatens its stability" (46). The "key to monster movies and the adolescents who understandably dote upon them," writes Walter Evans, "is the theme of horrible and mysterious psychological and physical change: the most important of these is the monstrous transformation which is directly associated with secondary sexual characteristics and with the onset of aggressive erotic behavior" (54). A monster like the creature in *Frankenstein*, he argues, "painfully embodies the adolescent's nightmare of being hated and hunted by the society which he desperately wishes to join" (55). The formulaic elements of these monster movies coincide with a series of adolescent symptoms, he suggests, including the uncontrollable body, menstruation, nocturnal emissions, struggle with reason, curiosity about hidden knowledge, rebellion, irrational desire, and homosexual experimentation. Indeed, in other teen horror films such as *Carrie* (1976), menstruation is portrayed as its own source of horror. Shelly Stamp Lindsey, for instance, argues that *Carrie* "presents female sexuality as monstrous" (281), owing to "[p]rohibitions surrounding first menstruation and menstruating women . . . grounded in fears that during menses a woman is polluted or possessed by dangerous spirits" (284). *Sleepaway Camp* also works its ways through all of these horrors and has at its disposal any number of ways of portraying Angela as abject, monstrous as a girl whose body is changing, whose body isn't yet changing, and whose body is actually, secretly, monstrously male, overlapping a troubling series of phobias onto body anxiety already embedded in the slasher story.

And yet, the trappings of the slasher film aside, *Sleepaway Camp* may go for shock in its final images and in its overall tone, but it nevertheless stumbles on something more complex along the way. I would go so far as to suggest that *Sleepaway Camp* has ingredients within it that place us more on the side of Angela than this final image suggests. Almost despite itself, despite how thoroughly *Sleepaway Camp* traffics in homophobic and transphobic terrors, despite the ways it is far more phobic than it is not, it also, in moments, participates more in what Benshoff calls "an opposing trend" (231). This he describes as a film where the "monster queers are closer to desirable human 'normality' than those patriarchal forces (religion, law, medicine) that had traditionally sought to demonize them" (231). Benshoff suggests, "Even the formal structures of many recent monster fictions permit their audiences the pleasures of identifying with the monster queer, and not the traditional normative pose of heterosexuality" (259). *Sleepaway Camp* certainly has its concerns with the way Angela deviates from the feminine norm, but it also turns the gaze from the female body to the structures, institutions, and individuals who monitor the female body, who are then subject to punishment. It does this in ways that other slasher films rarely ever dared.

Sleepaway Camp is less concerned with watching female bodies than it is about bullying as a theme, and it is here where the film does even more with its camp setting than these earlier films. It switches its attention from those bearers of the male gaze that punish the sexually curious to a sort of sympathy for those who are forced to be exposed in the first place, precisely because of the demands of the camp setting. Because so many strangers are made to live and play together in these sites, slasher films set at camp arguably play with these spaces and themes better than their typical slasher counterparts ever could. Just think of the iconography of the lake (where skinny dipping was always probable), bathrooms and showers (where groups of kids had to commune together), and beds (the site of undressing and perhaps even sex). In *Sleepaway Camp*, naturally, a teen is killed in the shower, in a bed, in a toilet stall, in an overturned canoe, and on the lakeshore, disrobed before sex. These are not simply places of vulnerability but places where gender is most on display, and in the case of teens and pre-teens, most awkwardly.

Because of her gender ambiguity, Angela spends much of the film refusing to speak or participate in some of the most common camp activities—swimming, tanning, making friends, dancing, kissing boys, or even speaking.

Angela has been murdering those people who have tried to make her take off her clothes, whether at the lake, in the shower, or at bedtime. Angela won't go swimming, in other words, because of her penis. *Sleepaway Camp* seems to address this topic, however unintentionally, through the pranks that appear throughout the film, which are often framed in noticeably homoerotic tones that at first glance seem to exist solely to increase the run-time but nevertheless emphasize the themes of vulnerability. It is downright surprising, in fact, how much time a film with a scant running time of 77 minutes (once you exclude the opening and closing credits) spends on the pranks that go on at camp. One of the younger boys, for instance, in an age-old prank, lies on his back and tries to rise up, only to find his face planted in the naked buttocks of another boy. This is typical for these sorts of slashers. In *The Burning*, several boys fire a pellet gun at another boy's buttocks, then pull their pants down for the camera to moon that same boy. Leslie Paris reminds us that this is a part of a long tradition at summer camps since their earliest days: "During the first few days of camp, veterans had opportunities to exploit their greater knowledge through pranks that demarcated them from the greenhorns. In a sign of the more explicitly aggressive nature of boys' culture, hazing rites, both official and unofficial, appear to have been far more prevalent at boys' camps" (104). It is remarkable how often teen horror movies feature moments of pranks and bullying. Bruce F. Kawin points to horror films like *The Funhouse* and *The Howling*, both from 1981, whose plots are about already mediated horrors (haunted houses at the circus, monster movies on television), to suggest that they "address . . . how to deal with real horrors when one has been encouraged, particularly by horror films, to expect any danger to be imaginary, to be fun" (105). Both films, like many slashers, feature jump scare pranks to create anxiety in the audience, with the camera sometimes taking on the perspective of a boy simply trying to give a girl a good scare. But *Sleepaway Camp*, like any good horror film, raises the stakes of these pranks, brutally punishing teens and children who are seemingly just goofing around. They instead are the focus of punishment in the film.

In *The Burning*, something of a predecessor to *Sleepaway Camp* and a far more typical slasher type, a chunk of the plot revolves around male counselors trying to get reluctant females to sneak away for sex in the woods. No less than two separate sequences in *The Burning* feature likeable female characters rejecting male advances and then reluctantly giving in. As such, the film aligns the predatory male point of view with what Christopher Sharrett calls the "destruction of the sexually curious" (264), as the killer dispatches females after they have indulged in sex, all while the general perspective of the film views women as objects of sexual conquest. Dika prefers to call these films "Stalker Films" for this very reason, because of the way the "killer's presence is indicated primarily by the musical score and a series of distinctive shots," most famously the "moving camera point-of-view shot, which stealthily approaches an unsuspecting victim" (88). Filmic conventions suggest that, typically, these point-of-view shots align the camera with the audience's point of view. Richard M. Gollin writes that the "subjective angle presents the point of view of another character, as if the camera and viewer had momentarily become the other character," such that "the angle provides an intense implication of the audience with a character's state of mind" (32). Because many horror films feature disturbed male killers dispatching women through overly sexualized and frighteningly violent means, slasher films are so often seen as troublingly misogynistic. The *Friday the 13th* series is similarly littered with such shots, moments where the gaze is shared by the killer, the male teens, and the male audience.

Some moments in *Sleepaway Camp*, for instance, take on the point of view of counselors as they watch female bodies, mostly from behind, play softball. But for every casual moment such as this, the film dwells on others that are seemingly designed to alienate the viewer. Early in the film, for instance, a cook carefully watches young girls get off the bus and run to their cabins. "Look at all that fresh young chicken," he snarls, a piece of grass between his teeth. "Where I come from we call them baldies," he continues, referring to their lack of pubic hair. "Makes your mouth water, don't it?" One of the other cooks gives him a sly smile, laughing, "They're too young to even understand what is on your mind." It's an exceptionally creepy moment and it is a reminder that *Sleepaway Camp* seems less concerned with the horror of the female body, and more with the horror of the male gaze. On the subject of this male gaze, Laura Mulvey famously writes:

> In a world ordered by sexual imbalance, pleasure in looking has been split between the active/male and passive/female. The determining male gaze projects its fantasy onto the female figure, which is stylized accordingly. In their traditional exhibitionist role women are simultaneously looked at and displayed, with their appearance coded for strong visual and erotic impact so that they can be said to connote *to-be-looked-at-ness*. (19, emphasis in original)

In *Sleepaway Camp*, by contrast, we are never asked as an audience to identify with this cook, to look at these young girls in this way, evidenced most
clearly in the way he is killed only moments later in the film.

In even your more straightforward slasher film, this predatory gaze is
rarely the stable, violent male point of view we might take for granted in
more mainstream fare. Benefiting from a visual style dominated by a point
of view, *Friday the 13th* for instance opens with a long point-of-view tracking shot as some figure, as yet unfamiliar to the audience, prowls around an
empty cabin, spies on campers, and then stalks a couple making out at the
top of a set of stairs. This same figure then murders the teens without
explanation. A surprising number of slasher films open in similar ways, a
predatory stalking point-of-view sequence meant to put the audience in
the killer's point of view. The gimmick of *Halloween* is that the opening
murderous point of view is actually a young child. In the case of *Friday the
13th*, a disgruntled mother is punishing surrogate teenagers like the ones
who neglected her son while he was swimming. So, importantly, the camera need not always mirror the killer's perspective. *Sleepaway Camp* employs
this first-person perspective and plays with the ambiguity already familiar
to the slasher genre. During one disturbing sequence, the cook described
previously takes Angela back to a food locker to show her some options for
dinner but also to molest her. He is thankfully interrupted. Moments later,
a shaky moving camera announces that we are in the killer's perspective as
two hands reach out to push this cook into a vat of boiling water, which tips
over and burns him badly. At this point in the film we have no idea who the
killer is, though we suspect it is Angela's outraged cousin. Elsewhere, the
film employs other similar conventions to keep the identity of the killer
hidden, such as placing the camera behind a figure wearing a hat or revealing only a pair of shadowed hands that kill a girl with a hair straightener.

Nothing is quite what it seems in *Sleepaway Camp* in several important
ways. First, the point-of-view camera that pursues and punishes the sexually curious in your typical slasher film is far less stable of a mechanism
here. As Peter Hutchings warns, "It is quite clear that this particular cinematic technique, far from having the singular meaning ascribed to it, often
involves a complex and sometimes decidedly ambiguous approach to the
material" (196). Again, the gimmick in *Sleepaway Camp*, as with the films
described earlier, is that the killer is not actually an adult male, as is most
often the case in slasher films, but a female child,[1] or at least the construct
of a female. As a result, the kind of audience identification that is meant to
recoil in shock at Angela's body at the film's end is blurred. It is difficult to

predict exactly how the audience might react, or even what is fully intended in this shot. This may seem like a strong claim, but Dika notes how bizarre audience identification plays out in real time for most slashers, as "manipulation of expectations has been known to elicit a voiced response from the audience," as spectators "greet the gruesome events on screen with open enthusiasm, cheering and laughing, and dividing their support primarily between the heroine *and* the killer" (emphasis in original, 88). The slasher is perhaps the ideal form for a queered horror story in that it blurs expectations of audience identification, in the sense that it doesn't quite conform to single perspectives. Benshoff describes how certain "horror films [can] work to position the spectator alongside or within the monster and/or the monster's point of view" (259), and even if the last shocking image of the film is troublingly transphobic, this makes sense in terms of thinking of Angela as both the slasher film's monster and killer.

Clover describes the killers in most slashers as "propelled by sexual fury" and "permanently locked in childhood" (28), and therefore more complex than, say, the aliens or radiated insects that populated sci-fi invasion and monster movies in the middle of the century. By the late 1950s, Mark Jancovich argues, "the distinction between the alien invader and the natural creature had either blurred or disappeared" (63), culminating in the general consensus that *Psycho*, the presumptive ancestor to the modern slasher, "supposedly presents its horrors not as the product of forces from outside American society, but as the product of the patriarchal family" (221). Jason Zinoman explains that by the seventies, "the werewolf had gone out of fashion in the movies, and the Frankenstein monster grumbled angrily less often than he once did" (135). In the new versions of horror, he continues, "clear motives and obvious metaphors were replaced by a more general sense of confusion" (136). It is no surprise that *Sleepaway Camp*, like other slashers but far more assertively, elicits more sympathy for the monster and also more distrust for the systems that surround her. The killers in slashers, in other words, are often the subject of our sympathy, scarred by terrible pranks or robbed of their development by circumstance, with only *Halloween* presenting a killer who is, at least according to his doctor, purely and simply evil. *Sleepaway Camp* takes sympathy to a whole new level, as Angela is thrown into a lake and harassed by bullies, pelted with water balloons, and constantly harassed by the increasingly aggressive Paul.

Angela is also, at least until the final image of the film, *Sleepaway Camp*'s final girl, surviving all of the murders that surround her very presence. Clover calls The Final Girl character "abject terror personified" (35), "watchful to the point of paranoia" (39), "not fully feminine" (40), containing all "qualities of character that enable her, of all the characters, to survive what has come to seem unsurvivable" (39). In *Halloween*, it is Laurie Strode (Jamie Lee Curtis). In *Friday the 13th*, the final girl is named Alice, then Ginny, then Chris, depending on the sequel. Importantly, Clover argues that these low-budget slasher films examine and play with gender in more subtle ways than one might expect, and are downright preoccupied with the *fluidity* of gender. They are the queer story, she suggests, of an overly masculinized female lead and a sexually confused male killer driven by sexual fury who swap places by the end of the film, when she picks up the killer's weapon and fights back. Clover argues that these are films where gender is "less a wall than a permeable membrane" (46), essentially "texts in which the categories of masculine and feminine, traditionally embodied in male and female, are collapsed into one and the same character" (61). *Sleepaway Camp* is perhaps most distinctive among its peers because there is no killer and heroine who do battle, only Angela, who stands in for both, who has blended into both by the film's end. Angela is queer in the way Steven Bruhm and Natasha Hurley explain that "the figure of the queer child is that which doesn't quite conform to the wished-for way that children are supposed to be in terms of gender and sexual roles" (x). Angela is neither child nor teen nor adult, neither male nor female, neither passive last girl nor quite the killer. She is both the subject of a romance and the monstrous block to that romance at the same time.

Again, in all of these ways, *Sleepaway Camp* is very hard to assess ideologically. Robin Wood divides horror films into what he calls the "reactionary wing," where monsters are designated as simply evil and necessarily defeated, and the more "progressive wing," progressive "in so far as their negativity is not recuperable into the dominant ideology" (191–92). Horror films, Wood contends, are about what civilization represses. "One might say," he proposes, "that the true subject of the horror genre is the struggle for recognition of all that our civilization represses or oppresses, its re-emergence dramatized, as in our nightmares, as an object of horror, a matter of terror, and the happy ending (when it exists) typically signifying the restoration of repression" (75). Wood lists the common subjects of repression as sexual norms (such as bisexuality and homosexuality), women, female sexuality, children, alternative ideologies, ethnic groups, and other cultures—all the standard subjects of horror films. There are hints that *Sleepaway Camp* leans toward the progressive in that its monster, Angela, is not simply evil and defeated. The final image, although decidedly transphobic, is inarguably arresting. "Horror films often present us with images that are painful, grotesque, awful—horrible to look at," notes Bruce Kawin, "but they regularly imply that these images somehow need to be looked at, that they will show us something we might be more comfortable not to see but ought to see nonetheless" (103). Zinoman talks about a similar effect with Tobe Hooper's cinematography in *The Texas Chainsaw Massacre*: "With his camera work, Hooper argues that that the most frightening thing is to see terrible violence happen and know there is nothing you can do about it. Drawing upon his experience in the emergency room, Hooper puts you in the position of complete, mystifying helplessness" (141). *Sleepaway Camp* thematizes this helplessness in the image of the primal scene. We discover in flashback that Angela and Peter used to walk in on their father in bed with another man and that later Angela and Peter used to sit on that same bed and look at each other's bodies, albeit clothed, presumably as a way of working through what they saw. Just as they are arrested by stumbling upon the primal scene, we are left with a final image that we, in turn, must wrestle with. How can a body be both male and female at the same time?[2]

And yet while there is a lot to admire about the gender fluidity that Clover describes, these films did appear during an especially conservative time. Though the roots of their conventions, plots, and overall tone can be traced back to politically progressive or at least culturally shocking films such as *Texas Chainsaw Massacre* (1974) and *Black Christmas* (1974), or even as far back as *Psycho* (1960), "most 1980s horror films," as Tony Williams reminds us, "brutally chastised those questioning or disobeying ideological norms" (165). These films, continues Williams, "serve as allegories to their adolescent audiences stressing vulnerability to parents, the adult world, and monstrous punitive avatars whether Jason, Michael, or Freddy" (173). Jon Lewis explains:

> Since horror films are about blame . . . the teen horror variety rather
> predictably points to the teenager's foundering parents . . . Teenagers
> are invariably depicted spending virtually all of their time unsupervised,
> given ample motive and opportunity to do precisely what their parents
> say they don't want them to do. Since parents fail to enforce their
> authority, social regulation emerges magically, from elsewhere. (67)

Though *Sleepaway Camp* evinces some sympathy for Angela and the teenagers in the film, it is hard to make claims that the film sustains any real progressive tendencies beyond these conventions. The several sequels to *Sleepaway Camp* take this idea to extremes, as a grown Angela returns to mercilessly kill any teenager who smokes, does drugs, has sex, or is simply disrespectful or petulant, pitfalls the original manages to avoid. Clover describes how the slasher film delivers a female story in such a way as to make it digestible for a predominantly male audience: Even in their best versions, the Final Girl is often depicted as thoroughly defeated by the end of the film, so insane that she needs to be hospitalized, or so fragile that she is quickly murdered in the sequel. "One of the last images of the stalker film," as Dika puts it, "is often that of the heroine, trapped within the confines of the frame and returned to her position as object" (95). *Sleepaway Camp* reminds us that the slasher film's progressive politics have limits.

Still, Wood distinguishes his example of a reactionary film, *The Omen* (1976), from his example of a progressive film, *Texas Chainsaw Massacre* (1974), in terms of taste and budget. He describes *The Omen* as "old-fashioned, traditional" (88), with a "big budget, glossy production values," and as "bourgeois entertainment" characterized by "Good Taste" (87). The latter film is, by contrast, "low budget, raw, unpolished" with "unknown actors" and characterized by "Bad Taste." There is something to be said about *Sleepaway Camp* in these terms. It is definitely a film in bad taste. Scott Tobias notes how *Sleepaway Camp* is the product of an aspiring filmmaker: "Writer-director Robert Hiltzik, a young NYU film-school grad seeking a path of least commercial resistance," who "opted to hop on the bandwagon by doing his own twist on the typical kids-getting-hacked-up-in-the-woods scenario" (n.p.). The film shows a surprising lack of competency in some of the basics of shot centering and editing. At many points throughout the film, especially when Angela is confronted by her aggressors, characters appear with far too much head-room above them, shots that appear curiously intentioned to be off-putting but are most likely a sign of amateurish cinematography. As Tobias remarks, "it's funny that one of the counselors is a bodybuilder who dashes around in mesh shirts and '80s short-shorts, but what to make of a shot of him pumping iron far in the background of a scene that has nothing to do with him?" (n.p.).

In its own clumsy and extremely messy way, *Sleepaway Camp* is a quirky reminder of that period when American cinema chose to set horror stories in a location that was otherwise idyllic, the summer camp. Its bizarre plot and infamous ending evoke a comment Clover makes of the horror films she watched to conduct her survey: "Like others before me, I discovered that there are in horror moments and works of great humor, formal brilliance, political intelligence, psychological depth, and above all a kind of kinky creativity that is simply not available in any other stripe of film-making" (20). It was a film that managed to take an already fairly inventive

genre and do something even more inventive with it. In Andrew Ross'
sense of camp, *Sleepaway Camp* participates in the "rediscovery of history's
waste" (151), that is, the slasher cycle that preceded it. Ross writes: "Camp
irreverently retrieves not only that which has been excluded from the serious high-cultural 'tradition,' but also the more unsalvageable material that
has been picked over and found wanting" (151). *Sleepaway Camp* is a
strangely creative film, one that managed to attend to anxieties of gender
in ways that few other slasher films like it dared, revealing in the process
why the summer camp was a perfect setting for queer, proto-campy horror
narratives in an especially conservative era.

Sleepaway Camp is, more than anything else, "campy," in the sense that
Susan Sontag describes naïve Camp, where "the essential element is seriousness, a seriousness that fails" (283). Scott Tobias captures this well in
his review of the film:

> It isn't really scary or atmospheric, but the implements of death, from
> a curling iron to a beehive, are exceedingly gruesome and unprece-
> dented. It doesn't announce itself as a horror-comedy, but the laughs
> come early and often, without a hint of self-awareness on the film-
> makers' part. Its summer-camp setting features actual teenagers, not
> overdeveloped twentysomethings masquerading as teenagers. And it
> has a psychosexual backstory like no other—one that not only
> accounts for the ending, but determines the hysterical pitch of the
> whole movie. (n.p.)

Sleepaway Camp is deeply earnest in almost every respect, especially as the
final image is played straight for maximum horror. This final image, after
all, simply shows us a young naked boy standing on a beach, not even
emphasizing the other boy he has killed, but the repeated cuts, the para-
lyzed onlookers, the shrieking music, the bizarre tint, all highlight a kind
of camp aesthetic that, as Chuck Kleinhans describes it, is more of "an
extravagant form that is out of proportion to its content, especially when
that content is banal or trivial" (186). Unlike self-aware kitsch, which Kleinhans defines as "highly self-conscious of their own debased status" (183),
Sleepaway Camp is overly committed to the horror of this tableau. Jack
Babuscio suggests that irony is the "subject matter of camp, and refers to
any highly incongruous contrast between an individual or thing and its
context or association" (22). And that sense echoes Sontag's insistence that
"Camp is the attempt to do something extraordinary. But extraordinary in
the sense, often, of being special, glamorous" (284).

As Sontag suggests, "Something is good not because it is achieved, but because another kind of truth about the human situation, another experience of what it is to be human—in short, another valid sensibility—is being revealed" (287). Or as Kleinhans puts it, "To get at the truth you have to put up with idiosyncrasies. It is excessive. It does not always work. But when it does, it says what no one else is saying" (192). *Sleepaway Camp* seems to get more deeply and bizarrely at a truth only hinted at in other slasher films, one Clover seems eager to identify as the slipperiness of clear-cut gender roles that circulate underneath the slasher film. Camp, through its emphasis on theatricality and performance, attends to "the absurdity of those roles that each of us is urged to step into with such a deadly seriousness" (Babuscio 26). *Sleepaway Camp* is deadly serious. It is also an infamously, notoriously bad slasher film that dramatizes those roles, makes a horror show of them, over-inflates their importance, and presents them more starkly than you might see in your typical slasher film. As a queer slasher film, and as a queer horror story, it remains among the best of them.

NOTES

1. It is a convention of slasher films that they are populated predominantly by teenagers who, in their last years of school, engage in a fair amount of drinking and sex. *Sleepaway Camp* is one of the rare slasher films that, even though it evokes all of the other conventions of the genre, features an array of children and pre-teens. Angela's age is never quite clear, though the actress who plays her, Felissa Rose, was fourteen when the film was shot, and many other characters in the film are clearly children.

2. It is important to be clear here. Peter is a boy who has been raised a girl, so I don't mean to imply that he has the body parts of a girl. I recognize the complexity of describing this. Yet the film does present Angela as *both* female and male in the sense that the actress's head was superimposed over the body of a male actor to achieve the effect in this last shot.

Striking Camp

Empowerment and Re-Presentation in *Lumberjanes*

Kyle Eveleth

I solemnly swear to do my best
Every day, and in all that I do,
To be brave and strong,
To be truthful and compassionate,
To be interesting and interested,
To pay attention and question
The world around me,
To think of others first,
To always help and protect my friends,
[line scribbled out; handwritten:] **then there's a line about God,**
or whatever
And to make the world a better place
For Lumberjane scouts
And for everyone else.

The *Lumberjanes* Pledge

The Eisner award–winning serial comics series *Lumberjanes* (2014–present), crafted by the Hardcore Lady–Type squad of writers Shannon Ellis, Grace

Waters, Noelle Stevenson, and a bevy of hardcore guest artists,[1] has been lauded by critics such as Alison Berry as "the book so many have asked for, both accessible and girl friendly without sacrificing entertainment value for the older set" (Berry).[2] Spinning the deep-woods tale of the eponymous Lumberjanes troop of Miss Quinzella Thiskwin Penniquiquill Thistle Crumpet's Camp for Girls Hardcore Lady Types ("Friendship to the Max"), *Lumberjanes* revitalizes and revises the century-old scouting girl genre of popular fiction that was made lucrative by the Edward Stratemeyer Syndicate in the late 1910s and thrived until the 1940s. At the same time, *Lumberjanes* confronts the problematic features of the scouting novel, such as its depictions of gender, sexuality, racial hierarchy, and American imperialism. Like other popular, yet clever reformulations of the summer camp story, such as Wes Anderson's critically acclaimed film *Moonrise Kingdom* (2012, see Mallan and McGillis's essay in this collection) and Katie Rice's award-winning webcomic *Camp Weedonwantcha* (2013–present), *Lumberjanes* challenges convention and revises the kids-at-camp genre through the campy humor of summer camp comedy.[3]

Scouting Out Camping: The Outdoor Panacea in Popular Culture

The scouting novel tradition from which *Lumberjanes* draws its form was short-lived but intensely influential for popular conceptions of what it meant—and, indeed, still means—to be a scout. Even today, beliefs about the benefits of the practical education afforded to children by the out-of-doors resonate in educational policy and theory. As popularity grew for scouting as a practice, media jumped in to capitalize on the fervor. Enjoying their heyday between the 1910s and the 1940s, scouting novels encapsulated and fictionalized the nascent scouting movement. Sarah L. Peters explains that the scouting movement aimed be an outdoor panacea for rising "fears that the forces of modernity had brought about a crisis of masculinity," a cure that would toughen up "boys [. . .] overcivilized and weakened by technological advances that distanced them from the natural world and their primitive drives" (57). Driven by these perceived threats to gender roles, the scouting movement was launched by such figures as Lord Robert Stephenson Smyth Baden-Powell, author of *Scouting for Boys* (1908) and Ernest Thompson Seton, creator of the Woodcraft Indians (1902), to reconnect boys and girls with their "natural" roles. Girls were eventually offered separate-but-equal scouting groups, Luther and Charlotte Gulick's Camp Fire Girls (1911) and Juliette Gordon Low's Girl Scouts (1912), which, despite their focus on outdoor activity and Theodore Roosevelt's

Kyle Eveleth

"strenuous life,"[4] were never meant to subvert gender norms (Inness 93).[5] Sherrie A. Inness historicizes boys' scouting, defining the movement's early groups as "pseudo-military organizations for boys that would provide the discipline of a military unit during a non-war period" (91). Susan A. Miller, analyzing Camp Fire Girls creator Luther Gulick's letters and other documents outlining the burgeoning Camp Fire Girls organization, notes that the goal of the Camp Fire Girls was to "develop womanly qualities in the girls" (15). Further, Helen Buckler, Mary F. Fiedler, and Martha F. Allen report in *Wo-He-Lo: The Story of Camp Fire Girls* (1961) that Gulick "wish[ed] to develop girls to be womanly" because "to copy the Boy Scout movement would be utterly and fundamentally evil, and would probably produce ultimately a moral and psychological involution" (qtd. in Buckler 22). Thus, though girls were allowed to be outdoors and take part in more strenuous activities than they would in, say, church groups, their excursions were always founded upon honing "womanly qualities"—skills like social mediation, community activism, and housekeeping rather than riflery, archery, or wayfinding.

Scouting novels, rarely officially sanctioned by the organizations they depicted, reified these conservative gender roles. They were not complex, thoughtful literature. Rather, they were a marketing ploy designed by the enormous Stratemeyer Syndicate (producers of other gendered works like *Nancy Drew* and *The Hardy Boys*) to capture the hearts, minds, and increasingly disposable allowances of middle-class white American youths. To that end, books for all the major players in the scouting world were published, but the most commonly available and widely read targeted Boy Scouts, Girl Scouts, and Camp Fire Girls. Riding on the coattails of the exploding scouting movement, the works were largely formulaic and moralistic adventure stories that affirmed the pioneer mythology of American culture while appealing to the essentialism of gender difference. Inness describes scouting novels as "churned out by the score by various obscure writers working for slim salaries" and as invariably "approximately 225 pages long, hardbound, [. . .] cost[ing] a nominal fifty to seventy-five cents" (93). The iconic Boy Scout, mobilized both by the mythology promoted by the organization itself and in the wildly popular but still unsanctioned "Boy Scout" books,[6] is invariably as good a shot as Wild Bill Hickok, as skilled a pioneer as Daniel Boone, and as courageous a woodsman as Paul Bunyan or, for maximal patriotism, as a young Teddy Roosevelt. He is a paragon of truth, justice, and the American way, his adventures taking him from perilous Pacific shining sea to patriotic Atlantic shining sea, and when he is not in the woods, he uses his impeccable marksmanship to save beautiful, virginal, white middle-class girls from "vile, leprous Chinamen" (Hoover 229).[7] The fictive "Girl Scout" or "Camp Fire Girl" was as peerlessly domestic as her brother was masculine. Real-life girl scouts, Inness explains, were roped into a "moral crusade" to keep an orderly, clean, and hygienic home (Inness 95). This ideology of "cleanliness is next to godliness" is reproduced in scouting fiction, which Inness argues is "very much aware of its responsibility to instruct young girls about socially acceptable gender behavior" (95). Thus, fictive Girl Scouts become "nicely trained little helpers for the home" (Garis 16; qtd. in Inness 95). Ellen Singleton explains that "girls went to camp to learn to keep house. If they did not want to be homemakers, they went to camp to learn why they should" (66). Carolyn Carpan notes that the books relentlessly championed "domesticity, femininity, and heterosexual romantic love" such that girls in the stories "learn such domestic skills as cooking and basic nursing care, even while they are camping" (39). Learning these skills is subordinate to the ultimate goal of finding a suitable husband (perhaps a Scout himself). Inness contends that the flash of outdoor activity represented in scouting fiction is merely a lure that "depicts scouting as offering [girls] escape from stereotypical gender roles" (93). But ultimately, Singleton reminds us, "romantic love and a life lived happily ever after were the incentives held out to 'womanly' females, and innumerable examples were presented in these stories to young readers" (67). The reward for learning domesticity and going on romps in the woods is a husband and domestic security.

As scouting groups across the nation saw their numbers explode, many parents nevertheless sought alternatives to the multiyear commitments required by scouting's paramilitary structure, especially after World War I. See, for example, Annebella Pollen's essay in this collection on alt-Scouting Woodcraft camping. Camping was a popular activity that had translated well from its Victorian roots to the wide open spaces of North America and, by the turn of the twentieth century, camping was one of the most popular activities for middle-class families. Building on the organized wellness resorts that thrived in the 1870s and 1880s thanks to efforts by health gurus like John Harvey Kellogg, Americans enjoyed the out-of-doors on their own, camping in tents on open tracts of land. By 1916, the U.S. government would officially sanction camping as a national pastime with the creation of the National Park Service and its territory, the National Parks. In 1927, the first modern recreational vehicle, the Airstream camper, made its debut; soon thereafter, mobile homes and camper vans would become common sights in the summer months.

Building on the popularity of camping in the United States as well as the growing need for summer outlets for children—especially as children stayed in school for longer than ever before—summer camps grew in number and popularity. With roots dating back to the 1870s and 1880s as correctives for "soft" urban children, the summer camp saw its cultural cachet grow extensively; between 1900 and 1918, the number of summer camps in the United States increased more than tenfold (Gershon). But, as camping itself modernized, so too did summer camps. By the 1930s, summer camps began to shift away from "roughing it" and toward ever more civilized pursuits: watching films, listening to radio broadcasts, learning to play tennis, and that camp standby, textile weaving.[8] Commentators at the time lamented the lack of actual "camping" in the woods, replaced by daily activities and cabins with amenities, but by the end of the Second World War, many Americans questioned the possibility of escape into Edenic pastoral gardens, even in the deep woods of North America (Gershon). Apparently, camp was no longer campy enough, and soon thereafter, themed summer camps emerged: space camp, swim camp, band camp, and all the possible interests beyond. The first summer camp comedy, *Meatballs*, appeared in 1979, starring Bill Murray, kicking off one of the most popular and campy comedic cinematic styles of the latter part of the twentieth century.

Summer camp comedies hinge upon the inherently ironic artifice of the summer camp as a location and as a venue for adolescent growth. In other words, they revel in—while mocking—the artificiality of the whole endeavor. As Jeff Brown notes in an interview with Everdeen Mason, in the early days of summer camp comedies, the target of the film's mockery was sex (Mason). Campers, kept in close proximity with little to no adult supervision, nevertheless were expected to maintain absolute abstinence from summer romances. In the summer-camp comedy, however, these repressive situations often yield embarrassing public displays of sexual promiscuity. In *Meatballs*, head counselor Tripper Harrison describes the final week of camp as Sexual Awareness Week, a competitive time when the camp will "import 200 hookers from around the world" so that "each camper, armed with only a Thermos of coffee and $2000 cash" can try to "visit as many countries as he can" to be crowned "King of Sexual Awareness Week." Later, Tripper and head female counselor Roxanne (Kate Lynch) are caught wrestling and making out on camp director Morty

Melnick's (Harvey Atkin) couch. "She came at me like an animal," Tripper gasps, safely positioned behind Morty. The irony lies in the summer camp's origins as a locus of control over male and female lives; segregation of the sexes was meant to curb adolescent desires, but, as the summer camp comedy's deployment of the interfacing counselors suggests, all camps did was heighten awareness of the tension. As Susan Sontag maintains in her seminal article on camp, "Camp sees everything in quotation marks," and it perceives "Being-as-Playing-a-Role" (280). Thus, in the summer camp comedy, "isolating" the sexes inevitably "isolates" sex—simultaneously setting it apart as taboo *and yet also* casting the viewer as the *voyeur* who watches it unfold. In this way, camp is both evocative and provocative, capable of evoking beauty while provoking distaste.

Making and Breaking Camp

Lumberjanes borrows many familiar elements of scouting novels, both male and female, while adding a campily comedic twist. Set in idyllic, pristine woodland camps, *Lumberjanes* depicts the iconic scout "always undaunted, always high-spirited"—always prepared, as it were—to safely negotiate "dangers that would be insurmountable to non-scouts" (Inness 93). The covers of most scouting girl novels feature a high-quality, "colored picture of a group of girls engaged in some scouting activity" (Inness 92). *Lumberjanes* continues this trend with its covers, featuring the ladies of the Lumberjanes—Jo, Molly, April, Mal, and Ripley—engaged in a myriad of scouting activities such as canoeing and navigating the woods in the dark, but it also "camps" them, mocking the impossible trials and tribulations scouting novel troops face. One of the best examples is the alternate cover for issue 4, in which the Lumberjanes are shown in profile, looking on in full scouting regalia as their camp fends off (plays with?) an albino sasquatch (see Figure 7). In the first four issues, the hardcore ladytypes battle supernatural foxes, eagles, sea-monsters, and possessed Scouting Lads. They also outwit and befriend hipster sasquatches, master ancient logic riddles, overcome stone guardians in feats of arm-wrestling strength, and take possession of divine implements of war like Artemis's fabled bow. Yet, like fictional female scouts, the Lumberjanes' friendships, camp spirit, and attire never waver nor fail during their trials and travails; like fictional male scouts, the girls manage to avoid receiving any major punishment or injury for breaking camp rules or engaging in outrageously dangerous behavior.

Figure 7. The Lumberjanes styled as if on the cover of a scouting novel. (*Lumberjanes* #4, alternate cover by Noelle Stephenson. © 2014, Boom Entertainment, Inc.)

By the same token, the iconic method of annotating a scout's progress, the merit badge, is at once maintained as important while openly mocked as banal. For deftly replying to Jo's request for final canoeing tips with "yeah, don't TIP over!" in issue 2, April is awarded with the "Pungeon Master Badge" ("The best kind of PUNishment"); Jo wins the "Everything under the Sum Badge" ("Math leads to a basic understanding of life") for her memorization of the Fibonacci sequence; Ripley wins the "Jail Break" badge ("Run as fast as you can") in a serious game of Capture the Flag (issue 6). The camping of scouting and summer camps goes beyond mere award, however: every issue is thematically linked to a badge, and each is presented by title card as an excerpt (complete with verbiage about the badge) from the *Lumberjanes Field Manual for the Intermediate Program, Tenth Edition, January 1984* (see Figure 8). This openly mocks the attenuated sanctity of the "camp manual" as a guide for camping activities.

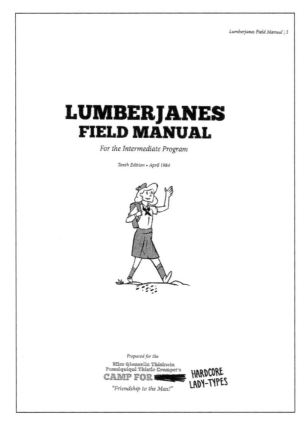

Figure 8. The *Lumberjanes* cover page, evoking scouting manuals. (*Lumberjanes* Vol. 1, page 3. © 2015, Boom Entertainment, Inc.)

Rounding out the low camp pastiche, character design in *Lumberjanes* is intended to evoke the iconic camp atmosphere and the history of outdoor exploration. The camp counselor, Rosie, is a lumberjack-inspired mashup of Paul Bunyan's flannel garb with Rosie-the-Riveter hair and biceps; the unnamed head counselor of the Scouting Lads camp (Mr. Theodore Tarquin Reginald Lancelot Herman Crumpet's Camp for Boys—"Be Watchful, Be Prepared") is an icon of camp hypermasculinity: hirsute and tanned, the head counselor wears the Stratton ranger hat perched atop his grizzled, eyepatched, square-jawed head, while beneath he dons a barely fitting olive drab camp suit, bedecked with patches, its sleeves rolled above watermelon-sized biceps, all barely containing enormous pectorals; below he sports high-rolled shorts, a Bowie knife in thigh-sheath, the outfit completed by muddy combat boots and a hatchet. He bursts in on the scene, asking what "the bejabbers" is going on in his camp, before admonishing his charges for their "pathetic" use of tea kettles and reminding them that girls are gross and stupid and that "real men should be splitting wood and smoking pipes" or "catch[ing] a fish by wrestling it away from a bear" (*LJ* #4, page 9; see Figure 9). Even the 'Janes themselves are outfitted according to common depictions of pioneering: Molly's outfit, with its living (?!) raccoon hat, Bubbles, calls to mind frontier representations of Daniel Boone, cutting his way westward through the Kentucky wilderness. Taken together, these visual nods to the material facets of camping and scouting culture reveal its performativity. In revealing the artifice of camping and scouting, *Lumberjanes* is able to begin deconstructing it as a farce.

Such deconstruction is especially important as a tool for critique and rehabilitation. At the same time as it recounts the familiar tropes of the adventurous scouting novel, *Lumberjanes* carefully navigates around the more problematic content these novels propagated in their earliest iterations. Specifically, *Lumberjanes* is dedicated both narratively and structurally to avoiding gender binarism—the belief that there are only two gender identities. Broadly, *Lumberjanes* disallows biological sex or gender identity any significant influence on a person's ability to achieve their goals. The girls run the visual gamut of possible gender expressions, from the exceedingly androgynous (Ripley, ostensibly the youngest) to non-binary (Mal, who half-shaves her head; Jo, who is transitioning) to the outwardly cisgender (April, Molly). Their lack of a commonly worn uniform, unheard of in real-world scouting, emphasizes the Lumberjanes' difference from one another. This allegiance to visual differentiation calls to mind the individualism of boys' scouting novels while destabilizing the misconception that women are naturally more communal—more uniform—than men. In

Figure 9. Apollo as the hypermasculine, action-hero camp counselor. (*Lumberjanes* #4, page 9. © 2014, Boom Entertainment, Inc.)

scouting novels, boys tend to come from a wide array of economic back-grounds and, though often white, are often portrayed as individual compo-nents of a team. Girl scouts, on the other hand, tend to be interchangeable; their power is as a mob, not a collection of individually empowered team-mates. In *Lumberjanes*, this expectation is inverted: The Scouting Lads appear uniform, undifferentiated, and domestic.

Beyond visual cues, *Lumberjanes* resists narrative expectation that girls prefer domestic spaces and boys prefer to be outdoors in the wild. Rather, gender differences are ablated, as Janes and Lads take part in a variety of tasks, domestic, rational, or pioneering, with aplomb. Many of the girls demonstrate the "feminine" traits of domesticity for which Girl Scouts in scouting fiction are renowned. April keeps a flawlessly detailed diary and is always equipped with the powerful but practical Scrunchie (*LJ* #1), while all the girls prove adept at the tried-and-true domestic camp activity of friendship-bracelet weaving (*LJ* #5). At the same time, their skills extend well into the outdoor fundamentals that were once limited to boys' scout-ing novels. Roanoke Cabin scout-leader Jen is an adept student of the natu-ral world, with peerless plant and animal recognition (by proper Latin nomenclature, *LJ* #4) undergirded with important anthropological uses of the flora and fauna she identifies. Her mastery of the night sky (*LJ* #7) and its secrets is ultimately what allows the Lumberjanes to save their little corner of the woods from certain domination by the warring divinities, Diana and Apollo (*LJ* #8). Molly, the quiet one, handles bows and arrows as nimbly as she can rearrange sentences into anagrams, both skills that end up saving the Janes' lives (*LJ* #6 and #8). Mal is a battlefield tactician of some renown with a rocket for an arm, to boot (*LJ* #6 and #8). Ripley leaps into scuffles both headlong and footlong, and ultimately channels the divine privilege over which Artemis and Apollo fight (which, of course, she wisely disperses into the universe to prevent its misuse, *LJ* #2 and #8). Even the outwardly "girly" April, red of hair and pink of shorts, has a tomboy streak: When Jo aptly comments that the pair are caught in a whitewater current, April triumphantly raises her canoe paddle overhead, saying, "YEAH WE ARE!" (*LJ* #2, p. 10). It is her arm-wrestling prowess ("It all comes down to leverage," *LJ* #3, p. 9) that aids the group in defeat-ing an ancient, muscle-bound stone guardian. Finally, in a scene reminis-cent of the "name of God" pit puzzle in *Indiana Jones and the Last Crusade* (1989), Jo's knack for mathematics—recognizing the Fibonacci sequence in a series of seemingly random numbers and remembering it to 233 (*LJ* #3, pp. 18–19) helps the girls navigate the correct path across the bottom-less pit. Perhaps the most gender-fluid of them all is Rosie, director of the camp. Styled as a flannel-clad Rosie the Riveter, Camp Director Rosie is an apt homemaker, offering the ladies hot chocolate after a late-night romp, as well as an accomplished woodcarver and, apparently, supernaturalist (*LJ* #1, 6, and 8). Interested in carving wood with any variety of bladed implements from hatchet to penknife and fond of woodland creatures, taxidermized or otherwise, Rosie is the quintessential Lumberjane: a mix of domestic gentleness and rustic tenacity. Her approach is, by turns, motherly and gruff: She (perhaps knowingly) gives the girls a long leash on which to explore and solve the mysteries of the woods around camp even as she offers Jen tough encouragement by pretending not to know the troop leader's name or care about her troop's misconduct (*LJ* #1, 6, and 8). Jen, the constant pushover, gets angrier about this as the series goes on until Rosie reveals that she had faith in Jen's leadership all along (*LJ* #8, p. 23).

Conversely, boys in *Lumberjanes* show a true knack for domesticity and nurturing. When Mal is rendered unconscious and not breathing as a result of water inhalation, the girls panic and don't know what to do. Molly flails her hands, cries, and is told to blow into Mal "like she's a balloon" before ineffectually kissing her. Quick-thinking Ripley saves the day by leaping feet-first onto Mal's diaphragm (*LJ* #2, p. 17). The boys, on the other hand, are apt nurses: they treat the Lumberjanes' poison ivy rashes with skin ointment, attentively serve their guests fresh cookies and hot tea, and keep an impossibly clean cabin (*LJ* #4, pp. 8 and 11). Jen gapes at the scene—her idea of perfect campers!—in which domesticity reigns supreme. It stands in stark contrast to the Lumberjanes' filthy cabin and the girls' poor manners. That the lads are so "orderly and obedient," the hallmarks of the perfectly socialized scouting novel lady, therefore reinforces how far the Lumberjanes are from that sexist ideal (*LJ* #4, p. 7). Unfortunately, the Lads are revealed to be feral boys when they turn into werewolves shortly thereafter (*LJ* #4, p. 18).[9]

It would be easy to say that *Lumberjanes* merely inverts traditional gender roles, making girls "tomboys" and boys "dandies." In a work that seeks to unsettle traditional gender norms, simple inversion is problematic because the work (perhaps unwittingly) makes more real the very gender roles it seeks to unsettle by perpetuating the use of binary gender categories. A work that unquestioningly inverts traditional binary conceptions of gender may actually *strengthen* the credibility of claims that some skills are *inherently* masculine or feminine, and that any non-normative gender expression is merely play-acting. The fear of women and men "playing at" gender informs Luther Gulick's concerns that allowing women access to knowledge and experiences once reserved for men would upset the fragile balance of the world (Buckler 22). For, if women and men can so easily "enact" gender, how can it be inherent or essential? Judith Butler, philosopher and critical theorist, is a pioneer in queer studies, a branch of cultural studies that seeks to destabilize, among other things, the intertwined notions that gender is binary, intrinsic, and determined solely by biological sex. Instead, queer theorists like Butler suggest that gender is performative, derived from a myriad of cultural norms and social expectations. For queer theorists, genders are not inherent or instinctual; instead, they are formed by a pastiche of actions that have been deemed appropriate to that gender. Thus, it is not enough to merely say that the genders are inverted, as the statement reinforces the fictional intrinsic nature of gender. In order to truly disturb normative ideas of gender, a work must expose binary and incommensurate gender roles, as Judith Butler does, revealing them as "cultural fictions" that are perpetuated by "tacit collective agreement to perform, produce, and sustain discrete and polar genders" (179). Put another way, a work must demonstrate that gender roles, traditional or not, are *all* cultural fictions. *Lumberjanes* does *not* invert traditional gender roles; rather, it shows that the supposedly incommensurate spheres of masculinity and femininity are deeply interwoven.

Perhaps the best example of how *Lumberjanes* achieves such exposure is through Rosie, the abovementioned head counselor. As noted before, Rosie's character design draws upon two important figures of self-reliance and personal strength: Paul Bunyan, the fictitious iconic lumberjack of North American lore, and Rosie the Riveter, the World War II–era propaganda figure of female empowerment and labor. The union of the two has an erasing effect on the gendered qualities of each figure; by absorbing the garb and woodsmanship of Bunyan while maintaining the domestic sensibilities often ascribed to women, Rosie the Counselor mitigates gender inversion. Referencing Rosie the Riveter, Rosie the Counselor likewise alludes to the primacy of female labor as a driving force of national survival in the Second World War. When it is mingled with the Bunyan-esque design, this primacy begins to look quite a lot like another female figure who was crucial to America's existence, the pioneer woman. And just as the pioneer lifestyle masked many of the markers that today inscribe gender difference, such as manual labor or childcare, Rosie's dual purpose as woodswoman and camp director strikes a dual pose between the gender poles. Most importantly, however, Rosie's figure unifies the assumed traits that often segregate men from women, especially notions of civility and domesticity. Rosie is *both* masculine/rough and feminine/tender; she is both

Figure 10. Rosie hard at work, featuring former head counselors. (*Lumberjanes* #7, page 1, panel 1. © 2014, Boom Entertainment, Inc.)

glamorous and tough. Even her décor, with its kitschy stuffed raccoons imploring visitors to wipe their feet mixed with prim portraits of proper Victorian ladies (see Figure 10) alludes to the closing of another distance often associated with Bunyan and Rosie: the distance between migrant labor class and middle-class housewife.[10]

The girls themselves should not be overlooked, however; their connection to the camping of gender expectation in scouting and camping deals more with the artifice of situations, rather than representations. For example, unlike the usual camp story in which a "nerdy" or otherwise intellectual child finds difficulty making friends in the natural world represented by the camp, the Lumberjanes' mastery in the sciences and the martial arts does not impede their ability to relate to one another and build strong homosocial relationships. And yet, unlike their scouting novel counterparts, the girls do not demonstrate an innate connection to domesticity, as evidenced by their poor caregiving skills (*LJ* #2, p. 17 and #3, p. 15). In fact, the girls' lack of domestic instincts is made a campy joke at the height of narrative tension. Jo has been turned to stone by an ancient curse. Through her logical anagramming skills, Molly discovers that the cure is the power of friendship (*LJ* #8, p. 11). The girls group hug Jo, heal her, and Mal metanarratively comments that she "can't believe that actually worked. 'The Power of Friendship?' Is this place for real?" (13). The camping here is on the pure artifice of the saccharine, after-school-special style of the message: Friendship is power.

Meanwhile, the feral boys, ostensibly representing innate masculine animalism, aren't so feral after all. In order to escape the boys, scoutmaster Jen spills food all over their cabin, causing them to immediately halt pursuit to clean up the mess (*LJ* #4, 19). *Lumberjanes* ultimately shows that such differentiations as male versus female are trivial and imposed—not essential. In the same story arc in which readers learn more about Jo's experience of transitioning from male to female (*LJ* vol. 4: *Out of Time*, issues 13–16), Scouting Lad Barney asks to tag along for the "different camp experience" that the Lumberjanes offer. Everyone welcomes him, and he takes part in the wayfinding and puzzle-solving inherent to Lumberjanes adventure. By the end of the arc, Jo makes it clear that sex or gender is not important in distinguishing between Lumberjane or Scouting Lad; what matters, as she reminds Barney, is where one feels they belong (*LJ* #16, p. 22). For the Lumberjanes, being a "Hardcore Lady-Type" has little to do with either biological sex or societal expectations of "ladylike" behavior. Rather, as the "high council" writes in the first volume's opening handbook selection, "this handbook is meant to guide you on your path as a Lumberjane, as a friend, and as a human being" (*LJ* vol. 1: *Beware the Kitten Holy*, 4). Though female pronouns are used and girlhood is discussed, *Lumberjanes* acts to defy common notions of what counts as "girlhood" by "learn[ing] to camp out."

This dismissal of binary gendering extends to *Lumberjanes'* narrative core via sibling rivalries. Such rivalries between cisgender males and cisgender females (both mundane and divine)[11] dramatize the polarizing effects of binary gender constructions. A camper with the Lumberjanes, Diane, is actually Artemis in disguise and reveals that she is locked in a struggle with her brother, Apollo, for control of supreme deific power over the universe. Diane/Artemis is a paragon of modern femininity: trendy, a self-styled "mean girl," too cool for camp and too aloof to participate in weaving friendship bracelets, learning astronomy, or the camp-wide game of capture the flag. When the Lumberjanes believe they have cracked her shell, she initially appears nurturing and caring, but it is quickly revealed to be a ruse to get her to the prize. Her presence alone begins to inspire catty in-fighting between close friends Jo and April. The "Camp Director," described earlier in this essay in all his hypermasculine goodness, turns out to be the adolescent Apollo. Put simply, Artemis and Apollo are caricatures of stereotypical femininity and masculinity. Such caricatures occur elsewhere, and with equal dismissal of importance: The statue that April arm-wrestles in issue 3 is muscle-bound, ridiculously proportioned, and poses at her as he lays down his challenge. The emphasis on typical masculinity heightens the campy hilarity of the statue's defeat to the "twig arms" April sports (*LJ* #3, p. 9). *Lumberjanes*'s frequent invocation and subsequent dismissal of exterior gender traits as indicators of interior features or identities act as an important part of its campy treatment of the often-gendered spaces of the woods.[12]

As much as Artemis and Apollo signify traditional gender difference, they also symbolize the inadequacy of gender polarity to describe modern identity. Their casting as irredeemable villains reinforces that they are untenable subject positions: nobody can live up to their expectations. Neither seems a strong candidate for ultimate deific controller of existence: through equivocation or duress, each has misled their charges, misrepresented their roles as leaders, and (most importantly to the campers) cheated in the contest for control of all creation. Faced with a seeming Gordian knot of whom to endorse, the Lumberjanes refuse to follow precut paths; they make their own way. Instead of allowing one of the siblings to take control of Zeus's supreme power, Mal hurls Ripley into the path of the power-granting lightning bolt. She steals the divine gift, taking from gods what was never meant from mortals: the power to re-shape reality (*LJ* #8, p. 18). For the Lumberjanes, that means dispelling the power so it can never be used against mortals again. Symbolically, Ripley casts aside the outmoded systems—binary gender norms, the conservative tradition of scouting novels, Imperialist messages of frontiersmanship and conquest—in favor of a new system, yet to be seen.

The use of Artemis and Apollo here is also an important opportunity for *Lumberjanes* to distance itself from the imperialist, racist stereotypes upon which many scouting trials and rituals were based. Jennifer Helgren, writing on the appropriation of Native American rituals for white consumption by Camp Fire Girls, explains that Camp Fire Girls co-owner Charlotte Vetter Gulick "intend[ed] to carry out, so far as possible, the ideal out-of-door Indian life" ("Camp Gulick on Lake Sebago"). For the Gulicks, the way to return lost (fictional) natural domesticity to Camp Fire Girls was via "making Indian jewelry and costumes, performing Indian dance and music, learning Indian myths and folklore, and using the Indian form of government" (Helgren 333). Racist, "noble savage" imagery and practice profoundly influenced scouting organizations, from the use of seemingly Native American naming conventions for camps and cabins to pseudo-native decorations on fringed leather dresses and eagle-feather headdresses (Helgren 334). Only a few decades after the cessation

of government-sanctioned violence against Native Americans, the appropriation of these forms allowed white Americans to redefine their blood-
spattered past: Shari Huhndorf writes that the "imperialist nostalgia" for
the noble savage symbol "veils the terrible violence marking the nation's
origins" (75–76). Helgren adds that these appropriations conveniently
"essentialized gender and created racial hierarchies within the nation"
(334). The staking out of once-held ideological territory became the new
frontier of Anglo-American conquest in the twentieth century; as more
and more white girls were called to "go native" in scouting organizations,
true native experience eroded. But the girls had recourse to resistance
even then; forced to "perform an idea of Indianness within a white institution not of their making," Camp Fire Girls were subversively empowered
to "[articulate] their own identities as modern girls" (334). "Sometimes
contesting and sometimes accommodating prevailing gender and racial
hierarchies," (334) Helgren argues that Camp Fire Girls, both white and
Indigenous, were empowered to articulate hybrid cultural practices. In a
similar way, *Lumberjanes* resists the purely indoctrinating ideology of the
imperial discourses that brought about the scouting movement, substitut-
ing hybridity for essentialism. The use of the twins Apollo and Artemis
replaces traditional "noble savage" mysticism; instead of appropriating
the mythology of a conquered victim, *Lumberjanes* rewrites Hellenic
myth, making the poetic and intelligent Apollo a gruff buffoon and the
huntress of the hills Artemis a mean girl with no outdoor sense.[13] Instead
of hiding the upper-crust origins of scouting behind pseudo-native naming, *Lumberjanes* foregrounds its roots in high-society England, as suggested by the long, Victorian-esque namesakes of its camps. The lone use
of a native name—Roanoke, the Lumberjanes' cabin—calls to mind
beneficial multicultural blending, hybridization by another name. In
popular conception, Roanoke colony was "lost" when settlers intermin-
gled with nearby tribes of Native Americans; according to historian Giles
Milton, evidence found at the former colony site supports this popular
belief (265–66), while, according to Glenn Ellen Starr Stilling, DNA test-
ing has shown significant intermixing in the Lumbee tribe near that area
("Lumbee Origins"). Even the opportunity given to (appropriated by)
Ripley functions as a hybridizing measure: The idea of "godliness" the
Lumberjanes have come to recognize is not an institution of their own
making, but instead has been shaped by Artemis's and Apollo's actions
throughout the course of the narrative. They are not native to the practices therein, so when Ripley chooses to utilize the power and dictates
her newly divine will, she subverts the dominant paradigms controlling

masculinity, femininity, scouting, and even relations between mortals and immortals.[14] Her choices range from silly to wise, but she ultimately resolves the sibling rivalry by destroying the divine gift (*LJ* #8, p. 21). Perhaps most importantly, the Lumberjanes represent diversity in race, economic background, gender identity, and sexual preference even as their adventures suggest an inward turn for exploration. Rather than colo-nizing the woods where they adventure, taking over and making their will the law of the land, the Lumberjanes attempt to live harmoniously within it; what few creatures they harm are mythical creatures put there by Artemis and Apollo to deter the other sibling. Even when they traverse the cave of trials, the girls make friends with the guardians rather than destroying them. When faced with opposition, such as the Scouting Lads-as-werewolves or a band of magical raptors (the dinosaur, not the bird of prey), the girls find a way to band together with the opposition. Ripley tames a raptor and rides it into battle at the end of volume two, and the Lads are saved with only minor injuries and the promise to team up again. The recurring message in Lumberjanes is "*friendship to the max*," but it may be fruitfully revised as "mutually beneficial" and "non-ablative of individual difference" friendship to the max.

The history of the scouting movement retold through the scouting novel has been, as Inness maintains, primarily "saccharine and uncritical" (Inness 98), failing to recognize the problematic gender constructions these movements outwardly perpetuated. However, critics have begun to note progressive undercurrents in some of the literature these groups produced. Rebekah E. Revzin and Laureen Tedesco challenge the traditional notion that all scouting materials reinforced early twentieth-century gender norms. Revzin argues that an ideological reading of Girl Scout handbooks and guides from the 1920s reveals that "[T]he Girl Scout organization (1) promoted feminist ideology to young girls in the early 1900s, (2) expected a woman's sphere to be restricted to the realm of children, religion, and the home, and (3) encouraged women to display independence either surrepti-tiously or overtly" (261). She admits that much of the content of official Girl Scout literature "promoted a traditional ideology of female domestic-ity," but she notes a "significant amount of material that challenges the more conventional feminine doctrine of the time" (268). In addition to traditionally feminine domesticity, Revzin reveals that the Girl Scouting handbooks espoused traditionally masculine virtues as well: to be "strong, educated, self-reliant, and goal-oriented, rather than timid, meek, subser-vient, and helpless" (268). As Mary Logan Rothschild puts it, "Girl Scout-ing emphasized both traditional feminine roles and a kind of practical feminism. At different times, one of these emphases has waxed and the other has waned, but neither has ever vanished from the program" (316). Tedesco maintains that such outwardly subversive cultural work was over-looked because "the Girl Scout program tried to solve some problems popularly believed to be immigrant problems—sanitation issues, ignorance about democratic processes, health deficiencies, inadequate maternal knowl-edge" (362). By visibly dedicating themselves as "home missionaries" (350), Tedesco argues, the Girl Scouts provided themselves with cultural cover. Appearing to solve issues that "resonated with the middle class, who had the leisure, money, and education to resolve them in their own lives" (362), Girl Scouts more likely "addressed those matters among the organizing class, not the class perceived as needing instruction" (362). And when "Progressive era interest in helping or besting the immigrant" ended, the Girl Scouts turned their collective eye to international peace, the next conservative talking point on a long list. By keeping questions of American conservation close to the surface, the Girl Scouts enjoyed "a measure of outdoor independence and soldierly role-play" (362). By the same token, Boy Scouting and boys' camps may have focused on traditional, if mytho-logical, markers of manliness, but a primary component of maintaining paramilitary orderliness, cleanliness, and hygiene lies squarely in the domestic sphere. Just as Gulick feared, allowing Girl Scouts access to the "masculine arts" produced an androgynous blurring of differences between Boy and Girl Scouts.

Lumberjanes is not a single piece of resistance against gender binarism in an otherwise hopeless quagmire. Other revisions of the scouting novel, such as the aforementioned *Moonrise Kingdom* and *Camp Weedonwantcha*, have made great strides in recovering this lost, once-popular genre from obscurity.[15] However, *Lumberjanes* is especially noteworthy because of its deployment of an ironic-yet-celebratory approach, one that simultane-ously revels in the fun, carefree atmosphere of vacation and summer camps while also prying open a critical space for reflection about how those camps have acted to stifle identity. Even as it employs ridiculous, garish, saccharine, and hyperbolic structures common to the scouting novel and the summer camp comedy, *Lumberjanes* is careful to always look to the side, to view these structures "in quotation marks," so to speak, with an obvious acknowledgment of their artifice or performativity. This is especially important because the camp has *always* functioned as a place where some societal norms are solidified and some are undermined. For example, in this chapter I have not broached the topic of lesbian romance, which threads throughout *Lumberjanes* in the innocent first love of Mal and Molly as well as in the bitter, lost love of former Lumberjanes Rosie and Abigail, and which is nevertheless a common feature of the summer camp comedy: new and lost romances. I have also not addressed the series' profound reliance upon reference and intertextuality. Frequent riffs on popular culture, such as April shouting "the cold never bothered us anyway" during a blizzard, or another Lumberjane scout telling Diane that "it's dangerous to go alone" into the woods firmly locate this text in the millennial period. At the same time, the use of historical women as exclamations—Holy Juliette Gordon Low (creator of the Girl Scouts)! Sweet Mae Jemison (first African-American woman in space)! By Great Anahareo's (Mohawk Canadian writer, animal rights activist, and conservationist) ghost!—refers the reader into a deeper historical record of women who defied gender expectations of their time, contributing to the "herstory" to which *Lumberjanes* owes a recognized and accounted debt. Finally, I have spent nearly no time discussing garishness, color, or other glitzy markers of camp sensibility, largely because to extricate those features from the glorious, tacky, and outlandish world of the *Lumberjanes* would be, as Sontag maintains about camp in general, to betray it by putting boundaries on it. And as the *Lumberjanes* are *always* concerned with pushing and breaking boundaries, I can think of no greater slight than to limit these Hardcore Lady Types.

NOTES

1. As a staunch proponent of equally recognizing all the contributors involved in large-scale comics creation, I list here the creative team that has worked on *Lumberjanes* issues 1 through 20. Writers: Noelle Stevenson, Grace Ellis, Shannon Watters, Faith Erin Hicks; Artists: Brooke A. Allen, Brittney Williams, Aimee Fleck, Faith Erin Hicks, Becca Tobin, Carolyn Nowak, Felicia Choo, T. Zysk; Letterer: Aubrey Aiese; Colorist: Maarta Laiho; Editor: Dafna Pleban.

2. *Lumberjanes* is a continuing comics series. As of October 2017, it is on its forty-third issue; the first twelve referenced in this essay are collected in trade paperbacks, cited at the end of this essay, but the best way to get the story in its entirety is to visit the local comic-book dispensary. As with most comics, they do not have page numbers; I have given issue number and approximate pagination where necessary. In addition, October will see the first *Lumberjanes* novel, written by Mariko Tamaki and illustrated by Brooke Allen primarily for middle-grade readers (between ages eight and twelve). Finally, a film directed by Emily Carmichael is in production through Twentieth Century Fox with no stable release date as of this writing.

3. My definition of camp is largely derived from Susan Sontag's work and that which follows it, including David Bergman's and Fabio Cleto's. Some suggestions for further reading on the subject are provided in the works cited.

4. The phrase comes from an April 1899 speech Roosevelt delivered at the Hamilton Club in Chicago, in which Roosevelt calls upon young Americans (men especially) to "lead clean, vigorous, healthy lives" of "toil and effort, of labor and strife." By turns profoundly racist, nativist, and pro-war—it is the speech from which the notion "the army and navy are the sword and the shield which this nation must carry if she is to do her duty among the nations of the earth"—Roosevelt's call to action preyed upon twin concerns in the greater American psyche: fear of being overrun by foreign hordes (the 1898 Treaty of Paris effectively ended the Spanish-American war and granted the United States Puerto Rico, Guam, and the Philippines) and fears of laziness driven by burgeoning modern ease.

5. Despite the largely oppressive gender expectations espoused by the scouting movement's major players, there has been a relatively recent trend since 1999 to examine individualized resistance within scouting. See Kathryn Kent, "'No Trespassing': Girl Scout Camp and the Limits of the Counterpublic Sphere" (reprinted in this collection); Susan Charles T. Groth's "Scouts' Own: Creativity, Tradition, and Empowerment in Girl Scout Ceremonies," Dissertation: University of Pennsylvania, 1999; Laureen Tedesco, "A Nostalgia for Home: Daring and Domesticity in Girl Scouting and Girls' Fiction, 1913–1933," Dissertation: Texas A&M, 1999; and Tedesco, "Progressive Era Girl Scouts and the Immigrant: *Scouting for Girls* (1920) as a Handbook for American Girlhood," *Children's Literature Association Quarterly* 31, no. 4 (2006): 346–68.

6. It is at first bewildering why organizations as concerned with preserving an image as scouting groups would not send takedown notices to the Stratemeyer Syndicate for clear copyright infringement. However, the popularity of the books correlated with booming Scouts enrollment despite severe economic downturn and two world wars, suggesting that longtime publisher and Boy Scouts co-creator, William D. Boyce, may have benefited from the free publicity the unsanctioned novels afforded.

7. For more on the intriguing relationship between the American fascination with sharpshooting, pioneer mythology, and the NRA, see Jay Mechling, "Boy Scouts, the National Rifle Association, and the Domestication of Rifle Shooting," *American Studies* 53, no. 1 (2014): 5–25.

8. Initially, this would probably have involved loom-weaving, knitting, lanyard-making, or basketry. By the 1970s, the epitome of camp banality, the "friendship bracelet," would be commandeered from pan-Central American

culture. All were designed as communal activities, in which (girls especially) would learn to work while socializing. For more on the appropriation of North-, Central-, and South-American practices in scouting and camping, see Jennifer Helgren, "Native American and White Camp Fire Girls Enact Modern Girlhood, 1910–39," *American Quarterly* 66, no. 2 (June 2014): 333–60.

9. For more on the American trope of the quasi-feral boy-child, see Kenneth B. Kidd, *Making American Boys: Boyology and the Feral Tale* (Minneapolis: University of Minnesota Press, 2004).

10. Lumberjacks were migrant laborers in the lumber trade, most often uneducated Quebecers who followed the logging season. The term itself is derogatory, with its original usage close to oaf or boor. Interestingly, *Lumberjanes* coined a new term for a female lumberjack—the typical usage is "Lumberjill," after the nursery rhyme "Jack and Jill." For more on Bunyan and his relationship to Camp masculinity, see Mielke and Trevarrow's essay in this volume.

11. Though it is not entirely clear if the namesakes of the Scouting Lads' and Lumberjanes' camps are related, the similarly lengthy pseudo-Victorian names and shared surnames suggest that Mr. Theodore Tarquin Reginald Lancelot Herman Crumpet's Camp for Boys and Miss Quinzella Thiskwin Penniquiquill Thistle Crumpet's Camp for Hardcore Lady Types are the result of sibling rivalry. They also hearken nostalgically back to a romanticized British history of genteel Imperial conquest.

12. For more on the gendering of the outdoors, particularly in Canadian cinema, see Kay Armatage, Kass Banning, Brenda Longfellow, and Janine Marchessault (eds.), *Gendering the Nation: Canadian Women's Cinema* (Toronto: University of Toronto Press, 1999). The gendering of outdoor space is a ripe area for examination; of particular interest on this topic are the fictional work of Margaret Atwood, especially *Surfacing* (1972), Lois Lowry's *Gathering Blue* (2000), and Suzanne Collins's *Hunger Games* trilogy (2008–2010).

13. As a Bakhtinian, I understand this revision as one with "a glance to the side"—the reader is expected to know the myth and laugh at the recasting of these mythic figures, not take it at face value. This kind of knowing reading suggests deeper engagement with the myth than scouting organizations would have done in appropriating Native American figures like the Crow.

14. Ripley's appearance in this section of book eight alludes to the shonen manga—comic books written specifically for teenage boys—*Dragon Ball* and *Dragon Ball Z*.

15. These works are complex enough that they deserve a much longer treatment than I could give them here. In particular, Wes Anderson's

ambivalent treatment of the "heteronormative first love" story alongside the dissolution of parental marriage is provocative; Katie Rice's webcomic is true to children's literary forms in that absolutely no adults are present, and the resulting wide-open space affords personal and interpersonal exploration that powerfully counteracts the highly structured form of scouting in which many contemporary children participate.

Escape to Moonrise Kingdom

Let's Go Camping!

Kerry Mallan and Roderick McGillis

A map of the world that does not include utopia
is not worth glancing at.

—OSCAR WILDE (40)

When we encounter camp, we live outdoors, as it were,
removed from commonality and conformity. We are,
strange as it may seem, good Scouts.

—RODERICK MCGILLIS (98–99)

Maps introduce us to places that might be unfamiliar. They are information and invitation. They can guide the journey from what we know to what we don't know. The cartographer's gaze shapes the form the map takes, its spaces and places. Storms alter and erase topography. Explorers and adventurers leave reminders of their presence, a campsite perhaps, and for some, they may indeed find utopia. It all depends on the eye of the beholder. Behind every map there is a story. Here is one of them.

A troop of "Khaki Scouts"—a fictionalization of the Boy Scouts—camps out on the also fictional island New Penzance with the requisite uniforms, badges, camping gear, and intrepid scoutmaster, Randy Ward. Randy is anything but randy; the same cannot be said for some of his charges, especially one, 12-year-old orphan Sam Shakusky. Sam strikes up a romance with Suzy Bishop, who lives on the island in a house named Summer's End. The two of them run away and make camp by themselves, intending to make a life together, two young people in love. Meanwhile, the scouts, Randy, Suzy's parents, the local constabulary, and the social services are all on the lookout for the young runaways. All of this takes place in 1965. All of this provides a nostalgic look at a time and place everyone has left behind, a time we remember but that never existed. All of this is parody of young love, coming of age, life in the camp. This is Moonrise Kingdom, the place longed for, remembered, completely fictional, and the titular setting of Wes Anderson's 2012 film.

The film is about an island that serves as camp to the few people who inhabit it. Camping out on the island is a summer activity for a nearby scout troop, the Khaki Scouts. Sam and Suzy fashion their own camp. The Bishop children camp in their own house. And the island itself is camp, in the sense of a sensibility that weaves color and texture into a nostalgic recreation of time and place that exists only in imagination, only in moonrise. As camp, the island offers escape from convention and normality and escape to a possibility. In short, the island is queer, a queer space in which forces of authority find purchase difficult, if not downright impossible. It also exists in a queer time—1965—the year that the first U.S. combat troops arrive in Vietnam and the battle of Ia Drang occurs: a temporal moment that adds to the film's inherent unsettledness. It might be no accident that the 1965 setting is one year after the appearance of Susan Sontag's famous "Notes on 'Camp.'"

Sontag's essay offers a purely aesthetic stance on Camp,[1] seeing it as a style or sensibility, disengaged, depoliticized, and apolitical (275–77), "a solvent of morality" that "neutralizes moral indignation" (290). Free of the burden of moral high-mindedness, camp "sponsors playfulness" (290) which offers an intimate pleasure for like-minded camp followers and participants. Writing in 1964, Sontag considered camp a benign, harmless pleasure devoid of political intent or sermonizing. For other writers, both before and after Sontag's "Notes on 'Camp,'" camp has a more political or at least a proto-political function: Newton notes camp's sarcastic humor and wit (106); for Babuscio camp is subversive and "challenges the status quo" (120); and Meyer says camp produces a "queer identity" (4). Queerness is a quality of both camp and *Moonrise Kingdom*, alongside deviance, humor, and aesthetics.

Our use of queer in the discussion of *Moonrise Kingdom* that follows is not intended to be synonymous with LGBTI identity or subjects. Rather, we use queer in a broader sense taking into account a range of social and institutional practices and rituals (camping, family, marriage, romance) that subvert norms or attempt to resignify normative ways of being and viewing the world. Judith Butler contends that norms work both ways: They can regulate and normalize power as well as form the basis for binding individuals together, along with their "ethical and political claims" (219). While a camp style is not (a) uniform, in the sense of having its own normative appearance and performance, it nevertheless does contain familial traces suggestive of belonging to a particular community (albeit a diverse one). Such is the nature of labels that certain rhetorical gestures and sartorial styles appear to mark affinity. This applies to "Boy Scouts" as much as it does to "drag queens." It is not too much of a stretch to see how Anderson turns scouting performance into something of a drag show: Boys and men perform as scouts, repeating a series of acts within a quasi-military frame, while disrupting the seriousness of the *doing*. *Moonrise Kingdom* fuses both camp and Camp—a double play that we explore in this chapter. While others have created lists of the hallmarks of camp—sarcasm, wit, parody, exaggeration, excess, impropriety, perverse pleasure, playfulness, aestheticism, seriously political—these defining features can be misunderstood as belonging exclusively to camp. Describing camp can easily become a cliché that is self-validating—"You know it when you see it." But camp seems to invite cliché, even flaunt it. Part of camp-cliché's success is its wide recognition and circulation through repeated performatives that are banal, kitschy, playful, and surreal.

In offering a camp reading of *Moonrise Kingdom*, we return to Sontag's early notion of camp but with a particular focus on how this style or sensibility can be read through the film's aesthetic composition and its queering of storytelling conventions for children. As we have noted elsewhere, camp aesthetics brings its own disruptive style of kitsch, nostalgia, and bad taste, inviting a "different kind of apprehension and consumption" (Mallan & McGillis 3). A key feature of how camp performs in this text is the way in which its distinctive humor infuses incongruous situations.

Setting Up Camp

If camp has a style, then its appeal must lie with its reception as much as with its performance. Whether Wes Anderson intended *Moonrise Kingdom* to be a Camp film is debatable. Regardless, it is the text itself that is of interest, as New Critics and Barthes's death of the author have insisted. Sontag, too, dismisses artistic intention reiterating that "the work tells all" (282). However, Anderson's deployment of a camp aesthetic and a queer perspective is a recognizable feature of his filmic style. This is not to say that Anderson set out to make a camp film. To do so would probably result in a heavy-handedness that would tip the "delicate relation between parody and self-parody in Camp" (Sontag 282). *Moonrise Kingdom*, like many of Anderson's films, exhibits a discernible quirkiness that infuses the story and characters. The classical-pop-country mix of music, color palettes, off-beat humor, and blurring between real and fake give his films a camp quality. And when the film is about boy scouts and summer camps, we are treated to a delightful playfulness that invites a double camp vision, which can transform the way the film is viewed and critiqued. In this film, camp and Camp come together. The scouts' summer camp offers an opportunity to "camp it up," as it were.

In the opening sequence of *Moonrise Kingdom*, we are presented with a series of tracking shots inside the Bishop household comprising Mr. and Mrs. Bishop, three young Bishop boys, and an adolescent girl, Suzy Bishop. The first image is a framed painting of the exterior of the Bishops' home with its distinctive red roof. Another interior scene follows where in the foreground we see a small dollhouse, with a similarly colored red roof. As the camera tracks from left to right across the different parts of the interior spaces, the filming process draws attention to itself by presenting the various spaces as contiguous film sets, as well as a *trompe l'oeil*; one painted wall with framed pictures and cupboards sits beside "real" images of sets and characters. Austerlitz remarks that many of Anderson's films are "cinematic dollhouses" (382), and this slow tracking of the interior of the house delivers such an effect, with the miniature dollhouse serving as a kind of in-joke to the knowing viewer. The camera's roving eye moves smoothly, changing directions—upwards, forward, panning around a room, giving us a glimpse into this domestic space, the relationships among the family members, their belongings. We see an old-fashioned record player, Suzy's binoculars, a pair of scissors, her books, bags, and kitten. Except for the Bishop boys, the mother, father, and Suzy are alone in their own spaces, and when Suzy moves into where her brothers are listening to their music, she appears detached, and settles into reading one of her fantasy books. The opening *mise-en-scène* communicates the emotional distance that appears to separate the Bishops from each other. When Mrs. Bishop calls the children to the table she speaks through a megaphone.

As the opening credits appear, Benjamin Britten's *The Young Person's Guide to the Orchestra* plays with the voice of a child presenter explaining that the orchestra is divided into "four different families"—which parallels the divisions within the Bishop family (boys, mother, father, Suzy) and their inhabiting of separate spaces in the home. Britten's music appears to be a favorite of the young Bishop boys who listen to this piece on a portable record player. Later we come to learn that the two young protagonists— Sam Shakusky and Suzy Bishop—first met at a performance of another of Britten's compositions, the children's opera *Noye's Fludde*. Based on a medieval play about Noah's Ark, *Noye's Fludde* and *The Young Person's Guide to the Orchestra* are fitting musical accompaniments to a story that is about young people, a great storm, and young love. While the thematic alignment of the music to the subject of the film becomes apparent as the story progresses, Britten's love of children, particularly adolescent boys, is a subtext that will likely be missed by child viewers. As Britten's biographer, John Bridcut, writes, 13-year-old boys were Britten's ideal, and he once explained that the reason he liked writing for children was because he felt that age himself: "I'm still thirteen" (8). Given that Sam and Suzy are 12 years old, and the boys of Troop 55 are of similar age, these characters come close to Britten's ideal. Youth is also a familiar subject in Anderson's films, and *Moonrise Kingdom* is about young love, and perhaps the loss of love and being young. Nostalgia is a companion of camp.

Nostalgia is an expression of longing for something left behind, something lost, something dearly desired. It casts an attractive light on that which is no longer within reach; it is wistful. Such wistfulness is apparent in the title of this film. A further element of nostalgia is the use of old technology—at least from the perspective of a new millennial audience. Suzy's brother has a portable record player, which she borrows when she embarks on her rendezvous/elopement with Sam. Nostalgia for old technology is a feature of Anderson's other films (for example, Mr. Fox's "walk sonic" portable radio in *Fantastic Mr. Fox*). Nostalgia is frequently discussed in the context of camp aesthetics. Sontag, for example, notes that with the passage of time the past can be appreciated anew: "Thus, things are campy, not when they become old—but when we become less involved with them, and can enjoy, instead of being frustrated by, the failure of the attempt" (285). While the record player is not anachronistic for the time setting of the film, for viewers (especially adults who lived through the 1960s) the portable record player, its old-fashioned controls, and the 45 RPM vinyl record bring a certain longing; for others these old technologies are enjoying a comeback due to what music commentator Simon Reynolds terms "retromania." At one point later in the film, Anderson even manages to evoke nostalgia from memories of Vietnam when scoutmaster Ward rescues Commander Pierce from the explosion at camp headquarters. Anderson's nostalgia is high camp in that it does not suggest critique so much as offer release.

In addition to infusing a sense of nostalgia, Anderson's careful selection and treatment of music is an "intrinsic part of his style" (Winters 46). Rather than use music to drive the narrative, Anderson, Winters contends, uses music to "provide an appropriate 'register' to characterize other events occurring on screen" (50–51). We can see this register later in the film when Suzy plays a record of popular sixties French singer Françoise Hardy singing *Le Temps De L'Amour.* The song supplies the appropriate romantic mood when she and Sam are alone on an isolated beach that becomes the eponymous Moonrise Kingdom.

The surface middle-class domesticity of the opening scenes carries the gloss of camp. This middlebrowing of camp is not a sophisticated, glamorous camp—a Hollywood camp—but one that is "naïve" in its lack of pretensions or self-awareness and worthy of Sontag's appellation of "pure camp" (282). As each scene unfolds we see different members of the household going about their day—mother is painting her toenails, then sitting under the dome-shaped hair dryer; father is in another room reading; the three young boys play a game under the table, run around the house, and listen to *The Young Person's Guide to the Orchestra.* All are objects of the viewer's gaze. But at the end of each tracking, Suzy uses her binoculars to make the viewer the object of her gaze. When she collects Sam's letter from the mailbox she puts it in a shoebox marked "Private." After reading its contents, she looks directly at the viewer, her blank expression conveying a subtle deviance. The as yet unrevealed significance of the letter is expressed through the music, which reaches a crescendo. Suzy's vivid blue eye-shadow, black eyeliner, yellow dress, and white knee-high socks remind us that this is a story set in the 1960s, but her youthful look with its pseudo-adult glamour sets her apart from the others in her family. We learn later that her parents see her as a troubled child, that she gets into fights at school, and she has no friends other than Sam. The yellow color palette evokes nostalgia for fashion trends of the sixties but also signifies "optimism" (Vreeland 41), which is apparent in Suzy's yellow suitcase, the uniforms of the scouts, and the tents. Yellow also brings to mind the golden days of summer and youth. With such longing, desire, and optimism, the questions "How do we get there?" and "Where is 'there'?" drive the utopian impulse in all of us, and especially in Sam and Suzy.

Queer Orientations

Orientations are "about starting points" (Ahmed 545), about proceeding from here to there. To orient oneself is to fix one's position prior to setting out on a journey: a journey that will take up space and time. However, a direction one follows does not necessarily stay fixed, as journeys have a way of taking unexpected twists and turns, leading to unknown paths. For Sara Ahmed, going off-course can bring rewards: "risking departure from the straight and narrow, makes new futures possible, which might involve going astray, getting lost, or even becoming queer" (554). Orientations are also about the ways bodies situate themselves in relation to each other, to objects and dwellings. Ahmed's idea of "queer orientations" offers a useful starting point for considering how *Moonrise Kingdom*'s camp aesthetic (its color, excess, humor, incongruities) mediates the queerness that disturbs the order of things in New Penzance.

While the opening *mise-en-scène* of *Moonrise Kingdom* lets us see what is inside the Bishops' house, a map gives us the perspective outside the house. In reference to the map, the voice of the anonymous Narrator tells us: "This is the island of New Penzance." The name of this fictional island recalls Gilbert and Sullivan's *The Pirates of Penzance*: an opera that conveys a camp sensibility through its extravagance, parody, and burlesque. The Narrator gives a roving tour and description of the island ("16 miles long") and information about its forests, tidal creeks, and Old Chickchaw Territory. The shift away from the Bishop household to the Narrator appears as an extra-diegetic commentary (another favorite technique of Anderson's, which *The Life Aquatic with Steve Zissou* exploits to good effect with its documentary within a documentary).

The narrator speaks directly to the camera. At one point, he stops moving and stands still on the edge of a rocky shoreline. He adopts a rather camp pose standing slightly turned to the side with one hand resting on his right leg which points to the front. His expression is serious and he announces dramatically that this is the spot ("the far edge of Black Beacon Sound") that was "famous for the ferocious and well documented storm that will strike from the east on the 5th September, in three days' time." (In November 1965, much of the northeast United States and parts of Canada experienced a blackout for nearly 13 hours.) The seriousness of this portentous speech and the mannered pose he adopts are at odds with his otherwise documentary-style delivery. The narrator serves to orient the audience to the place, the time, and the storm that will soon take place. His message is about the past and the future and his function is to set the scene and prepare us for the action that will unfold. The map and the background information of this scene orient us spatially (New Penzance) and temporally (1965). The storm that the Narrator forecasts parallels the disruption of the normal pace and stability of life on New Penzance caused by Sam and Suzy's escape.

Knowing how to read maps to find one's location and way are an important part of scout training. When scoutmaster Ward finds that Sam Shakusky has decided to resign from the Khaki Scouts and has gone missing from Camp Ivanhoe, he instructs his troop to find Sam and bring him back safely, reminding them to "use your orienteering and path-finding skills you have been practicing all summer." Sam's disappearance affords the troop the opportunity to *do* some serious scouting, and the doing depends on the repetition of norms and conventions, of skills and knowledge of routes and paths taken, and to be taken. But the boys' dislike of Sam drives them to inquire whether they can use force if he resists. In spite of Ward's warning that no one is to harm Sam, the troop sets off with a range of weapons—rifles, a wood club with nails, a hunting knife, an axe. Snoopy the camp dog leads the troop in their search. Ward expects his scouts to follow the straight (moral and dutiful) lines that the scouting tradition has already mapped out. There is no ambiguity about what is expected of a Boy Scout (the model for the film's scouts: "A Scout is trustworthy, loyal, help-ful, friendly, courteous, kind, obedient, cheerful, thrifty, brave, clean, and reverent" ("Scout Law"). The boys, however, have a different kind of law in mind: to find the fugitive and bring him back to camp—with force.

Sam also queers the way of being a straight scout. For Ahmed, queer is "what is oblique or off-line or just plain wonky"; queer is also "on a slant, the odd and strange one" (565, 566). The other scouts dislike Sam because he is an odd one, an outsider. Although he is a skillful and knowledgeable scout, Sam deviates from the straight scout uniform code: he wears a pearl broach that belonged to his mother on his shirt (a memento mori), a Davy Crockett hat, and he smokes a tobacco pipe. But despite the distance, the challenging terrain, and a violent encounter with the other scouts, Sam and Suzy arrive at their destination and with colonizing glee declare: "This is our land." Ahmed writes of "the magic of arrival," a feeling that makes one forget all the "work of arrival" (555). Sam reads his map well, follows directions, sets up camp, prepares meals with the supplies he brought, and shows Suzy how to fish for their supper. He is a good (queer) scout.

Suzy, too, resists the straight path that is mapped for her as a daughter. To borrow a phrase from Ahmed, she lives life "on a slant" (561). Ahmed suggests that when the queer body cannot orient itself in straight space, such failed orientation makes it seem as if it is "slanting, or oblique" (560). Suzy does not interact with others, except when arguing or fighting, and sits on the window seat apart from her brothers, with her legs bent. She views the outside world through binoculars—at one time seeing her mother sneaking off to have a secret liaison with Captain Sharp. In helping to see things closer, the binoculars also distance her from others. She likes to pretend the binoculars have "magical power." When she runs away with Sam, she is dressed in clothes that are more suited to Sunday school than trekking across the island. She also brings an assortment of impractical items—a basket with her kitten, bags, her fantasy novels, and her brother's record player—that contrasts with Sam's sensible camping kit.

Theirs is a kind of ludic temporality, although they treat their time together seriously. When they camp on what is marked on the map of the island as Meter 3.25 Tidal Inlet they swim, dance in their underwear, and kiss, with each declaring their love. The romantic clichés of the first kiss on a deserted beach and the performative language "I love you" fulfill the conventions of heteronormative romance and a palpable nostalgia for the adult viewer for a past which was innocent, young, and free of the burdens of adulthood. (The island romance is reminiscent of the 1980 film *The Blue Lagoon*.) The kiss, the dance, and the campfire create a *mise-en-scène* that employs romantic clichés to create a queer temporal and spatial effect. The two of them create a "queer [camp/Camp] space," a space described by Aaron Betsky as "useless, amoral, and sensual. . . . It is a space in between the body and technology, a space of pure artifice" (5). The film inverts the romance ideal (and idyll) of straight adult love to capture the transgressive sideways move of young straight love.[2]

Sam and Suzy choose to exist outside of the norms of childhood with its mapped life trajectory from childhood to young adulthood to adulthood. Their actions are risky—no money, no fixed address, limited supplies. When Suzy and Sam make the spontaneous decision to marry, they chart a course that veers away from the path that is mapped for adolescent development. The ceremony is carried out by "Cousin Ben," a profiteering scout master who runs the supply and resources store at Fort Lebanon. He is also a marriage celebrant. In agreeing to marry Sam and Suzy, Ben explains that he "can't offer a legally binding union . . . but the ritual does carry a very important world weight within yourselves." The ceremony queers contemporary, normative institutions of marriage and the law and offers instead an alternative alliance between an under-age couple. The film eschews any reductive moral binary of right/wrong but points to how desire is a site not only of regulation but also subversion. Despite the seriousness that Sam and Suzy give to their vows, the seriousness of the "marriage" ceremony "fails" as its theatricality and comic treatment bring to mind Sontag's comment that "Camp refuses both the harmonies of traditional seriousness, and the risks of fully identifying with extreme states of feeling" (1966: 287). Failure, too, as Halberstam suggests, brings its own rewards, one of which is that it "preserves some of the wondrous anarchy of childhood and disturbs the supposedly clean boundaries between adults and children, winners and losers" (2011: 3).

Sam and Suzy are not the only ones who live life on an oblique angle. Others, too, veer off-course. The Bishop family operates according to a schedule of isolation—different members live in different spaces, move around, pass one another, without any contact or communication, except via a megaphone when assembly is called. Scout leader Wade conducts a tour of the camp, checking on his troop's activities and handing out punishments for uniform violations and cautions against dangerous activities, all the while holding a lit cigarette. Captain Sharp fishes off the jetty with another resident. The relaxed nature of the activity is disrupted when Wade calls to say that a Khaki Scout has "escaped"—a word that conveys a breach of the rules, a movement across the boundary lines that mark out the camp's space. The scouts, too, go off-line and in doing so threaten the normative ways of being a Boy Scout.

The Boy Scouts thrive on uniformity. They are expected to follow the line of authority and responsibility that comes through the chain of command. The scout pack is a junior military without ordinance. They wear uniforms, they have reveille, they receive badges for various accomplishments, and they stick together through all sorts of weather. They camp out. They all wear shorts, even the scoutmaster. They bring childhood to the longing for manhood and vice versa. The first time we encounter the scouts from Troop 55, we notice that they like to be creative (building a tree house on a very high pole) and enjoy doing dangerous things (making explosives). Their actions are out of line even when Ward tries to keep them in line with threats and punishments. When the scouts eventually find Sam and Suzy, Scout Law seems the last thing on their minds, and the ensuing altercation results in one boy being stabbed with scissors by Suzy, and the dog, Snoopy, being accidentally killed by an arrow to its neck. When Suzy and Sam discover the dead dog, Suzy asks, "Was he a good dog?" to which Sam replies matter-of-factly: "Who's to say? But he didn't deserve to die." The clichéd exchange fills the emotional space but not with false platitudes. Instead, it offers a realistic assessment of a dog's right to live. The scene can also be read as an instance of camp's deployment of perverse wit that assumes a moral seriousness, only to expose it as a pretense by indulging in gratuitously graphic images of the damage caused by deviant actions.

When the Bishops learn of the violent encounter, Mr. Bishop attacks Ward's leadership and authority as a scoutmaster, shouting, "Why can't you control your scouts?" The implied accusation of weakness is accurate as Ward's position and authority are undercut by the scouts' actions, which contradict his commands. However, Bishop's heat-of-the-moment comment speaks to a key element of the film, namely, the incongruous relationships that characterize the disharmony between the characters—young and old alike. However, Ward recoups his honor when he rescues the Fort Lebanon Commander who has become trapped in a burning tent at the height of the storm. This rescue occurs only minutes after Ward has been stripped of his command. Then Ward successfully leads the scouts to safety as the storm rages. Troop 55 demonstrates that Ward's efforts in teaching them scouting skills were not lost as they successfully use their knowledge to locate Sam and Suzy and later carry out another rescue and escape.

In offering queer orientations where paths, actions, and desires are at angles to the straight lines of conformity, *Moonrise Kingdom* embodies a queerness that disrupts normative accounts of family, marriage, Boy Scouts, and the coming-of-age story. It makes the familiar look different and opens the possibility of arriving at a better place. Utopia evokes dreams of escape, transformation, and other ways of being in the world. Utopia is about hope that there is something better than what José Esteban Muñoz gloomily terms "the prison house" of the here and now (1). Sam and Suzy are trapped in their own prison houses—Sam's parents have died, and he has lived unhappily with a succession of foster families; Suzy lives isolated in her own family home and is unpopular at school. Together, Sam and Suzy dream of a better place, a no place. In his book *Cruising Utopia*, Muñoz maintains that queerness holds the potential for rejecting the here and now, for seeing the possibility of another world (1). Like Wilde's insistence that a map must include utopia, Sam is guided toward a point on a map, "Meter 3.25 Tidal Inlet," a place to which they can escape and possibly imagine a future.

Island/Eyeland

The film's final scenes stage a theatricality that is pure camp in its excessive display of dramatic tension. The setting is St Jude's Church where the night's performance of *Noye's Fludde* has been canceled because of the storm. The tension is heightened by the music of *Noye's Fludde*, a fitting accompaniment, as its own dramatic choral staging of human tensions (the building of the ark) is paralleled by the argument between Social Sciences, Ward, and Sharp over sending Sam to juvenile refuge. At the height of the tension, Sam and Suzy plan to jump from the church tower with the rising volume of bugles and repeated choruses of "Alleluia" playing in the background. Just as Britten wrote his opera so that the most dramatic moments were given to the congregation (who join the cast) so, too, does Anderson focus on professional and laypeople who argue what they consider to be best for Sam and Suzy, while the menagerie of children dressed as birds and animals observe and finally point to where Sam and Suzy have gone—up to the tower. After intense negotiations, Sam and Suzy agree to come down with Sharp, but at that dramatic moment a bolt of lightning strikes the tower. The result is an image of three blackened figures holding hands like interlinked paper-cutout figures. They are on a slant. Sharp utters the obvious—"Don't let go."

After the eye of the storm passes, the island is devastated, but eventually normality returns. Life appears to go along much the same as before. The closing scene of the film returns us to the beginning—the Bishop household. While Sam, dressed in the island police uniform, paints at an easel, Suzy reads her fantasy novels, and the Bishop boys listen to *The Young Person's Guide to the Orchestra*. Suddenly, Mrs. Bishop's voice is heard through the megaphone announcing that dinner is ready and everyone is to be downstairs immediately. The Bishop boys run downstairs, and Sam quickly moves to the window, tells Suzy he'll see her tomorrow, and climbs down to meet Sharp, who is his new foster father. Suzy is silent and looks through her binoculars as they drive away in the island police car. The camera moves to Sam's painting. It is of the beach, which has Moonrise Kingdom painted on its shoreline. The camera moves in for a close-up, and the painting transforms into the "real" beach. Sam and Suzy's utopia has been erased from the map of the island because of the storm's destructive force, but its fantasy remains. It all depends on the eye of the beholder.

NOTES

1. Sontag uses a capital *C*, which we follow when referring directly to her work. In other instances, we use a lowercase *c* as a way of distinguishing her work from our reading and those of others.

2. We thank Kenneth Kidd for his insight in shaping this observation.

"Finding We'Wha"

Indigenous Idylls in Queer Young Adult Literature

Joshua Whitehead

While the green world is no new invention, as Northrop Frye explores through the milieu of Shakespeare, I argue we see its enactment in queer young adult literature as a transformative space that bolsters the identities of non-native queer peoples. This green world is usually a forested space of wild abandon situated adjacent to the civilized spaces of the city, which are riddled with trauma, grief, politics, and social order. It is in this green space that the characters converge, undergo a metamorphosis, and return to their urban worlds with a newfound respect for civility. I have been tracking this green world trope through queer YA texts and argue that it transforms settler queerness through what I call an Indigiqueer idyll; this idyll becomes an illusive, precarious, and co-opted space that capitalizes on romanticized and necromantic[1] notions of Indigiqueer / Two-Spirit histories in order to consolidate settler queerness. There is something paradoxical at play in the desire to capitalize on Indigeneity as a transformative space for white adolescents to enter and emerge from as civilized adults. That is, the desire to masculinize and straighten adolescents (especially adolescent boys) runs counter to settler colonialism's reading of Indigeneity as inherently queered and potentially queering. In other words: How do you straighten queerness

in a space that is implicitly queer? Two-Spirit/Indigiqueers become sub-
jected to neocolonial observations and pale-ontology, or, the empty signification of the body—bodies of land, culture, history, and sexuality—and
the pale, or white, revisionism of the aforementioned body. Two-
Spirit/Indigiqueerness always lingers in the background of settler queer
texts that are set seemingly far from the frontier and feature no Indigenous
characters or thematic elements in problematic and unexamined ways.
Through this vanishing act, I have begun playing a game with settler queer
YA texts, a game I've called "Where's We'Wha."[2] I've been tracking the
peripheral NDN[3] throughout popular YA titles[4] in order to create a genealogy of dispossession and settler transformation, a genealogy that becomes
a means of both induction and invasion. Not only does Indigeneity open up
as a simulation that embeds settlers further into the nation-state; this simulation romanticizes Indigeneity as a queer idyll, a queer camp.

Playing Indigiqueer: Simulating Settler Ancestry

The trope of the vanishing NDN is ever-shifting, morphing into and
through various policies and mandates brought to Turtle Island (North
America) through conceptions such as manifest destiny and terra nullius—
one that creates what Jodi Byrd calls an "Indian without ancestry" (20).
Furthermore, as Gerald Vizenor argues in *Fugitive Poses*, "the simulation of
the *indian* is the absence of the native, and that absence is a presence of the
other, the eternal scapegoat, but not a native past; the native is a trace of
presence" (35). The simulation of the Indian, one without ancestry, one
deconstructed to the point of reconstruction, is a reoccurrence that reinforces the identity of settlers. To be even more specific, the vanishing NDN
takes on a different nuance when thought through queerness. In "Doubleweaving Two-Spirit Critiques: Building Alliances Between Native and
Queer Studies," Qwo-Li Driskill observes how "in queer studies, Native
people are largely ignored unless as 'subjects' of anthropological and historical research that demonstrate an idealized 'queer' past that can bolster
non-Native queer identities" (84). I ask: In what ways does this idealized
past, where Indigeneity becomes romanticized into a mystic queer-utopia,
world-make a space of simulation for settler queerness to play within, to
camp within, to be campy within, and/or to transform one's self from an
Enlightened universal into an individual with a genealogy? And how does
this simulated world untangle queerness from its fatalism[5] if only to redirect
that fatalism upon Two-Spirit/Indigiqueer literatures and livelihoods?

In her essay "Notes on 'Camp,'" Susan Sontag observes that camp "is not a natural mode of sensibility . . . indeed the essence of Camp is its love of the unnatural: of artifice and exaggeration. And Camp is esoteric— something of a private code, a badge of identity even" (275). I want to interrogate the distinctions and overlap between camp as a space and camp as a sensibility to flesh out this Indigiqueer idyll as a site of settler queer transformation. In what ways does the camp space camp up the "unnatural," and what means unnatural? As José Esteban Muñoz writes in *Cruising Utopia*, "Queerness is not yet here, the here and now is a prison house," but, as he argues, "We can glimpse the worlds proposed and promised by queerness in the realm of the aesthetic . . . the queer aesthetic frequently contains blueprints and schemata of a forward-dawning futurity. Both the ornamental and the quotidian can contain a map of the utopia that is queerness" (1). For the purpose of my argument, I combine Muñoz and Sontag, despite their differences, as collaborators of a world-building project, one that seeks to project queerness into its rightful futurism, into its utopia. For all of its optimism, I want to think about the problematic structures of such a conflation, both of which, I argue, figure through and by the spacings of camp. What does it mean to world-build a queer utopia and upon whose lands does such a space exist?

Both Sontag and Muñoz theorize and build through aestheticism, for Muñoz containing blueprints, and for Sontag a "way of seeing the world as an aesthetic phenomenon" (277). I argue that such aesthetics, in all of their promises for futurity, depend upon a cooptation of Indigenous land (literal and figurative), and through such a proximity, Indigiqueer bodies, as a type of blueprint, a type of primitive petroglyph. Furthermore, this cooptation materializes in and through the form of literature, and more specifically, queer young adult literature. For example, John Donovan's protagonist Davy[6] interpolates his queerness through the mirroring of a campy NDN feral-child while Emily M. Danforth's Cam Post's[7] queerness becomes inaugurated in the spacings of a Christian queer conversion camp through her conversations with and interpolations of the Two-Spirited Adam Red Eagle. The spaces of transformation for Cam and Davy are predicated upon a mystical notion of an Indigiqueer genealogy that is read as prehistoric; the path to a forward dawning-futurity, it seems, in order to avoid the "prison house of the now" depends wholly upon the campy aestheticism of Indigeneity that delimits and dispossesses Indigiqueerness by placing the immediate *now* into a forgotten *was*. My conflation of camp relies wholly on Byrd's "Indian without ancestry" (20), one that functions as a simulation, and perhaps even a stimulation, for settler queerness to don as a movement out of the past and into Muñoz's futurism.

Muñoz notes: "Futurity becomes history's dominant principle . . . I think of queerness as a temporal arrangement in which the past is a field of possibility in which subjects can act in the present in the service of a new futurity" (16). But whose past and which past? Again, the past that is here enacted is Indigenous. Muñoz's conceptions of utopia, while heartwarming, are akin to the benevolent interventions of boarding/residential schools and camp reformations, though, in this instance, entire histories, lands, and genealogies are reformed to benefit the identities and future prospects of queer settlers. These sentiments are mirrored in Muñoz's utopian methodologies, for which he draws upon the gay liberation journal *Gay Flames* and its demand that "We believe the land . . . belong[s] to the people and must be shared by the people collectively for the liberation of all" to frame his argument (19). The claiming of land, and the "we" invoked, are not attentive to Indigenous land claims whatsoever. In fact, the promise of a queer utopia is anti-relational and rather dystopian for Indigeneity as it further delimits Two-Spirit/Indigiqueer livelihoods. There is no Indigeneity in this collective "we" and there never was.

And while there is a sensibility for collectivity in this idyllic utopic camp, it is a sensibility that "converts the serious into the frivolous," which Sontag notes "are *grave* matters." More specifically, she notes that "most people think of sensibility or taste as the realm of purely subjective preferences, those mysterious attractions, mainly sensual, that have not been brought under *the sovereignty of reason*. They allow that considerations of taste play a part in their reactions to people and to works of art. But this attitude is *naïve*" (276). I place emphasis on Sontag's vocabulary to think through these sentiments, sentiments as a type of affect, affect as a type of feeling historical. Camp, in both of its iterations, morphs the "serious" into the "frivolous," or, it creates an "Indian without ancestry"—an asignifying event that truly becomes a "grave matter." Moreover, these transformations bring meaning and signification under the "sovereignty of reason," and this, as a utopic blueprint, further implicates queer utopias via the Indigiqueer idyll as a space of land theft where sovereignty is attributed not to the Indigeneity tied to the land but to the queer settler who places a rainbow flag in that very soil and calls it utopia—thus what Sontag labels the "naïve," I label the "native." These significations of taste also hail aestheticism not only in terms of preference but aestheticism as a craving for pre-contact hi/stories. If the camp becomes a space of transformation for settler queerness it only does so through the camping up of

Indigiqueerness as a mystical, romantic, ideal idyll that contains the "truth" of queerness as a genealogy untouched by the heteronormativity that maintains the prison house of the "now," a truth that posits Indigeneity as primitive, as feral and fatal. Camp places Indigeneity within quotation marks, marks its "Being-as-Playing-a-Role" (280). This being allows settler colonialism and, more specifically, settler queerness, to become, as Byrd notes, "a worlding anew . . . that decenters all static, grounding belongings and locates them instead in becomings: becoming-Indian, becoming-woman, becoming-America" and becoming-queer (13). In short, the ostensibly natural spaces of camp become the very spaces of an unnatural Indigiqueer becoming.

In *The Modern Age: Turn-of-the-Century American Culture and the Invention of Adolescence*, Kent Baxter offers a compelling perspective on the categories of adolescence and modernity—particularly in his chapters "Every Vigorous Race: Age and Indian Reform Movements" and "Playing Indian: The Rise and Fall of the Woodcraft Youth Movements." His arguments, in conversation with Philip J. Deloria's *Playing Indian*, Vizenor's *Fugitive Poses*, and Brian Dippie's *The Vanishing American*, tease out the braid of adolescence and Indigeneity through play and through camp. Baxter analyzes Ernest Thomas Seton's Woodcraft Indians and the creation of adolescence as an age category that points us wholly towards fantastical misconceptions of a vanishing Indigeneity. Baxter notes that the "process of becoming an adult was a type of artificial adolescence imposed upon Native American youth," thereby positing adolescence as an alter*native* temporality, a camp of sorts, that predisposes Indigeneity through the disposal of Indigenous peoples (74). This conflation, too, hearkens back to North America's ideology of killing the Indian in the child within Canada and the United States's mandate to kill the Indian and save the man. These ruminations direct us toward the ways in which interpellation into the nation-state as a full-fledged and civilized adult requires the death of the Indian, both the real NDN and the one that is inherited as one "native" to the Americas, one coded with ferality.

Baxter observes that Indigeneity is a "curious blend of fatalism and nostalgia" for settler colonialism to capitalize upon (79). This fatalism, when linked with the concept of the "Indian" as perpetually being a "simple child of nature," allows us to see a sort of fate that is fatal for the benefit of settlers (79). And it, too, is this fatalism that Muñoz asks queerness to avoid in the "prison house" of the now—a prison house that is as fated as it is fatal. "Queer fatalism," Sara Ahmed observes, "is how a queer demise is explained and made inevitable . . . queer fatalism = queer as fatal." Her theorizations place us back into the realm of queer young adult literature as she offers a reading of Nancy Garden's *Annie on My Mind* and the conflation of unhappiness with queerness through Lisa's father's statement that "I've never thought gay people can be very happy" (191). "Queer happiness," Ahmed writes, "[is] world making: we do not try to be faithful to what is fatal." This imperative to world-build a utopia, too, becomes a cooptation of Indigenous lands/bodies, Indigenous hi/stories, Indigenous sexualities— in not being faithful to the fatal are we being asked to not be conscious to the fatalism of Indigeneity, to instead focus, as Baxter points out, on the nostalgic? In this light, how does the romantic idyll as a space of refuge, asylum, and settler queer transformation not become a necromantic space for Indigeneity?

"The common construction of the impulsive, conflicted, and rebellious adolescent found its origin . . . at the turn of the century," Baxter argues, and that "this new age category came to represent all that was threatening about modern life" (3). Modernity, with its urbanization and industrialization, was the precursor for the formation of adolescence as a viable age category. With such modernization came specific and long-lasting effects on teenagers. "Rural labor traditions disintegrated," Baxter argues, and "enrollment in high schools doubled in the 1890s, and in that same period, there was a 38.4 percent increase in college enrollment" (4). The new demographic embodied a *fear* for "civilized" adults in that adolescents seemed more akin to stereotypes, such as the hoodlum or the wayward youth, or the "wild child" or "wolf boy" discussed by Kenneth Kidd. G. Stanley Hall viewed adolescence as a period of heightened storm and stress, which became, and remains, indicative of the teenage years in that the hoodlum-esque behavior of adolescence was attributed to conflict with parents, mood disruptions, and risky behavior. Thus, this storm and stress model, as Baxter argues, "put a name to this fear" of the adolescent (5). And this fear of the adolescent is linked with what Kidd, in *Making American Boys*, names as the feral tale. This tale, he argues, "guarantees the legibility of childhood itself, implying a usual path of development and deviation from such" (5). Thus, settlers are put through the idyll in order to manufacture themselves as members of civilization, to trump one's inner-Indigenous-saboteur, to play Indian in order to feel Indian and thereby kill the Indian in their child. The feral tale's lesson for settler colonialism is that the idyllic ferality inborn within the child becomes a concept that is more about "the white, middle-class male's perilous passage from nature to culture, from bestiality to humanity, from homosocial pack life to individual self-reliance and heterosexual prowess—that is, from boyhood to manhood" (Kidd 7).

Thereby the Indigiqueer idyll is formed out of a fear of the now, the *is*, that propels itself into a queer futurism, the *then*, that wholly depends on a nostalgic cooptation of the past, the *was*. The verb "to be" becomes a conjunction of these desires, to be, to be *is*, to be *now*, to be *soon*, all depend on a deflection of the *was*; to be or not to be NDN is the question. Or, as Jodi Byrd notes, "the prior calls into tension the non-presence of that present and the absent Other, past and future, against whom the 'present' aligns itself to come into Being" (8). I propose that the formulation of queered green spaces in queer YA is indicative of, and exemplifies, ingrained settler colonialism that intensifies at the turn of the century through the proximity to and/or the deployment of the "wild-child," "the wolf-boy," "street rats," and the "feral boy." Settler fear around the "wildness" or "ferality" of boyhood is quelled through boarding schools and youth organizations, a practice that requires a resignification of Indianness, a reformation of redness, where settler and settler queer nostalgia become the search for one's own individualism in an age of enlightenment, to kill the Indian in their child, and to remove the queer from universalism; these imperatives are fed via the Indigiqueer idyll: a gender-fluid pre-contact Indigenous hi/story that formulates where the camp and even "the slum become a sort of frontier space" (Kidd 99). Such spaces are used to link adolescence and Indigeneity as inextricably bound concepts within Turtle Island, link Indigeneity in all of its ferality as the "imago for the middle-class white man's inner self" (Kidd 88); these concepts demonstrate how pan-Indigenous hi/stories, cultural practices, spaces, sexualities, gender traditions, and bodies are used to bolster non-Native identities, queered and otherwise. Indigeneity serves as mirror for settler colonialism inasmuch as the Indigiqueer serves as mirror for the settler queer. These spaces become prime grounds for a resurrection of Indigiqueerness, for the settler queer to play within to find their own identity in a pseudo-settler-vision-quest, a calling by a spirit animal (read: *Grindr* tribologies), the queer desire for the feral in order to formulate a place of becoming.

Deferring the Come: Indigenizing Queerness

In moving us from the turn-of-the-century forward to Muñoz's utopic post-Stonewall world-building, we see a similar enactment of anxieties around masculinity and nationalism that are once again wholly dependent upon Indigeneity. John Donovan's *I'll Get There. It Better Be Worth the Trip*, the first young adult novel with visible gay content, exemplified this anxiety in 1969. The novel set a standard of queer suffering that would appear in the first wave of queer YA novels.[8] The trope of "vanishing" worked simultaneously with both queer YA protagonists and Indigeneity—though in vastly asymmetrical planes of power. Queer YA protagonists vanish even as they appear and are interpellated within Ahmed's notion of queer fatalism. Perhaps here is the sensibility of Muñoz's camp, in its love of the artifice, of the unnatural that intersects settler queerness with Indigiqueerness. Though this fatalism, as a shared affect between both, quickly becomes asymmetrical through the search for happiness, the quest for a settler queer utopia, inasmuch as this fatalism becomes deferred through a queer asylum in the Indigiqueer idyll, the green space as camp on unceded and/or stolen territories and hi/stories. Adolescence seemingly seeks to inaugurate settler queerness through the Indigenous idyllic camp, one that allows adolescence to idolize Indigiqueerness into a love-object, a mirror that reflects and grants genealogy and individualism. Indigiqueerness becomes the very aegis that protects and propels settler queerness into its utopic future.

I'll Get There. It Better Be Worth the Trip tells the story of Davy Ross, a lonely thirteen-year-old boy whose love-objects are his recently deceased grandmother, his dachshund Fred, and his classmate Douglas Altschuler. Davy, after his grandmother's death, is sent to live with his dysfunctional, alcoholic mother where he is more tolerated than loved. It is here that Davy is sent to the Episcopal school that becomes the setting for his homosocial and homosexual pairing with Altschuler. Davy's school is deployed as a reformative process through its instillation of virility and self-reliance; however, "wild child" anxieties are also bound up within queerness and the emergence of community-formation as we see through the kinship between the two boys and Davy's mother's horrified response to their relations.

There is a specific instance in *I'll Get There* that gives precedence and presence to Davy's queerness: his Indigenization. Davy comes to terms with his queer identity by making a stuffed coyote in the Museum of Natural History into his love object. Davy narrates:

> You [the coyote] must have had a name. You could have been . . . some Indian kid's pet . . . I think he sees me. Honestly. There is something in his eyes which makes me believe that he understands that I am there and talking to him as a friend . . . I lean over to the glass and kiss it close to his muzzle, and then I see some little kid standing there looking at me. I guess I get red in the face. (68)

Davy has an erotic connection with the coyote, which as a faux-trickster figure[9] is appropriated as an identity-formatting object. Davy leans in, he kisses the coyote, he watches it, and through the reflection of the mirror, he uses Indigeneity to see himself; Indigeneity is the catalyst and foundation of his non-Native queer identity. Davy later notes, "This coyote is a strange creature. He understands. I know he does" (196). The understanding the coyote offers is Davy's queerness, and in this formation of his teenage queerness, Davy gets "red in the face," or to be blunt: he Indigenizes himself in order to activate his queer imago. This pet coyote preserved as the love-object of an "Indian kid" is the reflection of Davy himself. Rather than killing the "Indian" in his child to straighten himself into civility, Davy Indigenizes himself in order to gain access to that same queerness, to remove himself from his imprisoned "now" and place himself into a utopic "then," both of which promise a better tomorrow. But recall Sontag here, for it is the Museum of Natural History that Davy visits, which "converts the serious into the frivolous," converting an Indigenous present into the pre-historic, which Davy reads through the museum's "dinosaur bones" (67). Davy observes that "there's a lot of stuff about American Indians which is pretty interesting, and so are the stuffed American wild animals . . . they are all fixed up so that they seem to be in places where they would be found *naturally*" (emphasis mine, 67). In addition to the coyote, Davy admires both bears and wolves—all sacred animals attributed to Plains Indigenous cultural and spiritual practices. What I find interesting is Davy's description of the coyote as "friendly looking" and the museum's narration that "coyotes become very tame and make attractive pets if they are caught young" (67). Davy's notes on the American Indian return us to the Indigiqueer idyll and my theorization of camp sensibilities. Not only are we bearing witness to the repetition of a wildness-turned-civilized through the taxonomy of these animals; also, they are placated as friendly, as dead, attractive through their availability. Moreover, the story of the youthful coyote made docile through capture can and should be read through the narrative of US/Canadian boarding schools. This Museum of Natural History becomes, what Sontag argues, a "way of seeing the world as an aesthetic phenomenon" (277) through the availability of such totemic and transferable taxonomic animals which signify a temporal removal from Turtle Island's genocidal history. Thereby the aesthetic of the museum and the coyote itself evinces a settler sensibility of an Indigenous disappearance, a way of feeling historical through a naïve and native affect. Thus I'd argue that the museum, in all of its simulations of naturalness and realness (re: unnatural) becomes a microcosm of the Indigiqueer idyll, one that allows a series of becomings, and in this case, queerness becomes palatable only through a series of becoming-animal—and that, too, is a grave matter.

Davy is able to enter the Indigiqueer idyll through transference and per-haps inheritance via the mirror, a tactic that allows him to signify queer-ness, however briefly, as an emerging queer individual. Davy's desire to romanticize in order to bolster a settler queer identity, one that creates a rather necromantic "now" for Indigiqueerness, becomes the foundation for a recycled and recirculated trope within queer YA novels. As he leans into the glass to kiss the coyote, which he observes as "some Indian kid's pet," and reddens his face, Davy's father continually calls him back: "come . . . come" (68). Leaving, Davy materializes the owner of the coyote, the "Indian" kid, which I read as a ghastly gay Indigiqueer, in the very mirror in which he sees himself—he re-members himself by placing queerness into an atemporality. As he is called back to civility from the Indigiqueer idyll, which has attracted him, Davy must placate his wildness in order to claim it; "'Coyotes are tame,' I tell the little kid and run after my father" (69). It is this proclamation that Davy makes that lays the groundwork for the claiming of settler queer identities in and through Indigenous lands and histories in several of the YA texts that will follow its publication; and it is this claiming that is done through camp. For, as Sontag notes, camp is a mysterious attraction that has not been "brought under the sovereignty of reason" (276). Thus, claiming sovereignty over the mysterious (re: wild-ness) creates an atemporal, ahistorical breeding ground for settler queer-ness to inaugurate itself as founder of, one that transforms a naïve attitude into a foundationally native aesthetic, that transforms the campy into a simulated camp. And is the constant calling of Davy's father for him to return from the museum not indicative of Muñoz's utopic blueprints? If Davy is continually in a state of "coming," is the inherent promise of a forward dawning futurity in Donovan's *I'll Get There. It Better Be Worth the Trip* too not a traversal through such an Indigiqueer simulation, a promise of be-coming? This continued space and state of delay becomes a means of preservation that depends wholly on a vanished and appropriated Indi-geneity. Thus, I argue that Davy sets the ground for queer transformation and settles the idyll as a frontier space, a *terra nullius*, and as much as the "Indian kid" and his coyote become filius nullius, so too does the very hi/story of Indigiqueerness.

The Promise of Preservation: A Necromance

The popularity of Emily Danforth's YA novel, *The Miseducation of Cameron Post*, published in 2012, resulted in a 2018 film adaptation. It tells the story of Cam Post and her attempted queer conversion at God's Promise, better known simply as Promise, a reformatory center functioning as a camp. At Promise, Cam befriends Jane, a lesbian with an amputated leg, and Adam Red Eagle, a winkte (Lakota terminology for Two-Spirit). Her friendship with both Jane and Adam leads to her eventual acceptance of her queerness and her induction into the queer life she so readily desires. Adam, introducing himself and Promise to a newly arrived Cam, notes that, "Promise has a way of making you forget yourself . . . [you] sort of disappear here" (310). Adam re-exhibits the trope of the "vanishing Indian" but in a revised fashion, for Adam, too, is at the same queer conversion camp as Cam. In accordance with cultural nationalisms that adopt heteropatriarchy as a means of survivance in a dystopic Indigenous "now"[10]—the revision, I would say, is that the "vanishing Indian" has now become the "vanishing Indigiqueer." Adam announces his slow but sure vanishing act, or his "disappear[ance]" and furthermore notes that Promise is the promise "to live in suspended time" (313).

Adam, in a scene with Cam, (inaccurately) calls himself a "two-souls person," much to Cam's curiosity and amazement (311). He notes that he does not want to be her "sacred and mysterious Injun" (311). Moreover, Cam, meditating on her placement in Promise and on her newfound relations with her campmates, is told that Promise is a place for you to forget your past, forget yourself. Hereafter, Cam argues:

> It's plastic living. It's living in a diorama. It's living the life of one of those prehistoric insects encased in amber: suspended, frozen, dead, but not, you don't know for sure. Those things could have a pulse inside that hard world of honey and orange, the ticking of some life force, and I'm not talking about *Jurassic Park* and dinosaur blood . . . but just the insect itself, trapped, waiting. But even if the amber could somehow be melted, and it could be freed, physically unharmed, how could it be expected to live in this new world without its past, without everything it knew from the world before, from its place in it? (313)

Cameron's ruminations on the prehistoric, by which I mean an Indigiqueer idyllic simulation, clash with her emerging queerness and her newfound relationship with Adam. In being asked to forget her queer past and "straighten" out, Cam begins to Indigenize herself, to play Indian, to skinwalk as an Indigiqueer. Rather than prehistoric, I argue Cam means to align herself with the precontact fantasy of a campy Indigenous queerness. That, I argue, is what is trapped within these amber bubbles. Indigiqueerness exists in an alter*native* (re: naïve) universe, a campy aesthetic; it is "suspended, frozen, dead." The chronotope of the idyll does not apply here;

this is the chronotope of a universe out of time, out of place, the chronotope of the Indigiqueer idyll. And Cam is correct in her observations: How *can* the insect encased in amber live in this new world without a past when that past is so readily coopted by her, the pseudo-Dr. Alan Grant greedily running his fingers over the genetically cloned eggs of an extinct species? In such a fashion, I would argue that institutions such as Promise—read as a camp, a reformative and transformative space—which are heteropatriarchal, religious, colonial, and nuclear, coexist with a queerness that adapts these same institutions. Both spaces collectively create for themselves a "diorama," or perhaps it is best to say they too create a faux Jurassic Park. This virtual world with cloned native ghosts and custom skins readily available to wear for whiteness, albeit queer or not, to don and play with in order to fully realize their detriment: They're white, not Indigenous, and therefore must grow up and straighten out.

In the final scene of the book Cam, alongside Adam and Jane, run away from Promise and return to Quake Lake, the newly formed lake made by an earthquake and a dammed river, also the place where Cam's parents died in a car accident. Coming to the lake, Cam observes a group of trees on the other side of the lake that are stuck in the water, barely visible. "They're like the ghosts of trees," Jane announces, to which Cam replies, "They're skeleton trees" (457). As they move closer Cam notes that "the closer [she] got, the stranger those skeleton trees looked . . . since the water had come and come and *settled* around them" (emphasis mine 458). Afterwards, Cam asks Adam about the Lakota people and their legends: "Who was that Lakota giant—the one who was supposed to be like visible to man forever ago, but isn't now?" (458). As Cam further questions Adam, she is informed: "This could be Yata territory. Yata is way into ceremonies. That's kind of what you're doing here, right" (459). Cam's faux-ceremonial performance functions to enable her to come to terms with her queerness and to absolve her guilt over her parents' deaths. She then takes a candle, lights it, strips naked, and walks into the freezing cold lake all the while holding the candle above the water. "If I wanted to make it to that skeleton forest," Cam announces, "I was going to have to swim" (465). Cam's desire is to enter the alter*native* space—the place beyond where the skeleton trees, the now unseen giants, and the dead Yata exist. Once fully emerged in the water Cam announces:

> I ha[ve]n't even become me yet. Maybe I still haven't become me. I don't know how you tell for sure when you finally have. I tilted the candle just so and let all the melted wax pooled around the wick spill

free and cascade down my knuckles, the trail at first translucent, then quickly hardening into a river of white on top of my skin. Lots of wax cascaded all the way down my hand, off the edge, and into the lake, and once there became magical. (468)

She realizes her queerness by performing a faux-ceremony, by giving herself a queer baptism into/with/beside her adolescence and desire to Indigenize, to fossilize herself. For, if we recall the earlier scene I quoted, the ideas of being encapsulated in amber and of being prehistoric/precontact are intertwined. While Cam allows the candle to melt over her hand, she forcibly inserts herself into this alter*native* world by Indigenizing herself—by becoming prehistoric/precontact, by making Indigiqueer into a certain type of camp, and by bringing a mysterious, wild, campy sensibility under her "sovereignty of reason." Cam, much like Davy, enters herself into a series of becomings (re: role-playing, simulations) through her insertion into this Indigiqueer idyll; becoming-Indigenous, becoming-dead, and thereby being reborn into a state of becoming-queer. And it is this becoming which seems to strategically preserve Cam; her "plastic living," that preservation, through Camp Promise allows her to bypass Muñoz's "prison house of the now" and project herself into the promise of a dawning futurity. By converting the Indigenous into the frivolous, she is able to forgo the grave-matters of both her immediate *now* and propel herself beyond the forgotten *was*, which seems to want to sing a genocidal song (re: the Yata), through the land(s) around her.

Is this romantic conception of the "Jurassic," by which I mean prehuman, not predicated upon Indigeneity? Even Gayatri Chakravorty Spivak has called Indigenous peoples the impossible prehistoric pterodactyl.[11] I am reminded of Chris Pratt's Owen Grady and ask that we look to *Jurassic World* for an answer. "I was in the navy," Grady proclaims, "not the Navajo." In conversation with Cam Post: What does it mean to shape-shift into an Indigenized prehistory? For she seems to bolster expectations of Indigeneity for settlers and various other global Indigenous groups to mold the NDN into a static being entrapped in amber as if it's some prehistoric Jurassic velociraptor. But what if Indigiqueerness were to reclaim the camp, to reterritorialize it, emphasis on the *terror* in that verb, where "to be" becomes an *is*, a *now* for the fatalism of a vanishing Indigiqueerness—what if we made campy this idyll to become our own badge of honor, as Sontag notes? What if we reclaimed our positions as "wolf-boys" and "feral kids" as a means of resurgence? Then doesn't this pre-historical, pre-human, pre-contact idyll coded with the Jurassic not become feral: to overwhelm with rapt, as in an overt fascination, or be carried away bodily to heaven (be raptured), or even to rapt, to seize, to plunder? And isn't velocity just another story of wind, another stressful storm?

Settler colonialism seeks to make Indigeneity biologically and essentially reproducible through vanishing acts and campy appropriations—what settlers do not know is that they have summoned ferality, summoned ghosts. Or, as Haraway argues, "bestiality has a new status in this cycle of marriage exchange" (11). Indigiqueer ferality is a means of procreation, of resurgence, of eroticism. If we exist in amber we, too, are ghosted into time, from the *was* into the *is*, from the then into the now, wreaking havoc as a mutated hybrid behemoth, Indominus (read: Indigenous) Rex procreated with an origin, produced without heterosexuality, without settler colonialism. Do we become the vessels for futurity and phase in the peripheries as Apache helicopters, as chemical concoctions (read: miniscule, atomic) made to entertain but choosing to eviscerate? I point us toward Desiree Akhavan's 2018 film adaptation of *Cameron Post*. The film features Forrest Goodluck as Adam Red Eagle—an interesting choice given Forrest played Hawk, Hugh Glass's Pawnee son, in *The Revenant*. Feral NDNS on the peripheries again.

In Cam's case, questions of "Who am I?" are answered by the space, which she observes: "My voice sound[ed] strange, like it belonged to the lake and not to me" (467). Cam, forcibly entering this alter*native* space, makes the subaltern speak and it says, "you are me." This, I would argue, is the function of settler queerness at large: to adapt, assimilate, and adopt Indigeneity to fit its own needs and to bolster its own identity. But what if the invisible Lakota giant struck and denied Cam? For, as the final paragraph explains, it is Adam who pulls Cam from the frigid and killing water, rebirthing her as a queer subject. The narrator notes that "Adam sloshed into the water . . . pulling me up fast and perfect as if he'd done it so many times before . . . [he] walked me to the shore, which was black and endless . . . and there was a whole world beyond that shoreline, beyond the forest . . . beyond, beyond, beyond" (470). Cam realizes the inherent terror in the Yata's territory; the beyond, she announces, seeks to create the machinations of Deleuze and Guatarri's desiring-machines which are built like a *Westworld*-esque camp made up of "and, and, and," again: simulation, stimulation, transformation. It is Adam who is accustomed to this terror, as well as this faux settler queer ceremony, and Adam who holds the agency in reviving or revoking Cam. Is Cam's repetition of "beyond" not a sort of paralysis? Having raised the veil and seen the simulation, does it not petrify/amberify her? Does Indigiqueerness not become a body snatcher or shape shifter in order to destroy space and thereby claim space?

Cam asks: What if "the amber could be melted, and it could be freed" (313)? As J Kēhaulani Kauanui tells us, "settler colonialism has historically deemed non-Christian concepts of the *sacred* as a form of *savage* superstition" (emphasis mine). What if we read the act of being sacred as the act of being *scared*? What if we embody the *terror* embedded in territorialisation? What if we rip apart that rainbow flag planted in Muñoz's utopia and replace it with our own Indigiqueer sovereignty of reason? I agree that, yes, without a past, Indigiqueerness has no means of surviving this "new world"—but what if we wrench our pasts from the identities we so happily accommodate? If Indigiqueerness is marked with fatalism, is it too feral? And if feral, is it too fatal? Does its resurgence rely upon retaliation? If it melts, does it emerge anew: taloned, clawed, feral, and Indigiqueer? There is a divide between Indigiqueer historical disappearance and its future re-emergence, that, I argue, is the alter*native* space, a graveyard, the Indigiqueer idyll where settler colonial identities enter and evolve, spaces that Indigenous cultural nationalisms have denied and buried—but that space is a space of becoming to and for Indigiqueerness, that space is haunted, that space is energized, that space is necromantic, not a romance. Cam's meditation relies wholly upon one thing: fear. The fear of a reverse colonization of a colonized queerness, the great fear of the Indigenous "beyond, beyond, beyond" and the fear of an emergence of an Indigiqueer revenant: feral and fatal.

On Indiginegativity: We'Wha Ex Nihilo

In attempting to formulate a methodology for Indigiqueerness as a praxis of resistance I want to turn us back to the child. To conclude, I propose a conceptual re-storying of settler queerness and Indigiqueerness as a means of procuring a theoretical framework for Two-Spirit survivance. If settler queerness bolsters itself through Muñoz's utopia and the Indigiqueer idyll as a space of literal and metaphorical camp, then ought Indigiqueerness rip a page from Lee Edelman's *No Future* to formulate a kind of negation of this appropriation? While Edelman discusses the Child as a formulation of reproductive futurisms, there is a sort of conceptual Child being crafted by and for settler queerness when I align Muñoz with my Indigiqueer. This type of utopic futurism, of removing the Child from the "prison house of the now" is a means of producing, perhaps, a nonreproductive futurism, but

one still predicated on the continued survival of the Child through reproductive futurisms. And this type of futurism, reproductive or nonreproductive, requires capitalism and settler colonialism to produce a sovereignty of
its own, a queer nation that settles Indigiqueerness. For in settler queerness's desire to move beyond, as with Edelman's queer negativity, or in
Muñoz's case a projection into a forward dawning futurity, both methodologies, without an Indigenous decolonial praxis, require desire and movement, both require a transit, albeit sideways or forward, that is wholly
embedded within and continually interpolated by empire.

And it is Edelman's "Child" whom I posit as the nexus of these settler
colonial fantasies. The Child, he argues, is "imagined as enjoying unmediated access to Imaginary wholeness" (10), and here, expanding further, I'd
also add the Child gains unmediated access to an Imaginary wildness. This
figural child, Edelman argues, "alone embodies the citizen as an ideal,
[one] entitled to claim full rights to its future share in the nation's good
[and here I'd also add the nation's land] through always at the cost of limiting the rights of 'real' citizens" (11). In what ways does this conceptual
child work against Indigeneity? A child who must master and settle its own
wildness in order to procure civility, or a child who must embrace its wildness in order to procure its queerness? To be even more specific, in what
ways does "the Child" dispossess Indigiqueerness? Can Edelman offer
Indigiqueerness a methodology to re-map our social, bodily, affective, and
national realities through negation? This negation I call Indiginegativity. I
say we take a note from Edelman, who claims, "rather than rejecting . . .
this ascription of negativity to the queer . . . [we] do better to consider
accepting and even embracing it" (4). If it is the fatalism of Indigeneity, and
moreover Indigiqueerness, to vanish and die, I say we perform our own
vanishing acts, that we reverse the imperative to "kill the Indian in the
child" and instead kill "the Child" in the NDN. I want to build upon Edelman's argument that we "begin again ex nihilo" (9). To world-destroy is to
make space to world-build, to perform our own vanishing acts is to produce identity as a "mortification" (25) but it, too, is a jouissance, a lovely
blossoming of sexed bodies, lives, and practices: My ectoplasm is a valiant
orgasm, my becoming is a series of comings. To be an Indigiqueer "wolf-
boy" or to craft an Indigiqueer feral fairy tale is a type of creationism, a
campy aesthetic, a pseudo-camp. We stimulate ourselves in order to simu-
late ourselves as self-sovereign, self-defined, methodologies of survivance.
I ask that we remember that we do not own the land, rather the land owns
itself, and we, by extension, own ourselves, our sexualities, our bodies, our
histories, our futurities. If we let *ex nihilo* become *creatio ex nihilo*, the camp

too can become an Indigiqueer creation story: There, I say, is We'Wha. So kill the Child in the NDN: Going feral can be an act of decolonialism.

NOTES

1. A term I use to braid together Northrop Frye's idyll and Achille Mbembe's "Necropolitics."

2. I deploy We'Wha, a Zuni Two-Spirit individual, as they often become the epitome of a pan-Two-Spirit/Indigiqueerness for settler queerness and Indigenous cultural nationalisms alike. See Will Roscoe's *The Zuni Man-Woman* (1991).

3. As a caveat, I deploy "Indian" in this essay in regard to the literature that names it as such. I use NDN as a reclamation, and Indigiqueer as a compound to further the self-determination of Two-Spirit (2S) people who may not use that terminology. Furthermore, Indigiqueer becomes a noun I use to fuse together both Indigenous and queer theory.

4. For more examples not included in this essay, see Isabelle Holland's *The Man Without a Face* (1972), Nancy Garden's *Annie on My Mind* (1982), and David Levithan's *Boy Meets Boy* (2003).

5. See Sara Ahmed's 2017 blogpost "Queer Fatalism."

6. *I'll Get There. It Better Be Worth the Trip* (1969).

7. *The Miseducation of Cameron Post* (2012).

8. See Michael Cart and Christine Jenkins's *The Heart Has Its Reasons* (2006) and Derritt Mason's "A Phallic Dog, A Stuffed Coyote, and the Boy Who Won't Come Out" (2016) for more on Donovan's novel.

9. See Thomas King's *Green Grass, Running Water* (1993) or Deanna Reder's *Troubling Tricksters: Revisioning Critical Conversations* (2010).

10. I deploy this claim due, in part, to the ongoing peripheral status of Indigiqueer/Two-Spirit livelihoods, histories, traditions, and literatures—for example, the illegalization of same-sex marriage in some sovereign nations, the removal of 2S from the national inquiry into MMIWG, and skirt-shaming and gendered ceremonies/traditions, as well as the lack of accountability for 2S health, lives, and sexualities in Canada's Truth and Reconciliation Commission.

11. *Death of a Discipline*, 80–81.

ACKNOWLEDGMENTS

Camp is a *tender* feeling

—SUSAN SONTAG, "Notes on 'Camp'"

KENNETH B. KIDD: I would like to thank Derritt, first of all, for being such a lovely and smart co-counselor. I would totally trust him on a 36-day canoe trip. I remain grateful to husband Martin, mother Doris, sister Kathryn, mother-in-law Carolyn, and the extended Smith-Provencher-Baumstark posse. I recognize also my Friday Mountain family, including but exceeding the Kidd clan. Fondly I remember and miss my grandparents, Von Catherine and Rodney J. "Captain" Kidd, and my father, Byron Lunsford Kidd, eighteen years old when Friday Mountain opened in 1947 and working as counselor and grocery boy. So many memories, personal and collective. While not all Friday Mountain alums will approve of my remarks or this project, I thank them all the same. Special thanks to former camper Andy Simpson for ongoing friendship, and to Scott Poteet, co-counselor, friend, life role model.

DERRITT MASON: In turn, I would like to thank Kenneth for being a dream collaborator and mentor. On top of his skill as a nature guide, Kenneth is adept at leading junior scholars like myself through their first editorial forays. He is truly worthy of the title "Honor Camper." I'm grateful to my parents, Bob and Sue, for sending me to camp—especially for having forced me back that second year, and never questioning it when I kept returning for another fourteen. Thanks to my sister Tamara for enduring any insufferable, sanctimonious behavior I may have demonstrated upon my annual return to the city. As I was co-writing the introduction, fellow camp-cademics Alexa Scully and Stuart Henderson were helpful interlocutors.

I'm especially indebted to my summer home for sixteen years, the Taylor Statten Camps. My network of former TSC campers and colleagues has been an enduring, vital source of friendship and support. I have benefited tremendously from and am deeply thankful for the leadership opportunities Taylor "Tike" Statten afforded me. TSC is situated on Anishinaabe land; this land includes the territories of the Ojibwe, Chippewa, Odawa, and Algonquin peoples. I am privileged to have spent so many summers as a guest on this land, and I am heartened to know that current staff members are working to address camp's colonial legacy. I also heard that the girls' camp hosted a Pride parade last summer. That's pretty cool. You're up next, boys!

Finally, I dedicate this book to Taylor, Jeff, Mark, Joe, and Jamie, the boys of Malibu Shores, my forever-friends and cabin mates in queer camping.

KK & DM: Together, we would like to thank our contributors for their compelling essays. It's not so easy to write about queer feelings and experiences, especially those drawn from childhood, and we appreciate all the enthusiasm, candor, and hard work. Gratitude and tender feeling also for the queer scholars who make possible this kind of scholarship, and to the global community of children's literature studies.

We are grateful to Daniel Mallory Ortberg for permission to reprint "Notes Home from Camp, by Susan Sontag," which first appeared on the website *The Toast*, and to Kyle Eveleth, for permission to publish a revised version of "Striking Camp: Empowerment and Re-Presentation in *Lumberjanes*," first published as part of *Good Grief! Children and Comics*, edited by Michelle Ann Abate and Joe Sutliff Sanders, an online companion volume to a 2016 exhibit at the Billy Ireland Cartoon Library and Museum at Ohio State University. We also acknowledge *Women and Performance: A Journal of Feminist Theory* for permission to reprint Kathryn R. Kent's "'No Trespassing': Girl Scout Camp and the Limits of the Counterpublic Sphere" (Issue 8.2, 1996, 185–202). Kathryn kindly wrote a new preface for her essay, as well.

Our thanks to the Faculty of Arts at the University of Calgary for funding these reprints, and to University of Calgary graduate students Paul Meunier and Emily Treppenhauer, who assisted with the preparation of the manuscript.

We have been fortunate indeed to call Fordham University Press home and are most grateful for the support of Richard Morrison, John Garza, and the whole Fordham team. Our two anonymous reviewers provided brilliant and generous feedback, and the volume is much improved thanks to their care.

Acker, Sandra. "Feminist Theory and the Study of Gender and Education." *International Review of Education* 33, no. 4 (1987): 419–35.

Adler, Melissa. *Cruising the Library: Perversities in the Organization of Knowledge.* New York: Fordham University Press, 2017.

Agamben, Giorgio. *Homo Sacer: Sovereign Power and Bare Life.* Translated by Daniel Heller-Roazen. Stanford: Stanford University Press, 1998.

———. "What Is a Camp?" In *Means without End: Notes on Politics.* Translated by Vincenzo Binetti and Cesare Casarino. Minneapolis: University of Minnesota Press (2000): 37–45.

Ahmed, Sara. *The Cultural Politics of Emotion.* Abingdon, UK: Routledge, 2004.

———. "Orientations: Toward a Queer Phenomenology." *GLQ: A Journal of Lesbian and Gay Studies* 12, no. 4 (2006): 543–74.

———. "Queer Fatalism." *Feministkilljoys.* Feministkilljoys (2017), https://feministkilljoys.com/2017/01/13/queer-fatalism/.

———. *Queer Phenomenology: Orientations, Objects, Others.* Durham, N.C.: Duke University Press, 2006.

The AIDS Memorial Quilt. The NAMES Project Foundation (2018). www.aidsquilt.org.

Akhavan, Desiree, dir. *The Miseducation of Cameron Post.* Parkville Pictures, 2017.

Allen, Arthur B. "The Sex-Rot Abroad." *The Flail: An Independent Kibbo Kift Magazine* 5, no. 1 (1927): 172–76.

Almaguer, Tomas. "Letter to Jackie Goldsby." *Out/Look: National Gay and Lesbian Quarterly* 13 (1991): 4–5.

Anderson, Robert Mapes. *Vision of the Disinherited: The Making of American Pentecostalism.* Oxford: Oxford University Press, 1979.

Anderson, Wes, dir. *Fantastic Mr. Fox.* Indian Paintbrush, 2009.

———. *The Life Aquatic with Steve Zissou.* Touchstone Pictures, 2004.

———. *Moonrise Kingdom.* Indian Paintbrush, 2012.

Austerlitz, Saul. *Another Fine Mess: A History of American Film Comedy.* Chicago: Review Press, 2012.

Babuscio, Jack. "Camp and the Gay Sensibility." In *Camp Grounds: Style and Homosexuality*, edited by David Bergman, 19–38. Amherst: University of Massachusetts Press, 1993.

———. "Camp and the Gay Sensibility." In *Gays and Film*, edited by Richard Dyer, 40–57. London: British Film Institute, 1977.

———. "Camp and the Gay Sensibility." In *Gays and Film*, edited by Richard Dyer, 40–57. New York: Zoetrope, 1984.

———. "The Cinema of Camp (AKA Camp and the Gay Sensibility)." In *Camp: Queer Aesthetics and the Performing Subject*, edited by Fabio Cleto, 116–35. Ann Arbor: University of Michigan Press, 1999.

Badley, J. H., et al. *Experiments in Sex Education*. London: Federation of Progressive Societies and Individuals, 1935.

Bakhtin, Mikhail. "The Idyllic Chronotope in the Novel." In *The Dialogic Imagination*, 224–36. Austin: University of Texas Press, 1981.

Baldwin, James. *The Fire Next Time*. New York: Vintage, 1993.

Baxter, Kent. *The Modern Age: Turn-of-the-Century American Culture and the Invention of Adolescence*. Tuscaloosa: University of Alabama Press, 2008.

Belfi, Barbara, et al. "The Effect of Class Composition by Gender and Ability on Secondary School Students' School Well-Being and Academic Self-Concept: A Literature Review." *Educational Research Review* 7, no. 1 (2012): 62–74.

Benjamin, Jessica. *The Bonds of Love: Psychoanalysis, Feminism & the Problem of Domination*. New York: Pantheon Books, 1988.

Bennett, Roger, and Jules Shell. *Camp Camp: Where Fantasy Island Meets Lord of the Flies*. New York: Crown Archetype, 2008.

Benshoff, Harry M. *Monsters in the Closet: Homosexuality and the Horror Film*. Manchester: Manchester University Press, 1997.

Bergman, David, ed. *Camp Grounds: Style and Homosexuality*. Amherst: University of Massachusetts Press, 1993.

Berlant, Lauren. "Slow Death (Sovereignty, Obesity, Lateral Agency)." *Critical Inquiry* 33, no. 4. Chicago: University of Chicago Press, 2007, 754–80.

Berry, Alison. "Review: *Lumberjanes #1*." *Comicosity* April 14, 2014, www.comicosity.com/review-lumberjanes-1/.

Bersani, Leo. *Homos*. Cambridge: Harvard University Press, 1995.

Betsky, Aaron. *Queer Space: Architecture and Same-Sex Desire*. New York: William Morrow, 1997.

Bey, Hakim. *T. A. Z.: The Temporary Autonomous Zone*. New York: Autonomedia, 1991.

Bildner, Elisa Spungen. *Our History*. Foundation for Jewish Camp, 2017, http://jewishcamp.org/about/history/.

Bloom, Harold. *The American Religion*. New York: Chu Hartley Publishers, 1992.

Bogdan, Robert C., and Sari Knopp Biklen. *Qualitative Research for Education: An Introduction to Theories and Methods*, 5th edition. Boston: Pearson, 2006.

Boldt, Gail Masuchika. "Sexist and Heterosexist Responses to Gender Bending in an Elementary Classroom." *Curriculum Inquiry* 26, no. 2 (1996): 113–31.

Booth, Mark. "Campe-toi! On the Origins and Definitions of Camp." In *Camp: Queer Aesthetics and the Performing Subject*, edited by Fabio Cleto, 66–79. Ann Arbor: University of Michigan Press, 1999.

Bourdieu, Pierre. *Distinction: A Social Critique of the Judgment of Taste*. Cambridge: Harvard University Press, 1984.

Bridcut, John. *Britten's Children*. London: Faber & Faber, 2006.

Brimhall, Traci. "Glossolalia." *New England Review* 30, no. 1 (2009): 71.

Britzman, Deborah P. "Is There a Queer Pedagogy?: Or, Stop Reading Straight." *Educational Theory* 45, no. 2 (1995): 151–65.

Brown, Gillian. *Domestic Individualism: Imagining Self in Nineteenth-Century America*. Berkeley: University of California Press, 1990.

Bruhm, Steven, and Natasha Hurley, eds. *Curiouser: On the Queerness of Children*. Minneapolis: University of Minnesota Press, 2004.

———, eds. Introduction to *Curiouser: On the Queerness of Children*, ix–xxxviii. Minneapolis: University of Minnesota Press, 2004.

Bryant, Marsha, and Douglas Mao. "Camp Modernism Introduction." *Modernism/Modernity* 23, no. 1. Baltimore: Johns Hopkins University Press, 2016, 1–4.

Bryson, Mary, and Suzanne De Castell. "Queer Pedagogy: Praxis Makes Im/Perfect." *Canadian Journal of Education/Revue Canadienne de L'éducation* 18, no. 3 (1993): 285–305.

Buckler, Helen, Mary F. Fiedler, and Marth F. Allen. *Wo-He-Lo: The Story of Camp Fire Girls 1910–1960*. New York: Holt, Rinehart and Winston, 1961.

Butler, Judith. *Bodies That Matter: On the Discursive Limits of "Sex."* London: Routledge, 1993.

———. *Gender Trouble: Feminism and the Subversion of Identity*. London: Routledge, 1990.

———. *Undoing Gender*. Abingdon, UK: Routledge, 2004.

Byam, Wally. "Wally Byam's Creed & Code of Ethics." WBCCI/The Airstream Club Caravans, http://wbccicaravan.wbcci.net/about-2/members/.

Byrd, Jodi A. *The Transit of Empire: Indigenous Critiques of Colonialism*. Minneapolis: University of Minnesota Press, 2011.

Campbell, Patricia B., and Ellen Wahl. "What's Sex Got to Do With It? Simplistic Questions, Complex Answers." In *Separated by Sex: A Critical Look at Single-Sex Education for Girls*, 63–73. Washington: American Association of University Women Educational Foundation, 1998.

Caplice, Kristin S. "The Case for Public Single-Sex Education." In *Harv. JL & Pub. Pol'y* 18 (1994): 227.

Carpan, Carolyn. *Sisters, Schoolgirls, and Sleuths: Girls' Series Books in America.* Lanham, Md.: Scarecrow Press, 2009.

Cart, Michael, and Christine A. Jenkins. *The Heart Has Its Reasons.* Lanham, Md.: Scarecrow Press, 2006.

Caruth, Cathy. Introduction to *Trauma: Explorations in Memory*, edited by Cathy Caruth, 1–12. Baltimore: John Hopkins University Press, 1995.

Chamberlain, Megan. "Revisiting Our History With a Modern Lens." *Farm & Wilderness*, 2017, www.farmandwilderness.org/2017/04/27/revisiting -history-modern-lens/.

Chattopaday, Tamo, and Linda Pennells. "Single-Sex Schools for Girls and Gender Equality in Education." *UNESCO Asia and Pacific Regional Bureau for Education*, UNESCO Bangkok, 2007.

Clark, Les, dir. *Paul Bunyan.* Walt Disney Pictures, 1958.

Clarke, Jackie, and John Flynn. "Showgirls. The Best Movie Ever Made. Ever!" *The Upright Citizen's Brigade, UCB Theatre*, directed by Jason Mant Zoukas, Upright Citizens Brigade Theatre New York, Sept. 2005–Apr. 2006.

Cleto, Fabio S. Introduction to *Camp: Queer Aesthetics and the Performing Subject*, edited by Fabio S. Cleto, 1–42. Ann Arbor: University of Michigan Press.

Cleto, Fabio S., ed. *Camp: Queer Aesthetics and the Performing Subject.* Ann Arbor: University of Michigan Press, 1999.

Clover, Carol. *Men, Women, and Chainsaws: Gender in The Modern Horror Film.* Princeton: Princeton University Press, 1992.

Cobb, Michael. *Single: Arguments for the Uncoupled.* New York: NYU Press, 2012.

Cohen Ferris, Marcie. "God First, You Second, Me Third: An Exploration of Quiet Jewishness at Camp Wah-Kon-Dah." *Southern Cultures* 18, no. 1 (2012): 58–70.

Cohen, G. A. *Why Not Socialism?* Princeton: Princeton University Press, 2009.

Cohen, Steven M., et al. "Camp Works: The Long-Term Impact of Jewish Overnight Camp." New York: Foundation for Jewish Camp, 2011.

Cook, Karen. "Regarding Harriet: Louise Fitzhugh Comes in from the Cold." *VLS* (1995): 12–15.

Core, Philip. *Camp: The Lie That Tells the Truth.* New York: Putnam, 1984.

The Course of Instruction. Woodcraft Folk, 1928, Woodcraft Folk archival collection, Folk House.

Creed, Barbara. "Horror and the Monstrous-Feminine: An Imaginary Abjection." In *The Dread of Difference: Gender and the Horror Film*, edited by Barry Keith Grant, 35–65. Austin: University of Texas Press, 1996.

Cvetkovich, Ann. *An Archive of Feelings: Trauma, Sexuality, and Lesbian Public Cultures.* Durham, N.C.: Duke University Press, 2003.

DaCosta, Morton, dir. *Auntie Mame*. Warner Brothers Pictures, 1958.

Danforth, Emily M. *The Miseducation of Cameron Post*. New York: Harper-Collins Publishers, 2012.

Davis, Mary. *Fashioning a New World: A History of the Woodcraft Folk*. Loughborough, UK: Holyoake Books, 2000.

de Abaitua, Matthew. *The Art of Camping: The History and Practice of Sleeping Under the Stars*. New York: Penguin, 2012.

de Lauretis, Teresa. *The Practice of Love: Lesbian Sexuality and Perverse Desire*. Bloomington: Indiana University Press, 1994.

de Leeuw, Sarah. "Writing as Righting: Truth and Reconciliation, Poetics, and New Geo-graphing in Colonial Canada." *The Canadian Geographer* 61, no. 3 (2017): 306–18.

Deleuze, Gilles, and Félix Guattari. *Anti-Oedipus: Capitalism and Schizophrenia*. New York: Viking Press, 1977.

———. "Becoming-Animal." In *The Animals Reader: The Essential Classic and Contemporary Writings*, edited by Linda Kalof and Amy Fitzgerald, 37–50. Oxford and New York: Berg, 2007.

———. *A Thousand Plateaus: Capitalism and Schizophrenia*. Minneapolis: University of Minnesota Press, 1987.

Deloria, Philip J. *Playing Indian*. New Haven, Conn.: Yale University Press, 1998.

Denisoff, Dennis. *Aestheticism and Sexual Parody, 1840–1940*. Cambridge: Cambridge University Press, 2001.

Dika, Vera. "The Stalker Film, 1978–81." In *American Horrors: Essays on the Modern American Horror Film*, edited by Gregory A. Waller, 86–202. Champaign: University of Illinois Press, 1987.

Dippie, Brian. *The Vanishing American*. Lawrence: University Press of Kansas, 1970.

Donovan, John. *I'll Get There. It Better Be Worth the Trip*. 1969, reprint, Woodbury, Minn.: Flux, 2010.

Driskill, Qwo-Li. "Doubleweaving Two-Spirit Critiques: Building Alliances Between Native and Queer Studies." *GLQ* 16, nos. 1–2 (2010): 69–92.

Duggan, Lisa. *The Twilight of Equality: Neoliberalism, Cultural Politics, and the Attack on Democracy*. Boston: Beacon Press, 2003.

Duggan, Lisa, and José Esteban Muñoz. "Hope and Hopelessness: A Dialogue." *Women & Performance: A Journal of Feminist Theory* 19, no. 2; *Between Psychoanalysis and Affect: A Public Feelings Project* (2009): 275–83.

Dyer, Richard. *Gays and Film*. London: British Film Institute, 1974, 1977.

———. *Heavenly Bodies: Film Stars and Society*. London: Routledge, 1986.

———. "It's Being So Camp as Keeps Us Going." *Body Politic* (1977): 11–13.

———. "It's Being So Camp as Keeps Us Going." *Camp: Queer Aesthetics and the Performing Subject*, edited by Fabio S. Cleto, 110–16. Ann Arbor: University of Michigan Press, 1999.

———. *White: Essays on Race and Culture*. London: Routledge, 1997.

Eager, William. *Making Men: A History of Boys' Clubs*. London: University of London Press, 1953.

Edelman, Lee. *No Future: Queer Theory and the Death Drive*. Durham, N.C.: Duke University Press, 2004.

Edgell, Derek. *The Order of Woodcraft Chivalry 1916–1949 as a New Age Alternative to the Boy Scouts*. Lewiston, N.Y.: Edwin Mellen Press, 1992.

Edmonds, Michael. *Out of the Northwoods: The Many Lives of Paul Bunyan*. Madison: Wisconsin Historical Society Press, 2009.

Eells, Eleanor. *Eleanor Eells' History of Organized Camping: The First 100 Years*. Martinsville, Ind.: American Camping Association, 1986.

Eisner, Michael D. *Camp*. New York: Warner Books, 2005.

Eliot, Charles. *Directions: Youth Development Outcomes of the Camp Experience*. 1922. Martinsville, Ind.: American Camping Association, 2005.

Evans, I. O. *Woodcraft and World Service*. London: Noel Douglas, 1930.

Evans, Walter. "Monster Movies: A Sexual Theory." In *Planks of Reason: Essays On The Horror Film*, edited by Barry Keith Grant, 53–64. Lanham, Md., and London: Scarecrow Press, 1996.

Fair, Henry. "Interview with Paul Bemrose, 1988." In *Fashioning a New World: A History of the Woodcraft Folk*, edited by Mary Davis. Loughborough, UK: Holyoake Books, 2000.

Faithfull, Theodore J. *Bisexuality: An Essay on Extraversion and Introversion*. London: John Bale, Sons & Danielsson, Ltd., 1927.

Farm & Wilderness. Farm & Wilderness Foundation, www.farmandwilderness.org.

Fegenbaum, Anna, Fabian Frenzel, and Patrick McCurdy. *Protest Camps*. London: Zed Books, 2013.

Feil, Ken. *Dying for a Laugh: Disaster Movies and the Camp Imagination*. Middletown, Conn.: Wesleyan University Press, 2005.

Feldman, Kiera. "The Romance of Birthright Israel." *The Nation*, 2011, www.thenation.com/article/romance-birthright-israel/.

Fernbach, David. *The Spiral Path: A Gay Contribution to Human Survival*. New York: Alyson Publications, 1981.

Ferrara, Peter J., and Margaret M. Ferrara. "Single-Gender Classrooms: Lessons from a New York Middle School." *ERS Spectrum* 22, no. 3 (2004): 26–32.

Field, Douglas. "Pentecostalism and All That Jazz: Tracing James Baldwin's Religion." *Literature and Theology* 22, no. 4 (2008): 436–57.

Fields, Noah. "Slave Chains and Faggots and Camp . . . Oh My!" *Bluestockings Magazine*, 2015, bluestockingsmag.com/2015/11/04/slave-chains-and-faggots-and-camp-oh-my/.

Finch, Mark. "Sex and Address in 'Dynasty.'" *Screen* 27, no. 6, (1986): 24–43.

Fitzhugh, Louise. *Harriet the Spy*. New York: Harper and Row, 1964.

Flinn, Caryl. "The Deaths of Camp." *Camera Obscura*, vol. 35. Bloomington: Indiana University Press, 1995.

Foucault, Michel. *The Archeology of Knowledge and the Discourse on Language*. New York: Vintage, 1982.

———. *Discipline & Punish: The Birth of the Prison*. New York: Vintage, 1979.

———. *The History of Sexuality: An Introduction*, vol. 1. New York: Penguin Books, 1978.

Foundation for Jewish Camp. 2016, www.jewishcamp.org/about/history/.

Fraser, Nancy. "Rethinking the Public Sphere: A Contribution to the Critique of Actually Existing Democracy." In *Habermas and the Public Sphere*, edited by Craig Calhoun, 109–42. Cambridge: MIT Press, 1993.

Freleng, Friz, dir. *Knighty Knight Bugs*. Warner Bros., 1958.

French, Robert. *Camping by a Billabong*. Sydney, AU: Blackwattle Press, 1993.

Freud, Sigmund. *Mass Psychology and Other Writings*. New York: Penguin Books, 2009.

Frye, Northrop. *Anatomy of Criticism: Four Essays*. 1957. Reprint, Toronto: University of Toronto Press, 2006.

Fuss, Diana. "Fashion and the Homospectatorial Look." *Critical Inquiry* 18 (1992): 713–37.

Garden, Nancy. *Annie on My Mind*. New York: Farrar, Straus, and Giroux, 1982.

Garis, Lilian. *The Girl Scout Pioneers or Winning the First B.C.* New York: Cupples & Leon, 1920.

Garner, Bill. *Born in a Tent: How Camping Makes Us Australian*. Sydney, AU: NewSouth Publishing, 2013.

Gershon, Livia. "Summer Camp, History of." *JSTOR Daily*, 2016. https://daily.jstor.org/history-summer-camp/.

Ginis, Liz. "Camping: The Classic Australian Experience." *Australian Geographic*, 2010, www.australiangeographic.com.au/topics/history-culture/2010/04/camping-the-classic-australian-experience/.

Goffman, Erving. *Asylums: Essays on the Social Situation of Mental Patients and Other Inmates*. New York: Anchor Books, 1961.

Gollin, Richard M. *A Viewer's Guide to Film: Arts, Artifices, and Issues*. New York: McGraw-Hill, 1991.

Green, Shelley. *Radical Juxtaposition: The Films of Yvonne Rainer*. Lanham, Md.: Scarecrow Press, 1994.

Griffin, Sean. *Tinker Belles and Evil Queens: The Walt Disney Company from the Inside Out*. New York: NYU Press, 2000.

Gulick, Charlotte V. "Camp Gulick on Lake Sebago." In *Camp Fire USA*, Kansas City, Mo.: CFUSA, 1910.

Gurian, Michael, Kathy Stevens, and Peggy Daniels. "Single-Sex Classrooms are Succeeding." *Educational Horizons* 87, no. 4 (2009): 234–45.

Haag, Pamela. "K-12 Single-Sex Education: What Does the Research Say?" *ERIC Digest*, 2000.

———. "Single-Sex Education in Grades K–12: What Does the Research Tell Us?" In *Separated by Sex: A Critical Look at Single-Sex Education for Girls*. Washington: American Association of University Women Educational Foundation, 1998, 13–38.

Hailey, Charlie. *Camps: A Guide to 21st-Century Space*. Cambridge: MIT Press, 2009.

———. *Campsite: Architectures of Duration and Place*. Baton Rouge: Louisiana State Press, 2008.

Halberstam, Judith (Jack). *In a Queer Time and Place: Transgender Bodies, Subcultural Lives*. New York: NYU Press, 2005.

———. *The Queer Art of Failure*. Durham, N.C.: Duke University Press, 2011.

Hall, Lesley A. *Sex, Gender and Social Change Since 1800*. 2nd ed. Basingstoke, UK: Palgrave Macmillan, 2013.

Hall, G. Stanley. *Youth: Its Education, Regimen, and Hygiene*. New York: D. Appleton and Co., 1906.

Halperin, David, and Valerie Traub. "Beyond Gay Pride." In *Gay Shame*, edited by David Halperin and Valerie Traub, 3–40. Chicago: University of Chicago Press, 2010.

Hansen, Miriam. *Babel to Babylon: Spectatorship in American Silent Film*. Cambridge: Harvard University Press, 1991.

———. Foreword to *Public Sphere and Experience*, by Oskar Negt and Alexander Kluge, 9–41. Minneapolis: University of Minnesota Press, 1993.

Haraway, Donna. *Manifestly Haraway*. Minneapolis: University of Minnesota Press, 2016.

Hardford, Margaret. "'Tondemonai' Staged by East-West Players." *Los Angeles Times*, May 30, 1970, A6.

Hargrave, John. *The Confession of the Kibbo Kift*. Glasgow: William Maclellan, 1927, 1979.

———. *The Great War Brings It Home: The Natural Reconstruction of an Unnatural Existence*. London: Constable and Company Ltd., 1919.

Harris, D. *The Rise and Fall of Gay Culture*. New York: Hyperion, 1997.

Hart, Laura C. "When 'Separate' May be Better: Exploring Single-Sex Learning as a Remedy for Social Anxieties in Female Middle School Students." *Middle School Journal* 47, no. 2 (2016): 32–40.

Haslanger, Sally. "Gender and Race: (What) Are They? (What) Do We Want Them to Be?" *Noûs* 34, no. 1 (2000): 31–55.

Helgren, Jennifer. "Native American and White Camp Fire Girls Enact Modern Girlhood, 1910–39." *American Quarterly* 66, no. 2 (2014): 333–60.

Herring, Scott. "The Sexual Objects of 'Parodistic' Camp." *Modernism/ Modernity* 23, no. 1 (January 2016): 5–8.

Hilal, Sandi, and Alessandro Petti. "Campus in Camps." In *Entry Points: The Vera List Center Field Guide on Art and Social Justice*, no. 1, edited by Carin Kuoni and Chelsea Haines, 118–19. Durham, N.C.: Duke University Press, 2015.

Hiltzik, Robert, dir. *Sleepaway Camp.* American Eagle, 1983.

Holland, Isabelle. *The Man Without a Face.* Philadelphia: J. B. Lippincott, 1972.

Hoover, Latharo. *The Camp-Fire Boys in the Philippines.* New York: A. L. Burt, 1930.

Hopper, Hedda. "Interview with Walt Disney." *Chicago Tribune*, May 9, 1948.

Houlbrook, Matt. "Thinking Queer: The Social and Sexual in Interwar Britain." In *British Queer History: New Approaches and Perspectives*, edited by Brian Lewis, 134–64. Manchester: Manchester University Press, 2013.

Howard, Shannon K. "Wilderness Laboratories: Rhetorical Acts of Surveillance at American Summer Camps." *The Journal of American Culture* 38, no. 4 (2015): 375–85.

Huhndorf, Shari. *Going Native: Indians in the American Cultural Imagination.* Ithaca, N.Y.: Cornell University Press, 2001.

Hutchison, Kay Bailey, and Barbara Mikulski. "A Right to Choose Single-Sex Education." *Education*, vol. 7 (2012): 11.

Hutchings, Peter. *The Horror Film.* Harlow, UK: Pearson Longman, 2004.

Iannello, Kathleen. "Women's Leadership and Third-Wave Feminism." In *Gender and Women's Leadership: A Reference Handbook*, edited by Karen O'Connor, 70–77. Thousand Oaks, Calif.: SAGE Publications, 2010.

Iñárritu, Alejandro González, ed. *The Revenant.* 20th Century Fox, 2015.

Inness, Sherrie A. "Girl Scouts, Camp Fire Girls, and Woodcraft Girls: The Ideology of Girls' Scouting Novels, 1910–1935." In *Nancy Drew and Company: Culture, Gender, and Girls' Series*, edited by Sherrie A. Inness, 89–100. Bowling Green, Ohio: Bowling Green State University Popular Press, 1997.

International Lesbian, Gay, Bisexual, Trans and Intersex Association (ILGA), www.ilga.org, 2017.

Isherwood, Christopher. *The World in the Evening.* London: Methuen, 1954, 1984.

It Gets Better Project. www.itgetsbetter.org, 2010.

Jackson, Janna. "'Dangerous Presumptions': How Single-Sex Schooling Rei-
fies False Notions of Sex, Gender, and Sexuality." *Gender and Education* 22,
no. 2 (2009): 227–38.

Jancovich, Mark. *Rational Fears: American Horrors in the 1950s*. Manchester:
Manchester University Press, 1996.

Jennings White, H. D. *The Biological Principles of Education*. Salisbury: Order
of Woodcraft Chivalry, 1928.

"Jew Camp." *Urban Dictionary*, www.urbandictionary.com/define.php?term
=Jew+Camp.

Kaminer, Wendy. "The Trouble with Single-Sex Schools." *Atlantic Monthly*
281, no. 4 (1998): 22–27.

Kauanui, Kēhaulani. "Jennifer Lawrence, Please Keep Your Butt Off Our
Ancestors." *The Guardian*, Guardian News and Media, 2016, www
.theguardian.com/commentisfree/2016/dec/09/jennifer-lawrence
-hawaii-shoot-sacred-rocks.

Kawin, Bruce F. "The Funhouse and The Howling." In *American Horrors:
Essays on the Modern American Horror Film*, edited by Gregory A. Waller,
102–13. Champaign: University of Illinois Press, 1987.

Kelner, Shaul. *Tours That Bind: Diaspora, Pilgrimage, and Israeli Birthright
Tourism*. New York: NYU Press, 2010.

Kent, Kathryn R. *Making Girls into Women: American Women's Writing and the
Rise of Lesbian Identity*. Durham, N.C.: Duke University Press, 2003.

———. *Making Girls into Women: Reading, Gender and Sexuality in American
Women's Writing, 1865–1940*. Dissertation, Duke University Press, 1995.

Kerber, Linda. "Separate Spheres, Female Worlds, Woman's Place: The
Rhetoric of Women's History." *Journal of American History* 75, no. 1
(1988): 9–39.

Kidd, Kenneth. *Making American Boys: Boyology and the Feral Tale*. Minneapolis: University of Minnesota Press, 2004.

King, Thomas. *Green Grass, Running Water*. New York: Bantam Books, 1994.

Kleinhans, Chuck. "Taking Out the Trash: Camp and the Politics of Parody."
In *The Politics and Poetics of Camp*, edited by Moe Meyer, 182–201. London
and New York: Routledge, 1994.

Kleiser, Randal, dir. *The Blue Lagoon*. Columbia Pictures, 1980.

Kruse, Anne-Mette. "' . . . We Have Learnt Not Just to Sit Back, Twiddle
Our Thumbs and Let Them Take Over': Single-Sex Settings and the
Development of a Pedagogy for Girls and a Pedagogy for Boys in Danish
Schools." *Gender and Education* 4, nos. 1–2 (1992): 81–103.

Kuoni, Carin, and Chelsea Haines, eds. *Entry Points: The Vera List Center Field
Guide on Art and Social Justice* 1, no. 1. Durham, N.C.: Duke University
Press, 2015.

Kurahashi, Yuko. *Asian-American Culture on Stage: The History of the East West Players*. New York and London: Garland Publishing, 1999.

LaBruce, Bruce. "Notes on Camp/Anti-Camp." *Bruce Labruce*, 2012, brucelabruce.com/2015/07/07/notes-on-camp-anti-camp/.

Lasky, Kyle. Personal interview by Alexis Mitchell. October 4, 2016.

Laughead, William B. *Introducing Mr. Paul Bunyan of Westwood, California*. Akeley, Minn.: Red River Lumber Co., 1914.

———. *The Marvelous Exploits of Paul Bunyan*. Akeley, Minn.: Red River Lumber Co., 1922.

———. *Tales About Paul Bunyan, Volume II*. Akeley, Minn.: Red River Lumber Co., 1916.

Lavell, Edith. *The Girl Scouts at Camp*. New York: A. L. Burt, 1922.

Lee, Esther Kim. "Transnational Legitimization of an Actor: The Life and Career of Soon-Tek Oh." *Modern Drama* 48, no. 2 (2005): 372–407.

Lee, Valerie E., and Anthony S. Bryk. "Effects of Single-Sex Secondary Schools on Student Achievement and Attitudes." *Journal of Educational Psychology* 78, no. 5 (1986): 381.

Lefebvre, Henri. *The Production of Space*. Malden, Mass.: Blackwell Publishing, 1991.

Levithan, David. *Boy Meets Boy*. New York: Alfred A. Knopf, 2003.

Levy, Harold P. *Building a Popular Movement: A Case Study of the Public Relations of the Boy Scouts of America*. New York: Russell Sage Foundation, 1944.

Lewis, Jon. *The Road to Romance and Ruin: Teen Films and Youth Culture*. London and New York: Routledge, 1992.

Lindsey, Shelly Stamp. "Horror, Femininity, and Carrie's Monstrous Puberty." *The Dread of Difference: Gender and the Horror Film*, edited by Barry Keith Grant, 279–95. Austin: University of Texas Press, 1996.

Lippit, Akira Mizuta, Noël Burch, Chon Noriega, Ara Osterweil, Linda Williams, Eric Shaefer, and Jeffrey Sconce. "Showgirls: Roundtable." *Film Quarterly* 56, no. 3 (2003): 32–46.

Lonzi, Carla. "Let's Spit on Hegel." In *Rivolta Femminile*, translated by Veronica Newman. 1970.

Lott, Eric. *Love & Theft: Blackface Minstrelsy and the American Working Class*. Oxford: Oxford University Press, 1993.

Luhmann, Susanne. "Queering/Querying Pedagogy? Or, Pedagogy Is a Pretty Queer Thing." In *Queer Theory in Education*, edited by William F. Pinar. New York: Routledge, 1998.

Macleod, David I. *Building Character in the American Boy: The Boy Scouts, YMCA, and Their Forerunners, 1870–1920*. Madison: University of Wisconsin Press, 1983.

Mael, Fred A. "Single-Sex and Coeducational Schooling: Relationships to Socioemotional and Academic Development." *Review of Educational Research*, 68, no. 2 (1998): 101–29.

Maher, Frances A. "Progressive Education and Feminist Pedagogies: Issues in Gender, Power, and Authority." *Teachers College Record* 101, no. 1 (1999): 35–59.

Mallan, Kerry, and Roderick McGillis. "Between a Frock and a Hard Place: Camp Aesthetics and Children's Culture." *Canadian Review of American Studies* 35, no. 1 (2005): 1–19.

Marsh, Jan. *Back to the Land*. London: Faber & Faber, 1982, 2010.

Mason, Derritt. "A Phallic Dog, a Stuffed Coyote, and the Boy Who Won't Come Out: Revisiting Queer Visibility in John Donovan's *I'll Get There. It Better Be Worth the Trip*." *Children's Literature Association Quarterly* 41, no. 3 (2016): 295–311.

Mason, Everdeen. "The Summer Camp Movie: The First Teen Sex Comedy?" *Refinery29*, 2014, http://www.refinery29.com/2014/06/69138/summer-camp-movies.

Mbembe, Achille. "Necropolitics." *Public Culture* 15, no. 1 (2003): 11–40.

———. *On the Postcolony*. Berkeley: University of California Press, 2001.

McDaniel, Judith. "The Juliette Low Legacy." In *Lavender Mansions: 40 Contemporary Lesbian and Gay Short Stories*, edited by Irene Zahava, 242–50. Boulder, Colo.: Westview Press, 1994.

McGillis, Roderick. *He Was Some Kind of a Man: Masculinities in the B Western*. Waterloo, Ontario: Wilfrid Laurier University Press, 2009.

McMahon, Gary. *Camp in Literature*. Jefferson, N.C.: McFarland, 2006.

Mechling, Jay. "Boy Scouts, the National Rifle Association, and the Domestication of Rifle Shooting." *American Studies* 53, no. 1 (2014), 5–25.

Medhurst, Andy. "Batman, Deviance and Camp." In *The Many Lives of Batman: Critical Approaches to a Superhero and His Media*, edited by Roberta Pearson and William Uricchio. New York: Routledge, 1991.

Men for Change. Woodcraft Folk papers, 1990. Collection of Chris Pyke.

Mermaid Café, and Andi D. "Gabey and Mike." Self-produced, 1990.

Meyer, Moe. "Introduction: Reclaiming the Discourse of Camp." *The Politics and Poetics of Camp*, 1–22. London and New York: Routledge, 1994.

Meyer, Moe, ed. *The Politics and Poetics of Camp*. London and New York: Routledge, 1994.

Miller, D. A. *The Novel and the Police*. Berkeley: University of California Press, 1988.

Miller, Susan A. *Growing Girls: The Natural Origins of Girls' Organizations in America*. New Brunswick, N.J.: Rutgers University Press, 2007.

Mishler, Paul C. *Raising Reds: The Young Pioneers, Radical Summer Camps, and Communist Political Culture in the United States.* New York: Columbia University Press, 1999.

"Moon on the Meadow." Anonymous, n.d. www.ultimatecampresource.com/site/camp-activity/moon-on-the-meadow.html.

Morrill, Cynthia. "Revamping the Gay Sensibility." In *The Poetics and Politics of Camp*, edited by Moe Meyer, 110–29. London and New York: Routledge, 1994.

Mulvey, Laura. *Visual and Other Pleasures.* Bloomington: Indiana University Press, 1989.

Muñoz, José Esteban. *Cruising Utopia: The Then and There of Queer Futurity.* New York: NYU Press, 2009.

———. *Disidentifications: Queers of Color and the Performance of Politics.* Minneapolis: University of Minnesota Press, 1999.

———. "Famous and Dandy Like B'n' Andy: Race, Pop, and Basquiat." In *Pop Out: Queer Warhol*, edited by Jennifer Doyle, Jonathan Flatley, and Jose Esteban Munoz, 144–79. Durham, N.C.: Duke University Press, 1996.

Nayman, Adam. *It Doesn't Suck: Showgirls.* Toronto: ECW Press, 2014.

Newton, Esther. *Mother Camp: Female Impersonators in America.* Chicago: University of Chicago Press, 1972, 1978.

Nunokawa, Jeff. "Queer Theory: Postmortem." *South Atlantic Quarterly* 106, no. 3, 2007.

Oh, Soon-Teck. *Tondemonai—Never Happen!* East West Players, 1970 (unpublished).

Oram, Alison. "'Sex Is an Accident': Feminism, Science and the Radical Sexual Theory of *Urania*, 1915–40." In *Sexology in Culture: Labelling Bodies and Desires*, edited by Lucy Bland and Laura Doan, 214–30. Cambridge: Polity Press, 1998.

Osterweil, Ara. "A Fan's Notes on Camp, or How to Stop Worrying and Learn to Love Showgirls." *Film Quarterly* 56, no. 3 (2003): 38.

Paris, Leslie. *Children's Nature: The Rise of the American Summer Camp.* New York: NYU Press, 2008.

Patton, Cindy. "Unmediated Lust: The Improbable Space of Lesbian Desires." In *Stolen Glances: Lesbians Take Photographs*, edited by Tessa Boffin and Jean Fraser, 233–40. Pandora Press, 1991.

Paul, Leslie. *The Training of Pioneers: The Educational Programme of the Woodcraft Folk.* London: The National Council of Woodcraft Folk, 1936.

Peaches. "Gay Bar." *Fatherfucker*, compact disk, Xl/Beggars Us Ada, 2003.

Pero, Allan. "A Fugue on Camp." *Modernism/Modernity* 23, no. 1 (2016): 28–36.

Peters, Sarah L. "'Moon Lake' and the American Summer Camp Movement." *Eudora Welty Review* 6 (2014): 55–67.

Pinar, William F., ed. *Queer Theory in Education*. New York: Routledge, 2012.

Pinzler, Isabelle Katz. "Separate But Equal Education in the Context of Gender." *New York Law School Law Review* 49 (2004): 785.

Phillips, Adam. *Missing Out: In Praise of the Unlived Life*. New York: Farrar, Straus and Giroux, 2012.

Phillips, John. *Transgender on Screen*. Basingstoke, UK: Palgrave Macmillan, 2006.

Pollen, Annebella. *The Kindred of the Kibbo Kift: Intellectual Barbarians*. London: Donlon Books, 2015.

Porter, Courtney. Personal interview by Flavia Musinsky. July 19, 2010.

Pryke, Sam. "The Control of Sexuality in the Early British Boy Scouts Movement." *Sex Education* 5, no. 1 (2005): 15–28.

Puar, Jasbir K. *Terrorist Assemblages: Homonationalism in Queer Times*. Durham, N.C.: Duke University Press, 2007.

"Queer Societies: Some Remarkable Institutions." *Northern Star* (1925): 7.

Quinlivan, Kathleen, and Shane Town. "Queer Pedagogy, Educational Practice and Lesbian and Gay Youth." *International Journal of Qualitative Studies in Education* 12, no. 5 (1999): 509–24.

Rainbow Resources: Compasito Companion on Sexuality and Gender. The International Falcon Movement-Socialist Educational International (IFM-SEI), 2014. www.ifm-sei.org/publications/rainbow-resources/.

Rand, Jennifer. "The Third Wave of Feminism Is Now, and It Is Intersectional." *The Huffington Post*, 2017. www.huffingtonpost.com/entry/the-third-wave-of-feminism-is-now-and-it-is-intersectional_us_586ac501e4b04d7df167d6a812.

Rasmussen, Mary, Eric Rofes, and Susan Talburt, eds. *Youth and Sexualities: Pleasure, Subversion, and Insubordination In and Out of Schools*. Basingstoke, UK: Palgrave Macmillan, 2016.

Reay, Diane. "Girls' Groups as a Component of Anti-Sexist Practice—One Primary School's Experience." *Gender and Education* 2, no. 1 (1990): 37–48.

Reder, Deanna, and Linda M. Morra, eds. *Troubling Tricksters: Revisioning Critical Conversations*. Waterloo, Ontario: Wilfred Laurier Press, 2010.

Redman, Jai. *This Is Camp X-Ray*. Installation in Manchester, England, sponsored by Arts Council England, Ultimate Holding Company, 2003. www.uhc.org.uk/about-us/an-introduction/.

Reitman, Ivan, dir. *Meatballs*. Performances by Bill Murray, Harvey Atkin, and Kate Lynch, Haliburton Films, 1979.

Report on the Implications of Learning by Doing. Order of Woodcraft Chivalry, 1930, Patrick Geddes papers, Special Collections, University of Strathclyde.

Revel, Dorothy. *Cheiron's Cave: The School of the Future: An Educational Synthesis Based on the New Psychology*. London: William Heinemann, 1928.

———. *Tented Schools: Camping as a Technique of Education*. London: Williams and Norgate, 1934.

———. "Woodcraft Discipline." *The Woodcraft Way Series*, no. 15. Salisbury: Order of Woodcraft Chivalry, 1930.

Revzin, Rebekah E. "American Girlhood in the Early Twentieth Century: The Ideology of Girl Scout Literature, 1913–1930." *The Library Quarterly: Information, Community, Policy* 68, no. 3 (1998): 261–75.

Reynolds, Simon. *Retromania: Pop Culture's Addition to Its Own Past*. London: Faber & Faber, 2011.

Rich, Adrienne. "Compulsory Heterosexuality and the Lesbian Existence." In *Blood, Bread, and Poetry: Selected Prose 1979–1985*. New York: Norton, 1986, 23–75.

Robinson, Douglas. *Estrangement and the Somatics of Literature*. Baltimore: John Hopkins University Press, 2008.

Robinson, Greg. "*Tondemonai-Never Happen!* (play)." *Densho Encyclopedia*, 2017, encyclopedia.densho.org/Tondemonai-Never%20Happen!%20(play)/.

Robinson, Smokey. *The Agony and the Ecstasy*. Motown, 1975.

Roen, Paul. *High Camp: A Gay Guide to Camp and Cult Films, Vol. 1*. New York: Leyland Publications, 1994.

Rogers, Richard A. "From Cultural Exchange to Transculturation: A Review and Reconceptualization of Cultural Appropriation." *Communication Theory* 16, no. 4 (2006): 474–503.

Roosevelt, Theodore. "The Strenuous Life." Hamilton Club, April 10, 1899, www.bartleby.com/58/1.html.

Roscoe, Will. *The Zuni Man-Woman*. Albuquerque: University of New Mexico Press, 1991.

Rose, Jacqueline. *The Last Resistance*. New York: Verso, 2007.

Ross, Andrew. "Uses of Camp." In *No Respect: Intellectuals and Popular Culture*. New York: Routledge (1989): 135–70.

Rothschild, Mary Logan. "Girl Scouts." In *Girl Culture: Studying Girl Culture: A Reader's Guide*, edited by Claudia Mitchell and Jacqueline Reid-Walsh, 314–17. Westport, Conn.: Greenwood Publishing, 2007.

Rowbotham, Sheila. *Edward Carpenter: A Life of Liberty and Love*. New York: Verso, 2009.

Roxworthy, Emily. *The Spectacle of Japanese-American Trauma: Racial Performativity in World War II*. Honolulu: University of Hawaii Press, 2008.

Ryan, Mary. *Women in Public: Between Banners and Ballots, 1825–1880.* Baltimore: Johns Hopkins University Press, 1990.

Sales, Amy L., and Leonard Saxe. *"How Goodly Are Thy Tents": Summer Camps as Jewish Socializing Experiences.* Lebanon, N.H.: Brandeis University Press, 2003.

Salomone, Rosemary C. "Feminist Voices in the Debate Over Single-Sex Schooling: Finding Common Ground." *Michigan Journal of Gender & Law.* 11 (2004): 63.

Salvato, Nick. "Tramp Sensibility and the Afterlife of *Showgirls.*" *Theatre Journal* 58, no. 4 (2006): 633–48.

Samarin, William J. "Variation and Variables in Religious Glossolalia." *Language in Society* 1, no. 1 (1972): 121–30.

Sarna, Jonathan. "The Crucial Decade in Jewish Camping." In *A Place of Our Own: The Rise of Reform Jewish Camping,* edited by Michael M. Lorge and Gary P. Zola, 27–51. Tuscaloosa: University of Alabama Press, 2006.

Sax, Leonard. *Girls on the Edge: The Four Factors Driving the New Crisis for Girls.* New York: Perseus Books Group, 2011.

Schaffer, David. *This Is Camp X-Ray.* BBC Manchester, 2003.

Sconce, Jeffrey. "I Have Grown Weary of Your Tiresome Cinema." *Film Quarterly* 56, no. 3, 2003.

Scott, A. O. "The Death of Adulthood in American Culture." *The New York Times Magazine,* 2014, www.nytimes.com/2014/09/14/magazine/the-death-of-adulthood-in-american-culture.html.

"Scout Law." *Boy Scouts of America,* 2017, beascout.scouting.org/?utm_source=scouting_top_nav&utm_medium=banner&utm_campaign=scouting_dot_org.

Sedgwick, Eve Kosofsky. *Epistemology of the Closet.* Berkeley: University of California Press, 1990.

———. "Privilege of Unknowing: Diderot's *The Nun.*" In *Tendencies,* 23–51. Durham, N.C.: Duke University Press, 1993.

Segal, Lynne. *Slow Motion: Changing Masculinities, Changing Men.* London: Virago Press, 1995.

Seltzer, Mark. *Bodies and Machines.* New York and London: Routledge, 1992.

Seton, Ernest Thompson. *Woodcraft and Indian Lore.* 1912. New York: Dover Publications, 2014.

Sharrett, Christopher. "The Horror Film in a Neoconservative Culture." In *The Dread of Difference: Gender and The Horror Film,* edited by Barry Kieth Grant, 253–76. Austin: University of Texas Press, 1996.

Shary, Timothy. *Teen Movies: American Youth on Screen.* New York: Wallflower Press, 2005.

Shire, Emily. "Hooking Up at Summer Camp." *Forward*, 2012, forward.com/
articles/161165/hooking-up-at-summer-camp/.

———. "Wet Hot American Jewish Sleepaway Camp." *Forward*, 2012, forward
.com/sisterhood/161285/wet-hot-american-jewish-sleepaway-camp/.

Shlasko, G. D. "Queer (v.) Pedagogy." *Equity & Excellence in Education* 38, no.
2, 2005, 123–34.

Shortchanging Girls, Shortchanging America: A Call to Action. Washington:
American Association of University Women, vol. 4792, 1991.

Shugart, Helen, and Catherine Egley Waggoner. *Making Camp: Rhetorics of
Transgression in U.S. Popular Culture*. Tuscaloosa: University of Alabama
Press, 2008.

Singleton, Ellen. "Camps and Tramps: Civilization, Culture, and the Use of
Leisure in the Early Twentieth-Century Outdoor Adventure Series Books
for Girls and Boys." *Leisure/Loisir* 29, no. 1 (2005): 49–70.

Smith-Rosenberg, Carroll. *Disorderly Conduct: Visions of Gender in Victorian
America*. Oxford: Oxford University Press, 1985.

Sontag, Susan. "Notes on 'Camp.'" 1964. In *Against Interpretation and Other
Essays*, 275–92. New York: Farrar, Straus and Giroux, 1966.

———. *Regarding the Pain of Others*. New York: Farrar, Straus and Giroux,
2003.

Spivak, Chakravorty Gayatri. *Death of a Discipline*. New York: Columbia University Press, 2003.

Stevenson, Noelle, Grace Ellis, and Brooke Allen. *Lumberjanes 1: Beware the
Kitten Holy*. Los Angeles: Boom! Studios, 2015.

Stockton, Kathryn Bond. *The Queer Child, or Growing Sideways in the Twentieth Century*. Durham, N.C.: Duke University Press, 2009.

"Student Success." *The Young Women's Leadership School (TYWLS)*. www.ywln.
org/student-success.

Summers, Darby. "Tondemonai, a Unique Theatre Experience." *The Advocate*
(1970): 12.

Tedesco, Laureen. "A Nostalgia for Home: Daring and Domesticity in Girl
Scouting and Girls' Fiction, 1913–1933." Dissertation, Texas A&M,
1999.

———. "Progressive Era Girl Scouts and the Immigrant: Scouting for Girls
(1920) as a Handbook for American Girlhood." *Children's Literature Association Quarterly* 31, no. 4 (2006): 346–68.

Thoreau, Henry David. *Walden or Life in the Woods*. Boston: Ticknor and
Fields, 1854.

Tobias, Scott. "Sleepaway Camp." *The Dissolve*, 2014. thedissolve.com/
reviews/820–sleepaway-camp/.

Tomczik, Adam. "'He-men Could Talk to He-Men in He-Men Language': Lumberjack Work Culture in Maine and Minnesota, 1840–1940." *The Historian* 70, no. 4 (2008): 697–715.

Trask, Michael. *Camp Sites: Sex, Politics, and Academic Style in Postwar America.* Stanford: Stanford University Press, 2013.

Trevorrow, Colin, dir. *Jurassic World.* Universal Pictures, 2015.

Tsolidis, Georgina, and Ian R. Dobson. "Single-Sex Schooling: Is It Simply a 'Class Act'?" *Gender and Education* 18, no. 2 (2006): 213–28.

"UNRWA in Figures 2017." United Nations Relief and Works Agency for Palestine Refugees (UNRWA), 2017. www.unrwa.org/resources/about-unrwa/unrwa-figures-2017.

van der Kolk, Bessel. *The Body Keeps the Score: Brain, Mind, and Body in the Healing of Trauma.* New York: Penguin, 2014.

Van Leer, David. *The Queening of America: Gay Culture in Straight Society.* New York: Routledge, 1995.

Van Slyck, Abigail A. *A Manufactured Wilderness: Summer Camps and the Shaping of American Youth, 1890–1960.* Minneapolis: University of Minnesota Press, 2006, 2010.

Verhoeven, Paul, dir. *Showgirls.* MGM, 1995, 2005.

Vincent, Andrew. *Nationalism and Particularity.* Cambridge: Cambridge University Press, 2002.

Vizenor, Gerald. *Fugitive Poses.* Lincoln: University of Nebraska Press, 1998.

Vreeland, Vaughn A. "Color Theory and Social Structure in the Films of Wes Anderson." *Elon Journal of Undergraduate Research in Communications* 6, no. 2 (2015): 35–44.

Wain, David, dir. *Wet Hot American Summer.* Eureka Pictures, 2001.

Wall, Sharon. *The Nurture of Nature: Childhood, Antimodernism, and Ontario Summer Camps, 1920–55.* Vancouver: UBC Press, 2009.

Waring, Sarah. Personal interview by Flavia Musinsky. July 24, 2010.

Warner, Michael. "Queer and Then." *Chronicle of Higher Education* (2012). www.chronicle.com/article/QueerThen-/130161/.

———. "Tongues Untied: Memoirs of a Pentecostal Boyhood." In *Curiouser: On the Queerness of Children*, edited by Steven Bruhm and Natasha Hurley, 215–24. Minneapolis: University of Minnesota Press, 2004.

Watters, Shannon, Grace Ellis, and Noelle Stevenson. *Lumberjanes Volume 1: Beware the Kitten Holy.* Collects issues 1–4. Los Angeles: Boom! Studios, 2014.

———. *Lumberjanes Volume 2: Friendship to the Max!* Collects issues 5–8. Los Angeles: Boom! Studios, 2015.

———. *Lumberjanes Volume 3: A Terrible Plan.* Collects issues 9–12. Los Angeles: Boom! Studios, 2016.

Watts, Steven. *The Magic Kingdom: Walt Disney and the American Way of Life.* Boston: Houghton Mifflin, 1997.

Weiner, Gaby. "Feminist Education and Equal Opportunities: Unity or Discord?" *British Journal of Sociology of Education* 7, no. 3 (1986): 265–74.

Weizman, Eyal. *The Politics of Verticality.* Open Democracy, 2002, www.open-democracy.net.

Westlake, Ernest. *The Forest School or Evolutionary Education.* Salisbury: Order of Woodcraft Chivalry, 1930.

Westworld. Created by Jonathan Nolan and Lisa Joy. Warner Bros. Television, 2016.

Wilde, Oscar. *The Soul of Man.* Arthur L. Humpreys, Project Gutenberg, 1900, www.gutenberg.org/files/1017/1017-h/1017-h.htm.

Williams, Raymond. *The Country and the City.* London: Chatto and Windus, 1973.

Williams, Tony. "Trying to Survive on the Darker Side: 1980s Family Horror." In *The Dread of Difference: Gender and The Horror Film*, edited by Barry Keith Grant, 164–80. Austin: University of Texas Press, 1996.

Wilsey, John D. *American Exceptionalism and Civil Religion: Reassessing the History of an Idea.* Westmont, Ill.: InterVarsity Press, 2015.

Winters, Ben. "'It's All Really Happening': Sonic Shaping in the Films of Wes Anderson." *Music, Sound and Filmmakers: Sonic Style in Cinema*, edited by James Wierzbicki, 45–60. New York: Routledge, 2012.

Wolf, John M. "Resurrecting Camp: Rethinking the Queer Sensibility." *Communication, Culture & Critique*, 6 (2013): 284–97.

Wood, Robin. *Hollywood from Vietnam to Reagan.* New York: Columbia University Press, 1986.

Woodhouse, Adrian. *Angus McBean: Facemaker.* Richmond, UK: Alma Books, 2006.

Woody, Elisabeth L. "Homophobia and Heterosexism in Public School Reform: Constructions of Gender and Sexuality in California's Single Gender academies." *Equity & Excellence in Education* 36, no. 2 (2003): 148–60.

Yates, Norris W. *William T. Porter and the Spirit of the Times: A Study in the Big Bear School of Humor.* Baton Rouge: Louisiana State University Press, 1957.

Zakim, Eric. *To Build and Be Built: Landscape, Literature and the Construction of Zionist Identity.* Philadelphia: University of Pennsylvania Press, 2006.

Zinoman, Jason. *Shock Value: How a Few Eccentric Outsiders Gave Us Nightmares, Conquered Hollywood, and Invented Modern Horror.* New York: Penguin, 2011.

CONTRIBUTORS

KYLE EVELETH is a Ronald E. McNair Postbaccalaureate Fellow and doctoral candidate at the University of Kentucky, where he specializes in twentieth- and twenty-first-century American literature, children's/young adult literature, and visual narrative. He has published on comics and narrative in *Critical Insights: The American Comic Book*, *Critical Insights: Neil Gaiman*, *disClosure: A Journal of Social Theory*, and *The South Central Review*. With Joseph Michael Sommers he is co-editor of *The Artistry of Neil Gaiman: Finding Light in the Shadows*.

D. GILSON is the author of *Jesus Freak* (2018), *I Will Say This Exactly One Time: Essays* (2015), *Crush* with Will Stockton (2014), and *Brit Lit* (2013). He is an Assistant Professor of English at Texas Tech University, and his work has appeared in *Quarterly Review of Film and Video*, *Journal of Popular Culture*, and as a notable essay in *Best American Essays*.

CHARLIE HAILEY is Professor of Architecture at the University of Florida. A registered architect and 2018 Guggenheim Fellow, Charlie is the author of *Design/Build with Jersey Devil* (2016), *Spoil Island: Reading the Makeshift Archipelago* (2013), *Camps: A Guide to 21st-Century Space* (2009), *Campsite: Architectures of Duration and Place* (2008), and *Slab City: Dispatches from the Last Free Place* (with photographer Donovan Wylie, 2018).

ANA M. JIMENEZ-MORENO is a Postdoctoral Fellow at the University of Notre Dame. She received a B.A. from Rutgers University and an M.A. and Ph.D. in English from the University of Notre Dame. Her dissertation, *Writing out of the Center: The Legacy of the Mexican Revolution on Interwar British Fiction*, focuses on the connections between post-colonial theory, phenomenology, the novel genre, and travel literature. Her article "Disgust as Redemptive Articulation: British Interwar Writers in Mexico" was published in the interdisciplinary journal *Atenea*.

KATHRYN R. KENT is Professor of English and Women's, Gender and Sexuality Studies at Williams College. Her chapter is part of a book-length project on sexuality and summer camp. Her recent publications include "Eve's Muse" in *Bathroom Songs: Eve Kosofksy Sedgwick as Poet*, ed. Jason Edwards, which is an excerpt from her book-in-progress, an experimental biography of Eve Kosofsky Sedgwick.

Kenneth B. Kidd is Professor of English at the University of Florida. He is the author of *Making American Boys: Boyology and the Feral Tale* (2004) and *Freud in Oz: At the Intersections of Psychoanalysis and Children's Literature* (2011). He is also coeditor of *Wild Things: Children's Culture and Ecocriticism* (2004), *Over the Rainbow: Queer Children's and Young Adult Literature* (2011), and *Prizing Children's Literature: The Cultural Politics of Children's Book Awards* (2017).

Mark Lipton is Professor in the School of English and Theatre Studies/Media Studies, University of Guelph. Lipton is the author of the media literacy textbook *Smoke Screens: From Tobacco Outrage to Media Activism* (with M. Dewing and Children's Media Project, Children's Health Initiative, 2002). He has written numerous monographs on the subject of communication, media, and education and is a coeditor of *Visualizing the Web: Evaluating Online Design from A Visual Communication Perspective* (2010), and author of *Research, Write, Create: Connecting Scholarship to Digital Media* (with T. Gibson, 2014). Research funding includes support from the Canadian Council on Learning, the Social Sciences and Humanities Research Council, the Mellon Foundation, the Ford Foundation, Children's Services Council, United Way, and others.

Chris McGee teaches children's literature, young adult literature, and film courses at Longwood University in Virginia. One of his primary areas of research and teaching is adolescent horror films, and his favorite movies are the eighties slasher films he'd watch at the local theaters with friends when he was a teenager. His other primary areas of interest are children's and young adult mystery fiction, contemporary American series fiction, and popular children's culture. He is currently at work on a manuscript on contemporary children's and young adult detective fiction.

Roderick McGillis is Emeritus Professor of English, the University of Calgary. He has collaborated with Kerry Mallan on several projects, including an earlier article on Camp aesthetics. Recent publications include a scholarly edition of George MacDonald's *Phantastes*, edited with John Pennington (2017) and a review in *The Wordsworth Circle*.

Kerry Mallan is Emeritus Professor, Faculty of Education, Queensland University of Technology, Australia. She has published widely on children's literature and film, with a special interest in gender and sexuality. Her books include *Gender Dilemmas in Children's Fiction* (2009), *Secrets, Lies and Children's Fiction* (2013), and *(Re)Imagining the World: Children's Literature's Response to Changing Times*, edited with Yan Wu and Roderick McGillis (2013). Her research also includes youth digital cultures and texts. A recent publication is *Digital Participation through Social Living Labs*, edited with Michael Dezuanni, Marcus Foth, and Hilary Hughes (2017).

DERRITT MASON is Assistant Professor of English at the University of Calgary, which is situated on the traditional territories of the people of the Treaty 7 region in Southern Alberta. Derritt teaches and researches at the intersections of children's and young adult literature, queer theory, and cultural studies. His monograph on queer young adult literature and culture is forthcoming from the University Press of Mississippi. Otherwise, Derritt's work has appeared in *Children's Literature Association Quarterly*, *ESC: English Studies in Canada*, and *Jeunesse: Young People, Texts, Cultures*. Derritt also coedited, with Ela Przybylo, a special issue of *ESC* (40.1) entitled *Hysteria Manifest: Cultural Lives of a Great Disorder*.

TAMMY L. MIELKE lectures in the Honors program at Northern Arizona University, specializing in children's and young adult literature. She taught elementary-age students for eleven years in areas with diverse populations. She researches the ways in which culture is reflected in literature.

ALEXIS MITCHELL is an award-winning artist and scholar whose works have shown at galleries and festivals internationally, including the Berlinale Film Festival, Gallery TPW, the Art Gallery of Windsor, and the Images Festival. Her projects make use of space and place to reconfigure relationships to memory, politics, and acts of belonging. She often works collaboratively alongside artist Sharlene Bamboat under the name Bambitchell. Mitchell earned her Ph.D. in Human Geography from the University of Toronto where she held a SSHRC Doctoral Fellowship and is a fellow of the Sommerakademie Paul Klee through Spring 2019. She has held artist residencies at Akademie Schloss Solitude, the Santa Fe Art Institute, and the MacDowell Colony, and is featured in a wide range of publications, including the *Los Angeles Review of Books*, *C Magazine*, and the recently published book *Contemporary Citizenship, Art and Visual Culture*. www.alexismitchell.com

FLAVIA MUSINSKY is a nonprofit professional with over ten years of experience working for organizations dedicated to the advancement of women and girls. Currently, she is the Member Acquisition Specialist for Girl Scouts of the USA, and has previously worked with Girl Scouts of Western PA, Strong Women Strong Girls, the Eileen Fisher Leadership Institute, Farm & Wilderness Camps, and MADRE. She has an MBA from Chatham University and a B.A. in Sociology and Gender Studies from New College of Florida, where she wrote a senior thesis from which her chapter is excerpted.

Daniel Mallory Ortberg is an American writer, blogger, editor, and co-founder of the feminist website *The Toast*. Previously, he wrote for *Gawker* and *The Hairpin*. His book *Texts from Jane Eyre* (2014) became a *New York Times* bestseller.

Annebella Pollen is a social and cultural historian who researches art, craft, design, dress, and photography across a range of periods and case studies. She is Principal Lecturer in Art and Design History at the University of Brighton, UK, the author of *The Kindred of the Kibbo Kift: Intellectual Barbarians* (Donlon Books), which won a 2015 Swiss Federal Office of Culture Most Beautiful Swiss Book award, and the co-curator of the accompanying 2015–2016 exhibition at Whitechapel Gallery, London. Her other books include *Mass Photography: Collective Histories of Everyday Life* (2015) and the co-edited collections *Dress History: New Directions in Theory and Practice* (2015) and *Photography Reframed: New Visions in Contemporary Photographic Culture* (2018).

Andrew Trevarrow is a doctoral student in the Literature for Children and Young Adults program at The Ohio State University. His research interests include critical theory, gender and sexuality studies, and LBGTQ literature for children and young adults.

Paul Venzo (Ph.D.) is a creative writer and academic working in Victoria, Australia. His research focuses on theories of in-between-ness, linguistic hybridity, and the poetics of identity. He has worked for more than a decade teaching child and young adult literature at tertiary level, and has published widely on translation, queer culture, and literary and popular media representations of children and young adults, as well as poetry and poetics. His recent creative work involves poetry-in-translation across English and Italian, in which he takes a contemporary flâneur's approach to mapping the Self into cultural, imagined, and literary geographies.

Joshua Whitehead is an Oji-Cree member of the Peguis First Nation on Treaty 1 territory in Manitoba, Canada, and he identifies as Two-Spirit/Indigiqueer. He is pursuing a Ph.D. in English Literature at the University of Calgary on Treaty 7 territory. Joshua is the author of *full-metal indigiqueer* (2017) and *Jonny Appleseed* (2018).

Index

Lightning Source UK Ltd.
Milton Keynes UK
UKHW010647140419
340989UK00001B/151/P